Virtual Private Networks

Virtual Private Networks
Second Edition

Charlie Scott, Paul Wolfe, and Mike Erwin

Beijing · Cambridge · Farnham · Köln · Paris · Sebastopol · Taipei · Tokyo

Virtual Private Networks, Second Edition

by Charlie Scott, Paul Wolfe, and Mike Erwin

Published by O'Reilly & Associates, Inc., 101 Morris Street, Sebastopol, CA 95472.

Editor: Andy Oram

Production Editor: Jane Ellin

Printing History:

| March 1998: | First Edition. |
| January 1999: | Second Edition. |

ISBN: 1-56592-529-7   [8/00]

[M]

Table of Contents

Preface

This book is about a very new area of computer technology: providing secure access between members of an organization who are cast far around the world. Both the technology providers and the users are feeling their way.

We approached the idea of the virtual private network (VPN) with some skepticism, since we own an Internet service provider. Security compromises are fairly common, as end users fail to understand the importance of password integrity and other basic protections. Though known cracks are not common, attempted cracks are; unfortunately, the successful cracks are those you never hear about.

Customers began approaching us with requests for solutions. How can we use the global reach of the Internet to access our various networks around the country and the world? Can we do it securely? Can we do it now? Charlie probably looked them square in the eye and said, "Oh, yeah, we can do that," then gave a cackle, to Mike's and Paul's dismay. In the course of trying to find solutions for these needy customers, and for our own nationally expanding networks, we turned to the virtual private network, and eventually wrote this book.

Although it doesn't fully represent the drama and tribulations of learning about and erecting a VPN, this book covers everything you need to know to get one up and running. The technology of the virtual private network is widely available; however, specific solutions are fairly slim. We cover the four that are currently available—Layer 2 tunneling through PPTP or L2TP, the Cisco PIX firewall, the AltaVista Tunnel, and the Secure Shell (SSH)—and other basics on how VPNs work, how much they cost, and why you should use one. (And when you shouldn't.)

Audience

We assume that you are a network administrator who has already set up local area networks and knows something about the Internet and remote access (dial-in use). VPN solutions are usually employed along with firewalls, which are discussed only briefly in this book. For help with firewall concepts and technologies, you can find a variety of useful books, including *Building Internet Firewalls,* by D. Brent Chapman and Elizabeth D. Zwicky, published by O'Reilly & Associates, Inc.

Contents of This Book

Chapter 1, *Why Build a Virtual Private Network?*
> Do you need a virtual private network? Good question. Read this chapter and find out. After we scare you with some common security breaches, you will find some comforting reasons why a virtual private network may be your solution.

Chapter 2, *Basic VPN Technologies*
> Still here? This chapter details the various pieces that make a VPN function and make it more secure. Firewalls, encryption/authentication, and some basic VPN protocols and standards are covered. Rounding out this chapter are some of the varied and fun encryption technologies, such as Data Encryption Standard (DES), the RSA Public Key Cryptosystem, IPSec, and Secure Socket Layer (SSL).

Chapter 3, *Wide Area, Remote Access, and the VPN*
> How much is this going to cost me? Justifying the cost of all these technologies is possible once you delve into the exciting world of VPN bean counting. In this chapter, the VPN's costs and benefits are weighed against the more traditional solutions: private lease-line Wide Area Network (WAN) and remote access. The three solutions are compared through a comprehensive breakdown of equipment, lines, personnel, and—most importantly—time. Prices may vary. Check your local listings for a showing near you.

Chapter 4, *Implementing Layer 2 Connections*
> What's a specific solution for my VPN? Well, there are several. We start with one of the cheapest versions (free!): Point-to-Point Tunneling Protocol, or, as we call it in the industry, PPTP. PPTP has recently been updated and broadened into the L2TP protocol—but the two are used the same way.

Chapter 5, *Configuring and Testing Layer 2 Connections*
> Okay, I've decided to use your PPTP or L2TP—but how? Here is everything you ever wanted to know about getting it running. We cover the protocols on Windows NT and Windows 95/98, as well as on Ascend remote access devices. Then we teach you how to test and troubleshoot the connections.

Chapter 6, *Implementing the AltaVista Tunnel 98*

PPTP/L2TP isn't enough for me—do you have anything else? Actually, yes. The AltaVista Tunnel is the newest entrant into the VPN world; it has proven to be a stable solution. Here we cover how the AltaVista Tunnel works, its advantages and limitations, and how it may fit into your VPN scenario.

Chapter 7, *Configuring and Testing the AltaVista Tunnel*

Okay, how do I make it work? We cover configuring server and client pieces on Windows NT and Windows 95, as well as mentioning a few Unix versions out there. We also cover testing and troubleshooting.

Chapter 8, *Creating a VPN with the Unix Secure Shell*

Years before commercial vendors offered the turn-key solutions described so far in this book, Unix administrators were securing connections through the Secure Shell (SSH). Implementing SSH requires a fair amount of building and cobbling together tools, but it's a proven solution.

Chapter 9, *The Cisco PIX Firewall*

What's the top of the line? For now, we've found Cisco PIX to offer the most features and bandwidth—an expensive choice, but perhaps the only one that large sites will find satisfactory. In this chapter we cover what PIX can do, as well as configuration of the firewall and the private network.

Chapter 10, *Managing and Maintaining Your VPN*

Now what's wrong? Someone can't dial in, or a connection that worked fine yesterday is down. This chapter takes you through the various points on the network (or your Internet provider's network) where access has failed. It also offers suggestions for policies that increase security on the VPN.

Chapter 11, *A VPN Scenario*

Okay, show me one that actually works. Well, here's a real live working VPN from a real live company, though the names are changed to protect everyone involved. This chapter shows a VPN scenario in all its glory, detailing the needs of a company and how the VPN saved the day. A description of the network topology and various required items is also included, as well as a handy network diagram.

Appendix A, *Emerging Internet Technologies*

This appendix covers IPv6 (the newest version of the IP protocol), IPsec, and Secure Wide Area Network (S/WAN).

Appendix B, *Resources, Online and Otherwise*

Technology and products for VPNs are evolving quickly. Here's a list of places we've found useful for the latest information.

Conventions Used in This Book

The following conventions are used in this book:

Italic

> Used for filenames, directory names, program names, URLs, and commands, as well as to introduce new terms.

`Constant width`

> Used for system output and excerpts from files, and to indicate options.

`Constant width bold`

> In some code examples, highlights the statements being discussed.

`Constant width italic`

> Indicates an element, such as a filename or variable, that you supply.

 The owl icon designates a note, which is an important aside to the nearby text.

 The turkey icon designates a warning related to the nearby text.

Comments and Questions

Please address comments and questions concerning this book to the publisher:

> O'Reilly & Associates
> 101 Morris Street
> Sebastopol, CA 95472
> 1-800-998-9938 (in the U.S. or Canada)
> 1-707-829-0515 (international or local)
> 1-707-829-0104 (FAX)

You can also send us messages electronically. To be put on our mailing list or to request a catalog, send email to:

> *info@oreilly.com*

To ask technical questions or comment on the book, send email to:

> *bookquestions@oreilly.com*

Updates

The technology of VPNs is evolving on a monthly basis. Since new products and new releases of old products appear constantly, the authors maintain a web site summarizing these developments. For information that has developed since the printing of this book, please visit:

http://www.vpn.outer.net

Any errors found in this book after publication are listed at the URL:

http://www.oreilly.com/catalog/vpn2/errata

Acknowledgments

The authors collectively wish to thank our insightful and understanding editor, Andy Oram. Without his direction, gentle reminders, and gracious deadline extensions, this book wouldn't be here.

Charlie would like to dedicate his portion of this book to his wife Mary, who has weathered the past three years of authoring exceptionally well. "You are my life." He'd also like to thank his co-authors Mike and Paul, for their help in making this book a reality.

Paul thanks his family (Brenda, Nikolaus, Lukas, and Rayna) for putting up with his long nights away from home. Thanks to OuterNet for their bulletproof network, without which this book would not be possible.

Mike would like to extend a hearty "thanks for everything you've done" to Kris Thompson, for lending him a Cisco PIX unit as well as his expert assistance in helping to get it configured and working. He'd like to further thank his friends and family, who put up with him as he tried to fit writing into his crazy schedule.

The authors would like to thank their many technical reviewers. First off, a special thank you for Scott Mullen, who helped shape the second edition with many useful comments on both technical matters and overall flow of material. Gracious thank yous also go out to Arlinda Sata, Tatu Ylönen, and Jani Hursti of SSH Communications for their help with the SSH chapter. Equally large thanks go to Arpad Magosanyi for authoring the Linux VPN HOWTO and allowing us to use it as a basis for the SSH chapter. Last but not least: here's to Jennifer Alexander, Gregg Lebovitz, Gordon C. Galligher, Matt Eackle, Sebastian Hassinger, Nat Makarevitch, and Alex deVries for their technical reviews, which mixed useful fixes and insightful general suggestions. The authors also wish to thank William Hurley for acting as their agent on this book.

The authors would also like to thank the production staff at O'Reilly & Associates. Jane Ellin was the production editor and proofreader. Ellie Maden was the copyeditor. Sarah Jane Shangraw, Madeleine Newell, and Sheryl Avruch performed quality control checks. Seth Maislin wrote the index. Edie Freedman designed the book's cover. Mike Sierra implemented the format in FrameMaker. Robert Romano created the illustrations. Betty Hugh and Jeff Liggett provided production support.

Finally, we thank the vendors that gave us products to test and document, as well as vendors who expressed interest in the book but could not get prototypes to us in time to write about them.

1

Why Build a Virtual Private Network?

Until now there has always been a clear division between public and private networks. A public network, like the public telephone system and the Internet, is a large collection of unrelated peers that exchange information more or less freely with each other. The people with access to the public network may or may not have anything in common, and any given person on that network may only communicate with a small fraction of his potential users.

A private network is composed of computers owned by a single organization that share information specifically with each other. They're assured that they are going to be the only ones using the network, and that information sent between them will (at worst) only be seen by others in the group. The typical corporate Local Area Network (LAN) or Wide Area Network (WAN) is an example of a private network. The line between a private and public network has always been drawn at the gateway router, where a company will erect a firewall to keep intruders from the public network out of their private network, or to keep their own internal users from perusing the public network.

There also was a time, not too long ago, when companies could allow their LANs to operate as separate, isolated islands. Each branch office might have its own LAN, with its own naming scheme, email system, and even its own favorite network protocol—none of which might be compatible with other offices' setups. As more company resources moved to computers, however, there came a need for these offices to interconnect. This was traditionally done using leased phone lines of varying speeds. By using leased lines, a company can be assured that the connection is always available, and private. Leased phone lines, however, can be expensive. They're typically billed based upon a flat monthly fee, plus mileage expenses. If a company has offices across the country, this cost can be prohibitive.

Private networks also have trouble handling roving users, such as traveling sales-people. If the salesperson doesn't happen to be near one of the corporate computers, he or she has to dial into a corporation's modem long-distance, which is an extremely expensive proposition.

This book is about the virtual private network (VPN), a concept that blurs the line between a public and private network. VPNs allow you to create a secure, private network over a public network such as the Internet. They can be created using software, hardware, or a combination of the two that creates a secure link between peers over a public network. This is done through encryption, authentication, packet tunneling, and firewalls. In this chapter we'll go over exactly what is meant by each of these and what roles they play in a VPN; we'll touch upon them again and again throughout the book. Because they skirt leased line costs by using the Internet as a WAN, VPNs are more cost-effective for large companies, and well within the reach of smaller ones.

In this chapter, we'll also talk about Intranets as the latest trend in corporate information systems, and how they were the impetus for VPNs.

What Does a VPN Do?

A virtual private network is a way to simulate a private network over a public network, such as the Internet. It is called "virtual" because it depends on the use of virtual connections—that is, temporary connections that have no real physical presence, but consist of packets routed over various machines on the Internet on an ad hoc basis. Secure virtual connections are created between two machines, a machine and a network, or two networks.

Using the Internet for remote access saves a lot of money. You'll be able to dial in wherever your Internet service provider (ISP) has a point-of-presence (POP). If you choose an ISP with nationwide POPs, there's a good chance your LAN will be a local phone call away. Some ISPs have expanded internationally as well, or have alliances with ISPs overseas. Even many of the smaller ISPs have toll-free numbers for their roaming users. At the time of this writing, unlimited access dial-up PPP accounts, suitable for business use, are around $25 per month per user. At any rate, well-chosen ISP accounts should be cheaper than setting up a modem pool for remote users and paying the long-distance bill for roaming users. Even toll-free access from an ISP is typically cheaper than having your own toll-free number, because ISPs purchase hours in bulk from the long-distance companies.

In many cases, long-haul connections of networks are done with a leased line, a connection to a frame relay network, or ISDN. We've already mentioned the costs of leasing a "high cap" leased line such as a T1. Frame relay lines can also give you high speeds without the mileage charges. You purchase a connection to a frame cloud, which connects you through switches to your destination. Unlike a leased line, the amount you pay is based more on the bandwidth that's committed to your circuit than distance. Frame connections are still somewhat expensive, however. ISDN, like the plain old telephone system, incurs long-distance charges. In many locations, the local telephone company charges per minute even for local calls, which again runs expenses up. For situations where corporate office networks are in separate cities, having each office get a T1, frame relay, or ISDN line to an ISP's local POP would be much cheaper than connecting the two offices using these technologies. A VPN could then be instituted between the routers at the two offices, over the Internet. In addition, a VPN will allow you to consolidate your Internet and WAN connections into a single router and single line, saving you money on equipment and telecommunications infrastructure.

The Rise of Intranets

By now you've probably heard of Intranets and the stir they've caused at many businesses. Companies are running TCP/IP networks, posting information to their internal web sites, and using web browsers as a common collaborative tool. An example of an Intranet application is a customer database accessible via the Web. Salespeople could use this database to contact current customers about new product offerings and send them quotes. The database could have a HyperText Mark-Up Language (HTML) front end, so that it would be accessible from any web browser.

The rise of Intranets was spurred on by the growth of the Internet and its popular information services, commonly known as the World Wide Web. It was as if the corporate sector had finally caught on to what the Internet community had been doing for years: using simple, platform-independent protocols to communicate more effectively. No matter how much marketing hype you hear, an Intranet is simply Internet technology put to use on a private network.

How VPNs relate to Intranets

Virtual private networks can be used to expand the reach of an Intranet. Since Intranets are typically used to communicate proprietary information, you don't want them accessible from the Internet. There may be cases, however, where you'll want far-flung offices to share data or remote users to connect to your Intranet, and these users may be using the Internet as their means of connection. A VPN will allow them to connect to the Intranet securely, so there are no fears of sensitive information leaving the network unprotected. You might see this type of connection also referred to as an "Extranet."

Using our previous example of the customer database, it's easy to see how a VPN could expand the Intranet application's functionality. Suppose most of your salespeople are on the road, or work from home. There's no reason why they shouldn't be able to use the Internet to access the web server that houses the customer database application. You don't want just anyone to be able to access the information, however, and you're also worried about the information itself flowing unencrypted over the Internet. A VPN can provide a secure link between the salesperson's laptop and the Intranet web server running the database, and encrypt the data going between them. VPNs give you flexibility, and allow practically any corporate network service to be used securely across the Internet.

Security Risks of the Internet

The risks associated with the Internet are advertised every day by the trade and mainstream media. Whether it's someone accessing your credit card numbers, prying into your legal troubles, or erasing your files, there's a new scare every month about the (supposedly) private information someone can find out about you on the Internet. (Not to mention the perceived risk that you might happen upon some information that you find offensive, or that you might not want your children to see.)

For corporations, the risks are even more real and apparent. Stolen or deleted corporate data can adversely affect people's livelihoods, and cost the company money. If a small company is robbed of its project files or customer database, it could put them out of business.

Since the Internet is a public network, you always risk having someone access any system you connect to it. It used to be that a system intruder would have to dial into your network to crack a system. This meant that they would have to find a phone number connected to a modem bank that would give them access, and risk the possibility of the line being traced. But if your corporate network is connected over the Internet and your security is lax, the system cracker might be able to access your network using any standard dial-up account from any ISP in the world. Even unsophisticated users can obtain and use automated "security check" tools to seek out holes in a company's network. What's worse is that, chances are, you'll never know that it's happening.

Before we put our private data out on the Internet, we'd better make sure a VPN is robust enough to protect it.

What Are We Protecting with Our VPN?

The first things that come to mind when you think of protection are the files on your networked computers: documents that contain your company's future plans, spreadsheets that detail the financial analysis of a new product introduction, databases of your payroll and tax records, or even a security assessment of your network pointing out holes and problematic machinery. These files are a good starting point, but don't forget about the other, less tangible assets that you connect to the Internet when you go online. These include the services that you grant your employees and customers, the computing resources that are available for use, and even your reputation. For instance, a security failure can cause your vendors' email to bounce back to them, or prevent your users from making connections to other sites.

The easiest thing would be to isolate, tabulate, and lock down your private data. Well over half the data you manage and distribute might call for some sort of security. Just think, even something as innocuous as customer records and addresses could be used against you in a negative advertising campaign; this might hurt you far worse than a negative campaign aimed at a random slice of the population.

Unfortunately, in the client-server world of telecommuters, field sales agents, and home offices, it's not so easy to keep all private data locked down in a single, protected area. The chief financial officer of a company may need to access financial information on the road, or a programmer working from home may need to access source code. VPNs help alleviate some of the worry of transmitting secure files outside of your network. In Chapter 2, *Basic VPN Technologies*, we will examine possible threats to your network and data, and explore the technologies that VPNs use to avoid them.

How VPNs Solve Internet Security Issues

There are several technologies that VPNs use to protect data travelling across the Internet. The most important concepts are firewalls, authentication, encryption, and tunneling. Here we will give them a cursory rundown, then go into more detail in Chapter 2.

Firewalls

An Internet firewall serves the same purpose as firewalls in buildings and cars: to protect a certain area from the spread of fire and a potentially catastrophic explosion. The spread of a fire from one part of a building is controlled by putting up retaining walls, which help to contain the damage and minimize the overall loss and exposure. An Internet firewall is no different. It uses such techniques as examining Internet addresses on packets or ports requested on incoming connections to decide what traffic is allowed into a network.

Although most VPN packages themselves don't implement firewalls directly, they are an integral part of a VPN. The idea is to use the firewall to keep unwanted visitors from entering your network, while allowing VPN users through. If you don't have a firewall protecting your network, don't bother with a VPN until you get one—you're already exposing yourself to considerable risk.

The most common firewall is a packet filtration firewall, which will block specified IP services (run on specific port numbers) from crossing the gateway router. Many routers that support VPN technologies, such as the Cisco Private Internet Exchange (PIX) and the 3Com/U.S. Robotics Total Control, also support packet filtration. Proxies are also a common method of protecting a network while allowing VPN services to enter. Proxy servers are typically a software solution run on top of a network operating system, such as Unix, Windows NT, or Novell Netware.

Authentication

Authentication techniques are essential to VPNs, as they ensure the communicating parties that they are exchanging data with the correct user or host. Authentication is analogous to "logging in" to a system with a username and password. VPNs, however, require more stringent authentication methods to validate identities. Most VPN authentication systems are based on a shared key system. The keys are run through a hashing algorithm, which generates a hash value. The other party holding the keys will generate its own hash value and compare it to the one it received from the other end. The hash value sent across the Internet is meaningless to an observer, so someone sniffing the network wouldn't be able to glean a password. The Challenge Handshake Authentication Protocol (CHAP) is a good example of an authentication method that uses this scheme. Another common authentication system is RSA.

Authentication is typically performed at the beginning of a session, and then at random during the course of a session to ensure that an impostor didn't "slip into" the conversation. Authentication can also be used to ensure data integrity. The data itself can be sent through a hashing algorithm to derive a value that is included as a checksum on the message. Any deviation in the checksum sent from one peer to the next means the data was corrupted during transmission, or intercepted and modified along the way.

Encryption

All VPNs support some type of encryption technology, which essentially packages data into a secure envelope. Encryption is often considered as essential as authentication, for it protects the transported data from packet sniffing. There are two popular encryption techniques employed in VPNs: secret (or private) key encryption and public key encryption.

In secret key encryption, there is a shared secret password or passphrase known to all parties that need access to the encrypted information. This single key is used to both encrypt and decrypt the information. The data encryption standard (DES), which the Unix *crypt* system call uses to encrypt passwords, is an example of a private key encryption method.

One problem with using secret key encryption for shared data is that all parties needing access to the encrypted data must know the secret key. While this is fine for a small workgroup of people, it can become unmanageable for a large network. What if one of the people leaves the company? Then you're going to have to revoke the old shared key, institute a new one, and somehow securely notify all the users that it has changed.

Public key encryption involves a public key and a private key. You publish your public key to everyone, while only you know your private key. If you want to send someone sensitive data, you encrypt it with a combination of your private key and their public key. When they receive it, they'll decrypt it using your public key and their private key. Depending on the software, public and private keys can be large—too large for anyone to remember. Therefore, they're often stored on the machine of the person using the encryption scheme. Because of this, private keys are typically stored using a secret key encryption method, such as DES, and a password or passphrase you can remember, so that even if someone gets on your system, they won't be able to see what your private key looks like. Pretty Good Privacy (PGP) is a well-known data security program that uses public key encryption; RSA is another public key system that is particularly popular in commercial products. The main disadvantage of public key encryption is that, for an equal amount of data, the encryption process is typically slower than with secret key encryption.

VPNs, however, need to encrypt data in real time, rather than storing the data as a file like you would with PGP. Because of this, encrypted streams over a network, such as VPNs, are encrypted using secret key encryption with a key that's good only for that streaming session. The session secret itself (typically smaller than the data) is encrypted using public key encryption and is sent over the link. The secret keys are often negotiated using a key management protocol.

The next step for VPNs is secure IP, or IPSec. IPSec is a series of proposals from the IETF outlining a secure IP protocol for IPv4 and IPv6. These extensions would provide encryption at the IP level, rather than at the higher levels that SSL and most VPN packages provide.

IPSec creates an open standard for VPNs. Currently, some of the primary VPN contenders use proprietary encryption, or open standards that only a few vendors adhere to. Rather than seeing IPSec as a threat to their current products, most vendors see it as a way to augment their own security, essentially adding another interoperable level to their current tunneling and encryption methods.

We'll go into detail about the power, politics, and use of various encryption techniques in Chapter 2.

Tunneling

Many VPN packages use tunneling to create a private network, including several that we review in this book: the AltaVista Tunnel, the Point-to-Point Tunneling Protocol (PPTP), the Layer 2 Forwarding Protocol, and IPSec's tunnel mode. VPNs allow you to connect to a remote network over the Internet, which is an IP network. The fact is, though, that many corporate LANs don't exclusively use IP (although the trend is moving in that direction). Networks with Windows NT servers, for instance, might use NetBEUI, while Novell servers use IPX. Tunneling allows you to encapsulate a packet within a packet to accommodate incompatible protocols. The packet within the packet could be of the same protocol or of a completely foreign one. For example, tunneling can be used to send IPX packets over the Internet so that a user can connect to an IPX-only Novell server remotely.

With tunneling you can also encapsulate an IP packet within another IP packet. This means you can send packets with arbitrary source and destination addresses across the Internet within a packet that has Internet-routable source and destination addresses. The practical upshot of this is that you can use the reserved (not Internet-routable) IP address space set aside by the Internet Assigned Numbers Authority (IANA) for private networks on your LAN, and still access your hosts across the Internet. We will look at how and why you would do this in later chapters.

Other standards that many VPN devices use are X.509 certificates, the Lightweight Directory Access Protocol (LDAP), and RADIUS for authentication.

VPN Solutions

A VPN is a conglomerate of useful technologies that originally were assembled by hand. Now the networking companies and ISPs have realized the value of a VPN and are offering products that do the hard work for you. In addition, there is an assortment of free software available on the Internet (usually for Unix systems) that can be used to create a VPN. In this book, we're going to look at some of the commercial and free solutions in detail. Which one you choose for your network will depend on the resources available to you, the platforms you run, your network topology, the time you wish to spend installing and configuring the software, and whether or not you want commercial-level support. We can't cover every vendor and product in this book; they change too quickly. Instead, we offer guidelines you can use on all networks and details on a few stable products that were available when we were writing this edition—we don't mean to imply that there's anything less valuable about competing products.

VPN packages range from software solutions that run on or integrate with a network operating system (such as the AltaVista Tunnel or CheckPoint Firewall-1 on Windows NT or Unix), to hardware routers/firewalls (such as those from Cisco and Ascend), to integrated hardware solutions designed specifically for VPN functions (such as VPNet and the Bay Networks Extranet Switch). Some VPN protocols, like SSH or SSL, gained popularity for performing other functions, but have since become used for VPNs as well.

In addition to products, ISPs are also offering VPN services to their customers. The tunneling usually takes place on the ISP's equipment. If both ends of the connection are through the same ISP, that ISP might offer a Service Level Agreement (SLA) guaranteeing a certain maximum amount of latency and uptime.

Quality of Service Issues

Running a virtual private network over the Internet raises an easily forgotten issue of reliability. Let's face it: the Internet isn't always the most reliable network, by nature. Tracing a packet from one point to another, you may pass through a half-dozen different networks of varying speeds, reliability, and utilization—each run by a different company. Any one of these networks could cause problems for a VPN.

The lack of reliability of the Internet, and the fact that no one entity controls it, makes troubleshooting VPN problems difficult for a network administrator. If a user can't dial into a remote access server at the corporate headquarters, or there's a problem with a leased line connection, the network administrator knows there are a limited number of possibilities for where the problem may occur: the machine or router on the far end, the telecommunications company providing the link, or the machine or router at the corporate headquarters. For a VPN over the Internet, the problem could be with the machine on the far end, with the ISP on the far end, with one of the networks in between, with the corporate headquarters' ISP, or with the machine or router at the corporate headquarters itself. Although a few large ISPs are offering quality of service guarantees with their VPN service (if all parties involved are connected to their network), smaller ISPs can't make such a guarantee—and there will always be times when the network administrator is left to her own resources. This book will help you isolate and identify the problem when something goes wrong on your VPN.

A Note on IP Address and Domain Name Conventions Used in This Book

The notation 1.0.0.0/24 is commonly used in describing IP address ranges. It means "start with the address 1.0.0.0 and allow the right-most 8 bits to vary." The 8 is calculated by using 32 bits (the maximum for an IP address) minus 24 (the size specified after the "/"). So 1.0.0.0/24 means all addresses from 1.0.0.0 to 1.0.0.255.

We've elected to use the same IP address ranges and domain name throughout this book. For Internet-routable IP address ranges, we're using the blocks 1.0.0.0–1.255.255.255 (or 1.0.0.0/8) and 2.0.0.0–2.255.255.255 (2.0.0.0/8), which we subnet to suit our needs. These ranges were chosen because they are designated as Internet routable, but are reserved by the IANA and aren't currently being used. We hope that using these ranges, rather than randomly picking some or choosing them from "active" registered networks, will makes examples and figures easier to understand while protecting the innocent. We found that this helped us maintain our own sanity while writing the book.

For internal networks, we use the IP ranges set aside in RFC 1918 for use on private networks. These ranges are 10.0.0.0–10.255.255.255 (or 10.0.0.0/8), 172.16.0.0–172.31.255.255 (or 172.16.0.0/12), and 192.168.0.0–192.168.255.255 (or 192.168.0.0/16). We also subnet these as we deem necessary for an example.

The domain name we use for our examples is *ora-vpn.com*. Within this domain, however, we don't have a hostname convention, because we typically create a hostname to match whatever solution we are writing about in a given chapter.

2

Basic VPN Technologies

This chapter focuses on the background technologies used to build a virtual private network. As we discussed in Chapter 1, *Why Build a Virtual Private Network?*, there are two competing camps at work when we talk about connecting networks. The first camp places the highest worth on the accessibility of data anywhere the user might be, and anywhere the data might be. The second emphasizes that the protection of the data itself, the content, is most important and must be protected to prevent unauthorized persons from using it. As you can see, these two concepts are not at all mutually exclusive, but more of a yin-yang. As you focus on sharing more and more information so that everyone can get what they need, you must also remain focused on the security of that information so that others will not take advantage of you.

Because the Internet is a vast collection of resources, it is clear that sharing your information with other participants can help you prosper. It is not clear, however, at what risk you place yourself when you actually connect. It is our opinion that some companies see the Net as a huge untapped marketplace, full of consumers and advertising opportunities, but don't realize that the Internet has its own version of an "underworld" as well. It is this, above all else, that compels us to protect our data, and where the emergence of the virtual private network presents itself is a stepping stone into the 21st century. The protection of private data is the core of the virtual private network, and the two most relevant technologies (encryption and firewalls) are what make it all possible.

In this chapter we will present an overview and background of the technologies used to build a VPN, and how they are incorporated into the products and services covered in this book. We will start with a discussion of how firewall techniques are used to protect an entire network at its gateway routers. Next, we will present you with a general background on encryption: how it is used in a traditional sense, plus how it will be deployed using a VPN. Following this, we will discuss authentication techniques and how they are used in conjunction with the encryption algorithms with VPNs. Also, we will delve into the protocols that have arisen from the growth of the VPN industry. Lastly, we will briefly cover various compromise methodologies that a potential assailant may use to try to gain access to your private network or data.

Firewall Deployment

The first of the security-related technologies that we cover in this book is the firewall. A firewall is a system that stands between your internal network and the world outside. Firewalls have been employed on large public networks for many years and are a great starting place in the development of a security strategy. The reason to start with firewalls is that they are generally placed at the point at which your network interconnects with a public network, like the Internet. Although not a perfect strategy, a firewall is easy to configure; it requires only the modification of one gateway router. Of course, if you have a large, multiply-connected WAN, with many paths to the Internet, then it should be noted that you will need to create a firewall for each interconnection point. The complexity of this process increases dramatically from the single point gateway to the multiple point gateway.

What Is a Firewall?

The U.S. Department of Defense, probably the world's authority on data sensitivity and security controls, used a system of confidences defined as security levels to restrict access to classified documents. The criteria for determining how a governmental computer should be protected were detailed in the fabled "Orange Book." It stated that to secure highly sensitive data, one must never connect the computer to an exterior network. This is of course the best firewall strategy that exists, but it is too restrictive to be practical. We know the value of interconnection like the rest of you; we just want you to realize that the best firewall for *extremely* sensitive materials is to isolate them on a computer without a network connection at all.

Firewalls usually serve two main functions for a network administrator. The first is to control which machines an outsider can see and the services on those machines with which he can converse. The second controls what machines on the Internet an internal user can see, as well as what services he can use. A firewall is much like a traffic cop, organizing which paths network traffic can take, and stopping some altogether. Internet firewalls usually do this by inspecting every packet that tranverses the gateway router, which is why they are usually referred to as "packet filtration" systems.

Watch out for possible circumvention techniques. The best firewall in the world won't do you a bit of good if there is some backdoor or circumnavigational route the attacker can take. Take care to protect the remote access systems (such as PPP, SLIP, and ARA servers) that allow users to dial directly into your private network. Remember that hackers will try to take these avenues into your site if you allow them. By avoiding the gateway firewalls and all of your cleverly erected traps and pitfalls, a system cracker has only to dial in with a compromised account to gain access to services against which your exterior gateway firewall can't protect. Remember that your firewall is only as strong as its weakest point. No one security package is a comprehensive solution for all of the services your network provides. It is important to conduct an ongoing audit of your access policies and police your site regularly in concert with researching vulnerabilities as they become discovered.

For this chapter, we will use our large branch network as an example. We will further assume that we have a Cisco 2500 series router and 40 workstations. Of the 40 computers, three are servers: one FTP server, one mail server, and one web server. We have a full class C address (2.48.29.0/24) allocated to us from the NIC (Network Information Center); we will be presenting examples throughout this section on how to set up different firewall topologies using our 40 machines and the network provided earlier. Figure 2-1 illustrates what the firewall will be doing in a basic sense for both our large branch as well as our main corporate network (at the top).

What Types of Firewalls Are There?

Since almost all firewalling techniques are designed around a similar model, a centralized point of control, there are only a few variations at the top level that need to be explored. You are probably already familiar with the packet filtration firewall; most people are these days, given the recent attention paid to it by the news media. In this section we will discuss the operation and configuration of four architectures of firewall design. There are many variations of the four that you may have seen implemented, and certainly we are omitting several of the most complex and advanced architectures. But we hope to familiarize you with what a firewall is, how it works, how to set one up, and, most relevant to this book, how it fits into the world of the virtual private network.

Packet restriction or packet filtering routers

Routers and computers that conduct packet filtration choose to send traffic to a network based on a predefined table of rules. The router does not make decisions

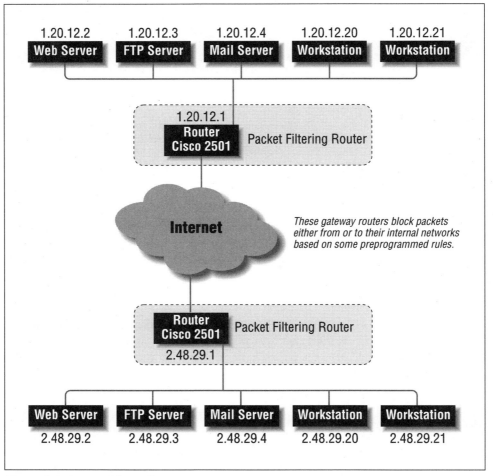

Figure 2-1. A typical firewall

based on what's inside the packet's payload, but rather on where it is coming from and where it is destined. It only considers that if the packet matches a set of parameters, it should take appropriate action to either allow or deny the transit. These allow and deny tables are set up to conform to the overall network security policies put in place by the network administrator or security coordinator.

A peek into the operation of a packet filter shows us that the router never even looks at any of the packet's payload, but only at the TCP/IP header information, to make its screening decisions. Thus, as shown in Figure 2-2, if a router were asked to allow all traffic from network 1.34.21.0/24, it would check all packets for a matching source address and pass them across. Should a packet be received from another network, the filter would disallow the transit, and the packet would be thrown away. So, in essence, this is how the entire operation of this firewall affords security to the site.

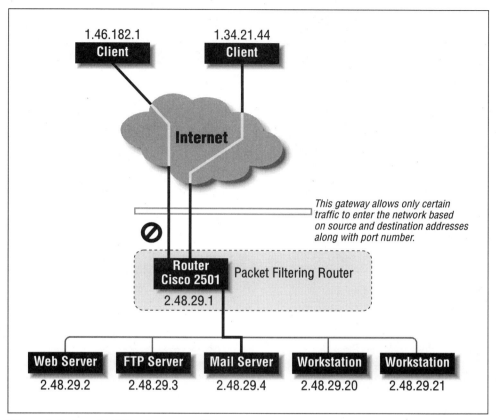

Figure 2-2. A packet filtration router filter

Packet filtering can take on two basic forms. First is an open network with selective filtering of unwanted traffic. For each type of network attack, an appropriate filter must be put in place on the router. Second is the closed network with selective filtering of desired traffic. Although affording greater security, even for those attacks that haven't been thought of yet, the drawback for the network administrator is having to update the firewall as new computers or services are added or changed

As you can guess, a packet filter suffers from several inadequacies. First off, there's no way to do user authentication; either a peer pair is allowed, or it's not. For example, either machine 1.34.21.44 can pass mail traffic (ports 25 and 110) to our mail server on our large network (2.48.29.4), or it can't. There's no provision for *who* is trying to send the mail. Shouldn't it be possible for Bob, one of our employees who is visiting the ZZZ Cyber Coffee Shop (the owners of network 1.34.21.44), to be able to check his email and have a coffee?

Further, be glad for performance reasons that the router doesn't actually open all the packets it gets. Routers these days are asked to perform miracles, especially with the race for more and more bandwidth. The router's job is to decide where to send the traffic, not really to catch and throw away packets that are security risks.

What we're suggesting, of course, is that there will be a marked change in what gateway networks will look like in the future. We believe that there will be a decoupling of routing equipment and packet filtration (or even security equipment, for that matter) in the very near term. Actually, this may already be the case. New products are already coming out that support dynamic authentication through a packet filtering router directly to the user level, even across an encrypted link.

A last impediment is that frequent changes to the network may require wholesale reconfiguration of the gateway router and the packet filtration firewall that lives on it. This can be time-consuming and disaster-prone if either an uncaught mistake leaves most of the network wide open, or a subtle change leaves the router crippled and unable to perform its first duty as a network traffic director.

Bastion host

A bastion host or screening host, as it is sometimes called, uses both a packet filtering mechanism provided by the router plus a secured host. A secured host is one that has had its operating system and major services combed over by a security expert. The primary security is provided by a packet filtering router, and the secured host is used to stage information flow in either direction. The bastion host is a security-checked machine that is connected to the Internet with the same method as other machines. The gateway allows traffic to pass to it in a less restricted fashion. Bastion hosts are typically used in combination with filtering routers because simple packet filtration systems can't filter on the protocol or the application layer. (See Figure 2-3 for a sample configuration.)

A bastion host is much easier to configure than a distributed server and tons easier to maintain, because the bulk of the traffic is being sent to one system. Since the bastion host is situated on the internal wire, it needs no special exemptions from other locally connected equipment. The site's security policy will dictate what needs to be configured on the packet filtering router, which will be as restrictive as necessary. It's not uncommon at all for an administrator to use a combination of strategies, employing both the packet filtering router and a bastion host.One of the great things about the configuration of a bastion host for security measures is that configuration of the packet filter becomes a generic "deny everything" statement, preceded by some very specific allow statements that pertain *only* to the bastion host. For large and quickly changing networks, you can see that this reduces the

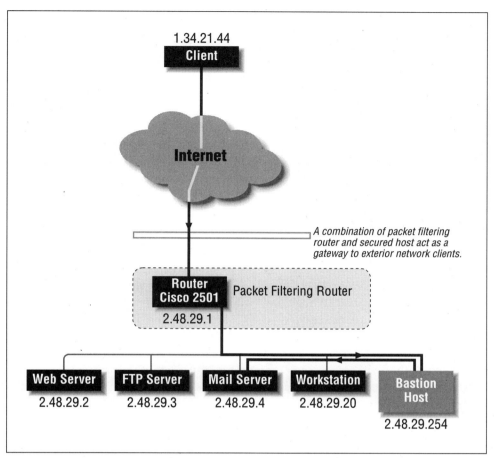

Figure 2-3. A bastion host firewall

load of the security personnel. Adding new machines or having users install poorly secured equipment does not affect the firewall or the protection afforded by the bastion host.

Of course, having a centralized point of control does have its disadvantages. For one, a large, busy network would need several machines acting as bastion hosts (making the administration of them more time-consuming), or even better, a perimeter network of bastion hosts might be required (see the next section). Each machine needs its own section in the packet filtration firewall, piling on complexity, and with each machine comes the headache of having to test and double test it for purity. Along with the need for multiple hosts to prevent network congestion, the centralization of information at the bastion will tend to draw attack attention there, making it ever more important to secure and monitor it around the clock. It should go without saying that a major drawback to this type of firewall configuration is that it can lead to a tragic security hazard should an assailant get system operator privileges on the bastion host. Thus, a single point of control equals a single point of failure.

DMZ or perimeter zone network

A popular ploy to separate large corporate internal networks from the hostile environment of the Net is to erect a "routing network" on which all inbound and outbound traffic must travel. Huge installations normally have such networks already set up so that they can effectively separate the local traffic from the metropolitan traffic from the wide-area or worldwide traffic. As you might have guessed, a routing network consists of only routers, including those both internally and externally connected, and usually goes by the term "backbone." A sample configuration is shown in Figure 2-4.

You might be wondering why the term DMZ is sometimes used interchangeably for a *perimeter zone network*. DMZ stands for "demilitarized zone" and serves the same purpose as it does in areas of geographical conflict: it's a buffer zone between two hostile parties that must coexist in close proximity. In creating a perimeter zone network, the added security you get is multifold. First, there are at least two routers involved in protecting your internal network. One router sits as the gateway to the Internet, and one sits as the gateway to your internal network. The network the two routers share should not have any other host equipment on it other than routing equipment and trusted host equipment (used as a bastion host, detailed earlier).

The second security feature inherent in the DMZ architecture involves a security breach at the outside perimeter router level or at any host on the perimeter network; intruders can sniff only packets transiting through, and nothing else. To gain access to the internal network, they would then have to crack the internal perimeter router, which should dishearten them enough to make them disappear. Plus, a VPN solution from the internal network would almost certainly involve encrypting packets, further complicating a compromise attempt.

In a standard perimeter zone construction, the most complex and careful controls are placed on the internal router, which is the one that separates the internal network from both the perimeter network and the external network. It is a very common practice to erect the DMZ network in this fashion, because this configuration can be likened to tiers of concentric circles—each one further out provides less security. Also, it is becoming common practice to use Network Address Translation (NAT) at the internal router to further complicate locating and hijacking internal communications. NAT provides security by translating non-routable addresses (like the 192.168.0.0 range) into real Internet addresses in a dynamic fashion.

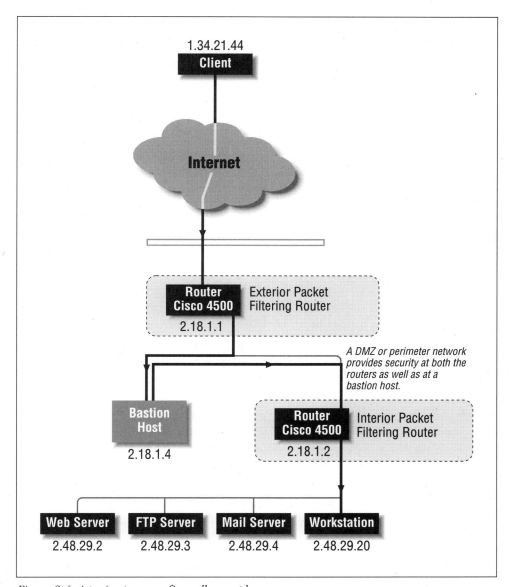

Figure 2-4. A perimeter zone firewall example

There is no easy way to exchange traffic with internal hosts except by circumventing the machine doing the NAT translation.

The tightest security you can make with a DMZ would be to disallow all traffic outbound from the internal network from the exterior router, and to disallow all traffic inbound to the internal network from the Internet. In essence, this makes all traffic a two-step process. Clients on the Internet can peer only with machines that are located on your perimeter network, and clients that are deep inside the internal network can't see the Internet directly; they too need to use a middleman through a bastion host on the DMZ. You can see why this can really ruin an attacker's day. As we stated earlier, most acts of compromise are done by convenience. The harder you make it for the snoops to snoop, the harder you make it for them even to assess the steps required in their warfare, and the more difficult you make their ultimate goal, the faster they are going to evaporate.

Proxy servers

Proxies act much like bastion hosts, and in some firewall texts, the two overlap almost completely. We use the term "bastion host" to refer to a computer that acts as a staging area for information that is in transit either to or from the Internet. We use the term "proxy server" to refer to a type of bastion host that is running specialized software that masquerades as an internal machine to an external one. In the following example, we contrast a typical bastion host and typical proxy server.

A good illustration of an application for a bastion host is email. A bastion host is typically set up to act as the "delivery point" for email inbound from the Internet. Hence a DNS mail exchanger record (MX) is traditionally set up to point traffic to the bastion for delivery. From there, the bastion may re-deliver the mail to an interior mail host (which it can see due to its position in the firewall), or it could hold onto the mail, waiting for the client to read it with a POP mail client. A whole selection of different firewalls can be constructed in this manner.

By contrast, a proxy service is more of an "in-transit" checkpoint than an information staging area. The proxy pretends to be one end of a connection, but protects the true sender or recipient from unwanted traffic. The service that presents the greatest trouble to a security manager's life is the standard file transfer protocol (FTP). It's insecure because it uses random, high-numbered ports to establish a peer-to-peer session with the client. Having a service that operates on more than one port, and especially one that operates on most any port greater than 1023, provides a real nightmare to the security administrator. To address this, a "passive" FTP session can be established (using the control and data ports [20 and 21] for actual data transit rather than one greater than 1023), but not all clients support it.

Using a proxy, as shown in Figure 2-5, is another option for establishing FTP across a firewall. After you set up a host machine on a perimeter network that acts for the client, which is located on the internal network, a full connection can be made with little security to give up. The FTP proxy lives on the perimeter network and is granted access through the exterior firewall to conduct FTP sessions. Special software must be installed on the proxy so that it can accept incoming requests from an FTP client beyond the interior gateway and masquerade as the client in talking to the outside world.

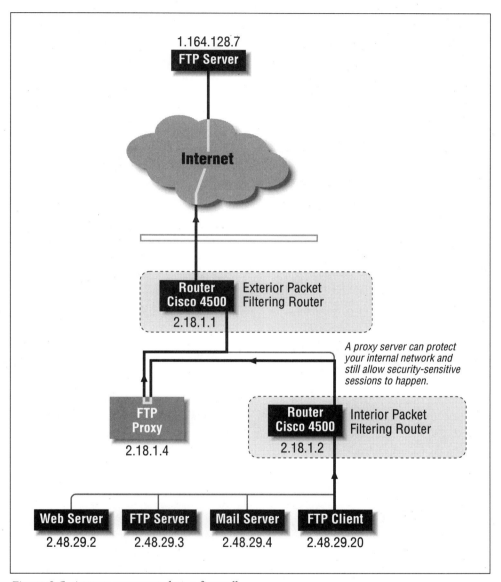

1.164.128.7
FTP Server

Internet

Router
Cisco 4500
2.18.1.1

Exterior Packet
Filtering Router

A proxy server can protect your internal network and still allow security-sensitive sessions to happen.

FTP
Proxy
2.18.1.4

Router
Cisco 4500
2.18.1.2

Interior Packet
Filtering Router

Web Server	FTP Server	Mail Server	FTP Client
2.48.29.2	2.48.29.3	2.48.29.4	2.48.29.20

Figure 2-5. A proxy server used as a firewall

The same security model using proxy servers can be tooled using a dynamic firewall filtration router such as the Cisco PIX or the Firewall-1 system. A more complete description of the PIX's abilities can be found in Chapter 9, *The Cisco PIX Firewall*.

Because a proxy service is more like a host computer than any sort of firewall, special care must be given to ensure that the proxy server is well protected by the site's security policy. Plus, it is important to note that a proxy service is an additional measure of protection and certainly should not be considered a total solution. The shield of a packet filtration firewall can help keep things segregated, and/or the network can be segmented in different subnets, isolating high-risk units from low-risk ones.

Use of Firewalling in a VPN

The importance of firewalling to a virtual private network is straightforward and to the point. Since a VPN is an interconnection of two or more disconnected networks utilizing public resources (such as the Internet) for transit, it follows that these networks individually must be protected in and of themselves. Imagine each network that needs to be placed in a VPN as a separate bubble, with its own connections and users.

Viewed this way, each separate bubble needs a protective wall around it to make it safe from invasion. The concept behind using firewalls with a VPN is to secure the networks as if they were isolated; then the system administrator opens specific ports in the packet filtering router to allow the encrypted data to stream from one bubble to the next. Thus, a private and secure communication (based on the type and implementation of the cryptographic routines used) is set up in a channel between two sites. The VPN software provides the security and the application layer routing, so that the networks in question will appear to be as one when presented to users at either end.

Firewall techniques are the first line of protection in the fabric of a VPN, and they must be developed and tested before the benefits of the VPN can be fully harvested. Even if the VPN software or hardware you deploy has built-in firewalling that seems to be everything you would ever need, chances are that you will need to follow some security guidelines on your network anyway, just to stay on the safe side.

Encryption and Authentication

The configuration and deployment of a virtual private network obviously involves more than just a packet filtration router. Otherwise, all you would have is a smoked glass window hiding your data from the rest of the world. The real concept of this book, and that of the VPN, is the secure communication between two distinct networks over a public medium, done in such a way that they seem to be sharing a LAN from either end. Thus far, our discussion of firewalling techniques only covers half of the equation. Firewalls either allow or deny traffic based on the source and destination, but once the traffic makes it into your network, the disciplines of authentication and encryption add further protection by securing the conversation.

Encryption can be regarded as a method for altering data into a form that is unusable by anyone other than the intended recipient, who has the means necessary to decrypt it. The input to an encryption algorithm is typically called *clear text,* while the output is referred to as *ciphertext* or *crypt text.* The encryption process protects the data by making the assailant work too hard or too long to get at what's being hidden. As we will discover, cryptographic routines use mathematics to alter the data in such a way that the process is difficult and expensive to reverse. As with all things, there are sometimes several ways to peel a banana.

Another important topic that we will discuss in this section—a topic that is closely linked with cryptography—is the art and science of authentication. Where encryption and cryptography deal with the conversion of data into a protected form for transmission to a trusted party in a hostile environment, authentication is the identity checking and confirmation of that entity, which guarantees their claim with a great degree of certainty. The notion of authentication is very important to the concepts employed by creating a VPN. Without knowing with certainty the identity of a participant, how could you entrust a data communication channel to them? It would be like inviting them over to your office and giving them the keys to the filing cabinet and access to a photocopier.

A Brief History of Cryptography

A major tenet of the art and science of cryptography is that the transformation process must be a fairly quick one for the owner of the data (the encryptor)—otherwise it would be too slow to be useful—yet computationally difficult (if intercepted) for a hostile third party to reverse. Hence, most algorithms that morph data for security purposes do so in a way that is programmatically complex. In this section, we will explore the world of ciphers from about five thousand feet up. We will cover some of the nastier mathematics that make encryption work, but we aim to do so in a fashion that won't leave you wanting a degree in higher math.

The algorithms discussed here fall into three basic categories.

The first category of algorithms uses a one-way transformation process to alter the clear text into ciphertext. These transformation programs are typically referred to as *hash* algorithms. The value of hashes and message digests is that they are easy to compute but hard to reverse, and rarely repeat. Hashes don't normally have keys associated with them, as do the next two types of encryption techniques.

The second and third types of encryption algorithms are the *private key* and *public key* cryptosystems. There are other common names for these encryption procedures, including *asymmetric* and *symmetric* algorithms, or *one-key* and *two-key* systems. All these terms refer to the same processes. The *hash* algorithms briefly discussed in the previous paragraph are sometimes referred to as *no-key* or *zero-key* encryption operations because, as the name would suggest, hash algorithms do not use a key.

This brings us to the topic of *randomness* and why pure random numbers are extremely important to the application of these cryptographic concepts. The transmission of encrypted data over a network in a VPN typically requires a key exchange. This means that for each separate transaction between a client and a server, a new set of keys would be produced. Although this may seem unnecessary, it would be disastrous if the same fixed keys were always used and a third party were to gain access to them without the knowledge of either party, or if the message was recorded, cracked, and the keys reused. In essence, the key snoop would be able to decrypt all conversations until the key files were changed, which wouldn't happen unless the parties recognized the attack.

To produce a "cryptographically strong key" on the fly, a computer must have access to a good pool of random numbers. Using something seemingly random, like transformations based on clock time, seconds past a certain fixed date, or other easily obtainable environmental conditions, proves to be an inadequate solution. If the attacker knows that the key generator uses the time of day for the key, it is highly likely that a constrained brute force approach could be used to help narrow the scope of the problem to one that is not computationally infeasible.

Now let's discuss network security and the use of encryption with networking protocols to secure a data transit stream. We know that firewalls aren't 100% airtight: attackers can still use social engineering like password guessing to gain access, circumvent your routers altogether by dialing in directly, or just stubbornly probe all avenues for entry in an exhaustive fashion. So it's wise to add an additional layer of protection: encrypt the data transfer so that even if a snoop were tapping the line, all they would see is "garbage."

One serious flaw (or design element) in using cryptography to seal up data is that it is only a temporary fix. The real comparison should be to use a suitable key length or encryption algorithm that outpaces the ever-increasing advance in technological capabilities. Also, the lifetime of that data itself should be compared in a similar fashion. Using small keys and weak (but fast) encryption techniques is fine for data that will be worthless in 24 hours, especially since it will take a would-be cipher hack more time than that to crack it.

Cryptography: How to Keep a Secret

A good starting point for illustration is the code system generally attributed to Julius Caesar. Caesar swapped each letter in the alphabet for another letter some distance away. Hence, all 26 letters of the standard western alphabet would have a complementary cipher letter which would be used for a coded transmission. For example, the letter "I" could represent "A," the letter "J" could stand for "B," and the letter "K" for "C." The entire alphabet would have such a transposition wrapping from "Z" around to "A" where necessary. As you can see, each letter is replaced by another 8 letters away. Hence, by knowing only one letter transposition, you know them all.

Several modifications make the code more complex, but no harder to break. By assigning random letters to stand for other letters, and by not repeating them, one would need the entire translation table to decrypt a message, rather than just knowing the replacement distance (as in our previous example). But it turns out that knowing the language the clear text is in gives valuable insight into cracking the code. A simple frequency chart plotting letter occurrence produces the clear text with ease.

One protection factor that strengthens the algorithm is not being able to reverse the process. Using variations on the mathematical modulo operation is essential for this. The *mod* operation on two numbers produces the remainder when the first number is divided by the second. For example, 17 mod 3 would be 2, because 17 divided by 3 is 5, with a remainder of 2. It is possible to have a mod value of zero; this would be the case if the operation was, for example, 15 mod 5.

An interesting thing to note about using the mod operation is that ridiculously large numbers can be reduced dramatically by simply moding them by a smaller number. A possibly non-obvious truth to mod math is that the result can never be larger than the second operand in the mod equation less one. Thus, in our first example (17 mod 3), without even knowing the answer, we can guarantee that the answer will *never* be larger than 2. If you produced 5 for an answer, then it too would have been divisible by 3, while still leaving 2 for the answer. In this manner, you can see that even 923897958729349872356 mod 3 still leaves only 0, 1, and 2 for possible answers.

An important point with using the modulo operation is that given one of the operators and the answer, it is impossible to know what the other operand was. For example, if we told you that some number mod 3 produced the answer of 2, could you guess what number we were referring to? Remember that 5 mod 3 = 2, and 8 mod 3 = 2, and 11 mod 3 = 2. You can see the pattern developing easily from here. This (even if simply put) is one reason why it is impossible to reverse a mod equation with exact certainty, and why a decent amount of protection is provided by cipher equations.

Cryptography in Network Communications

Protecting a network conversation is almost as fundamental as having one. The protection part comes from the need to send data over an unknown public network. This is commonly referred to as the "transmission over an insecure channel" problem, and is almost always solved by one of two methods.

The easiest solution is, of course, to make the channel secure by privatizing the medium. If you make sure that third parties do not have access to the physical line, snooping becomes extraordinarily difficult, so the connection is solid. As usual, this is not always the best approach, for several reasons. It is expensive to secure an entire media delivery system, which may be unfeasible as well as impractical to alter in a timely fashion, not to mention that sometimes it is impossible to secure a delivery system to a user's complete satisfaction.

This is exactly the reason why the virtual private network will be deployed on a large scale in the coming years. Since the solution is not to privatize an existing delivery system, it must be to secure the data itself on the insecure channel. In other words, make it accessible for everyone, but transform it in a way (using cryptography) that only an affiliate can undo it.

Cryptographic Algorithms

In the following section we cover the three basic types of encryption algorithms that can be used to protect data. Some of these systems are marginally unsuitable for VPNs, or present administration troubles, and others seem like they were made exactly for protecting network communications.

Hash algorithms

Hash algorithms, which are usually known as message digests or one-way hashes, take an arbitrarily large string and mathematically convert it into a fixed-length, one-way number. Hashes are typically used to check the validity of a particular message or password. A good scenario is one where a system needs to be able to check the authentication of a particular user, but does not want to store an unencrypted password on the disk. Doing so would compromise security for every user on the whole system at once. When the system hashes the passwords and then stores the hash, the attacker who gains access to the password file still has nothing with which to help him. But, he can engage in brute force attacks against all the users at once, which provides adequate reason for the system administrator to keep the hashed password file as safe as possible.

The process of hashing must be fast and reliable, and must produce a result that is fundamentally difficult to reverse. Because there is a loss of data in the production of the hash (e.g., the transformation of a potentially large value into a smaller fixed-length one), a cryptoanalyst has only the tools of brute force attacks, social engineering, or algorithm-specific attacks. It is possible for there to be more than one input value that hashes to the same result. A robust algorithm makes it computationally unfeasible to find two such values easily.

An example of a hash would be to take an input password, multiply it by π (3.1415), divide by e (2.71828), mod the result by 7654321, and take the middle eight bytes. It would certainly be nasty to reverse this process without knowing anything about it.

The NIST's (National Institute of Standards and Technology) proposed message digest function (hash) is called SHA, which stands for "Secure Hash Algorithm." Ron Rivest (he's the "R" in RSA) created a set of hash algorithms, "MD2" through "MD5," which stand for "Message Digests."

Secret key systems

The secret key cryptosystem takes as input a message of a variable length and a secret key by which the message is transformed into the ciphertext. In fact, from a distance the transformation is very similar to the hash algorithms. An important distinction is that a separate user-controlled variable is supplied to help encipher the data. Further, where the hash algorithm creates a fixed length result from a variable length input, the secret key system operates on successive fixed blocks of input using the fixed length key to produce a variable length result. Hash systems are for one-way checks, and secret key systems preserve the entire clear text so that the original text can be produced when needed.

Because the secret key used in the equation is of a fixed length, using a key that is too short reduces the overall security of the system. Imagine using a key that is one byte long (8 bits); it shouldn't take a cryptoanalyst too long to run through the 256 possible keys that could be used to decrypt the data. Since the operation of encrypting the message uses fixed blocks of input, using a message block size of one byte would also be insecure because the cracker would only have to create a table of clear text to ciphertext pairs, once he knows that he could send his own data through the algorithm.

As with hashing systems, the secret key system is designed to take a variable length clear text input and produce a random-looking similarly sized output. Further, changing the input by only one bit should change the output so that there is no way to trace a transformation from bit to bit. The randomness of the ciphered message suggests that at any given time, about half of all the bits in the resulting sequence are on and the other half are off.

Secret key cryptography uses algorithms that effectively disperse the bits completely across the resulting output, and then mix them up by looping multiple

times so that it becomes impossible to trace a given bit through the process and
have any idea of what happened to it along the way. Typically, during the encryption process, there are several operations that can be found in use, including the
substitution of input bits for other input bits, and the swapping of bit positions
with other bit positions.

DES, which stands for the Data Encryption Standard, was developed in 1977 by
the National Bureau of Standards for low-grade U.S. government work and commercial applications. The standard was based on work done earlier by IBM that
was codenamed the "Lucifer Cipher." DES uses a 64-bit key, but trims the last bit
off each of the eight bytes (8 bits each) as a parity check, making the actual key
size only 56 bits. Originally, DES was designed to be used in a hardware-only
implementation, but since there has been phenomenal growth in semiconductor
speeds in just the last few years, it is now just as practical to conduct in software.
This was obviously beyond the intentions of its designers, who had their own
agendas in mind.

IDEA, the International Data Encryption Standard, was originally developed by
Xuejia Lai and James Massey of ETH Zuria. Contrary to DES, IDEA was designed to
be much more efficient when implemented as a software application. Instead of
operating on a 64-bit message block size, with a corresponding 64-bit key size, the
IDEA code uses a 128-bit key to transform a 64-bit message block into a 64-bit
result. Although the algorithm is very new compared with DES and even other
secret key systems, it has proven to be quite secure, and probably superior to DES
in the long run. Both DES and IDEA are similar in that they operate on data one
chunk at a time, performing mathematical transforms based on substitutions and
permutations.

Public key cryptosystems

Public key systems, on the other hand, are a collection of ciphers that do many
different things. Some do digital signatures, some do key exchange, some do
authentication but no encryption, and some do everything. However, they all have
one general concept in common: there are always two components that are used
for operation on the input data. One of the components is the *private* piece and
one is dubbed the *public* piece. An interesting nugget of trivia is that it is irrele-
vant which actual piece is which mathematically, since the two are inverse operations of one another. The thing that separates the two is that the "private" piece is
the part that is secreted away, while the other is distributed. Distributing both
pieces would be like giving away your secret key with each bit of encrypted data
you send.

Diffie-Hellman

The Diffie-Hellman algorithm, generally regarded as the oldest public key system, was based on the problem of how two entities could agree on a secret by using only public channels. It was the genesis of RSA, which we will discuss next, but it provides only a bare skeleton of secret exchange. Diffie-Hellman supports neither encryption nor digital signatures. You might be wondering, without those features, what value could it have?

The Diffie-Hellman algorithm is typically used for quick key exchange. When software is programmed to change its key values every once in a while, or even with every transaction, having a quick way of producing a secret key that both parties know, even by using only a public channel, is required. This is where Diffie- Hellman excels. Imagine two famous people at either end of a restaurant, passing notes to each other that anyone can read along the way. These notes contain the information necessary for the two parties to agree upon a secret key, but it's done so that no one looking at the slips of paper could know what that secret was. Nifty trick, eh? The Diffie-Hellman algorithm is based on a principle involving the concept of a strong prime number.

Diffie-Hellman's weakness is that even though two parties can establish a secret key in a public arena, there could be a masquerader who effectively middlemans between the two parties, completely unobserved. By placing himself in the path, and by catching the right messages, the middleman doesn't need to actually know the secrets, but he can masquerade as the other by misdirection. Suppose an interloping party (let's call him "M") could listen to party A's initial request to B, and respond with M's code pretending to be B. Further, M could copy the message, replace his code for A's, and forward the message on to B to establish a faked conversation that way as well. In this manner, M would have successfully exchanged two secrets (one with both A and B) but without the knowledge of either. A and B think they are talking to each other, but they are really talking indirectly through M.

RSA

RSA gets its name from its inventors: Rivest, Shamir, and Adleman. It is a public key system supporting both encryption and decryption with a variable length key. Using a long key increases security, but at the cost of performance; likewise, a short key is quick to compute, but is less secure. The RSA algorithm, as implemented, typically uses a 512-bit key, with an upper range of about 4K bits. Larger keys than that become unwieldy to use given today's computing power. It's nice to know that as long as the underlying principles of the algorithm are safe, meaning that no one has been able to break the fundamental problem of factoring quickly, then as computing power increases, both attacker and protector enjoy an equal gain in performance.

Unlike private key encryption, the message block length (i.e., the size of the chunk of message to be operated on) is also variable. Unlike DES and IDEA, RSA's message block length can be almost anything. However, it must be equal to or smaller than the size of the key to prevent an easy security breach via a brute force search of the possible ciphered alphabet. Regardless of message block size, the ciphertext block size will always equal the size of the key.

Because RSA uses the principles of gigantic prime numbers to base its equations on, as well as modulo exponentiation arithmetic, the RSA algorithm is much slower than almost any of the popular secret key systems (including the ones discussed previously, DES and IDEA).

To use the RSA algorithm, one generates what is commonly referred to as a key pair. The first step in doing this is to choose two large prime numbers. Numbers in the 50 to 100 digit range are typical. Call these p and q. Multiply them together to get the result n. From there, using mathematical magic, you would choose a number e that is relatively prime with respect to the totient function of n.* We won't bore you with the mechanical intricacies of how exactly this is done. Suffice to say that a pair of numbers is produced, e and d, with the odd property that one is the multiplicative inverse of the other with respect to an equation where mod n is used. From here the combination of $\{d,n\}$ is referred to as the private key, and the set $\{e,n\}$ is the public key. In actuality, since one is the exact inverse of the other (given the equation $de = 1$ mod totient(n)), it doesn't matter at all which is the public one and which is the private one. The one that you keep hidden is the private one.

The RSA algorithm used for encryption and decryption is essentially the same. Given that e and d are inverses, encryption is the process of running the message with the public key forward through the algorithm, while the act of decryption is also running the ciphertext through the algorithm with the other key. Specifically, the encryption routine consists of taking the clear text chunk and raising it to the power of e mod n, and decryption is essentially taking the ciphertext and raising it to the power of d mod n.

How Secure Is It Really?

Given the explosive increase in computing resource power every year, data stored in encrypted form gets less and less secure. As we discussed earlier, the life of a particular piece of encrypted data or even the life of an encryption algorithm itself is governed by the raw processing power that can be leveled against it. The

---

* When n is a positive integer, Euler's totient function is defined to be the number of positive integers not greater than n and relatively prime to n.

greater the MIPs rating, the greater the threat and the faster the data falls to a simple brute force attack.

DES, in particular, has been the focus of some discussion concerning its security into the 21st century. One of the reasons for its waning protection is that it uses only 56 of the 64 bits of its key. Although it cannot be considered academic for another few years yet, the possibility of creating a simple and widely distributed software brute force crack of DES is looking quite real just on the horizon. As of July 1998, a cheap hardware DES cracker was demonstrated by the Electronic Frontier Foundation, constructed of off-the-shelf components. One way to combat these threats is to multiply encrypt the inputs. The "triple-DES" standard is such an implementation, and given that it increases the number of possible keys, it effectively removes any threat for the foreseeable future.

RSA's strength is derived from the inability to factor a huge number quickly. As we discussed in the explanation of the RSA algorithm earlier, the sheer size of the numbers that are used is enormous, large enough that it surpasses that number of bits that even large computers use to store numbers internally. Think about it in terms of how many digits you could put into a calculator. The bigger problem is that even if you could represent the numbers in a way that a computer can handle, the act of factoring is a long and tedious process without shortcuts and without easy, simplifiable steps. Because of this, you could spend a great deal of time just looking through billions of numbers and never finding a factor of n. Remember that if you wanted to crack RSA, the surefire way of doing it would be to recreate the original inputs used to calculate d and e. That means factoring n.

Use of Cryptosystems and Authentication in a VPN

As with all secure communications, all protection systems have three important functions in common. Secure communications first protects the data in transit so that hostile or curious third parties in the middle are not able to intercept and read the transmission (this is the concept of *encryption*). Popular encryption techniques used in VPNs include DES, Triple DES, RC2, and RC4.

Second, both parties must know with confidence that they are speaking to one another. In other words, Alice is certain she is speaking with Bob, and vice versa, even though they can not see each other (this is the idea of *authentication*).

Lastly, both Alice and Bob need to be able to detect if any third party is trying to tamper with the messages, either with a destructive goal (like the insertion of many messages to prevent Alice from reaching Bob) or even a benign one (like infrequently inserting garbage to test a hypothesis). This is the concept of *message integrity*, and is sometimes referred to as a *message digest* (for example: MD5 or SHA).

How all of this ties together can be illustrated by a short scenario. When Bob wants to send a message to Alice, he would first run his clear text through a message digest function that would produce a hash code or a message authentication code (MAC code), which would be encrypted with his own private key, then included with the message itself, and then the whole thing would be encrypted with the receiver's public key. After transmission, the receiver would decrypt the whole package with her private key, compute her own MAC code from the now clear text document, decrypt the sender's MAC code with his public key, then compare the MAC code she locally created to the one sent in transit. If they differ, tampering has occurred.

Sun's SKIP protocol is a fairly popular implementation of encryption and authentication, comparable to the IPSec standard discussed later in this chapter. SKIP is available from various vendors on a number of Unix operating systems as well as Windows. Each host using SKIP maintains an access control list specifying which hosts it's willing to receive traffic from and what type of encryption to use for each one. When an IP packet is sent from one SKIP host to another, the sender encrypts the packet with the SKIP protocol and then wraps another IP packet around it so it can go over the general Internet.

The keys to erecting a private data exchange or a secured data store rely on being able to fence out unwanted people and place locking boxes around what you wish to protect. Without firewalls, a VPN could exist, albeit without the same security philosophy. But, without encryption, a VPN most certainly could not exist. Cipher routines solve the fundamental problem of secure communication over an insecure channel in a hostile environment.

Using the components of encryption, authentication, and integrity, we will next explore the different protocols that are used to build VPNs. After that, we will briefly delve into the different compromise methodologies that can be leveled against these security schemes.

VPN Protocols

Coming from different directions and supporting different products and services, several security protocols have been in development over the last few years. We will start with one that has firmed up only recently, but will probably become nearly universal—the IPSec standard.

IPSec

Over the years as vendor after vendor labored over reinventing wheels, trying to hide IP packets in a secure protocol, people began to wonder why the TCP/IP protocol itself wasn't updated to support authentication and encryption. That way, the network itself is secure and everything built upon it must also be secure. IPSec is the answer to this question.

The Internet Security Protocol (IPSec) is a generic structure initiated and maintained by a working group of the Internet Engineering Task Force (IETF) to provide various security services for the Internet Protocol (IP), for both IPv4 (the current standard) and IPv6 (the upcoming one). IPSec presents design goals for a top-level component-oriented structure, rather than detailing specific encryption algorithms or key-exchange methodologies.

Conceptually, IPSec was created to secure the network itself, presenting no real changes to the applications that run above it. Since the TCP/IP protocol is so ubiquitous, it is a natural evolution to produce a secure network system developed almost in parallel to the existing system. Upgrading to IPSec products and services will only enhance security, as current network-oriented applications can still be used to transport data.

The IPSec documents produced by the IETF are predominantly concerned with three basic areas of securing the IP protocol: encryption algorithms, authentication algorithms, and key management. These components help define the entire architecture of a security scheme, generically making the IPSec structure insensitive to the fast-paced, changing world of authentication and encryption algorithms. It is expected that new algorithms will be presented for use as times change and computing services emerge. IPSec is designed so that new methods can be added to the suite with very little work and little effect upon previous implementations.

The two key benefits derived from IPSec compliance are that products or services sporting IPSec gain additional security features as well as interoperability with other IPSec products. Enhanced security means that only the most comprehensive and most robust authentication, key-exchange, and encryption algorithms, hardened for use in the real world, will be used. Interoperability is also a must in today's world, where many different products will be expected to communicate securely with one another.

Although IPSec is still undergoing change, much of the basic framework has been frozen enough for vendors to finalize, test, and distribute their VPN products. It is a common consensus that the "finalized" IPSec standard won't be solidified until the end of 1998 or the beginning of 1999.

IPSec was designed to support two encryption modes. The *transport* mode protects only the payload portion of each packet, while the *tunnel* mode encrypts both the header and the payload. Logically enough, the tunnel mode is more secure, as it protects the identity of the sender and receiver, along with hiding certain other IP fields that may give a middleman useful information.

For IPSec to work as expected, all devices must share a common key. Even though the protocols used to cipher the data are very important to the overall success of the system, a great deal of work has gone into the authentication and exchange of keys by the sender and the receiver. Of course, this effort wasn't done in a vacuum, as it builds upon the body of work done to create and swap keys using public digital certificates. This is largely accomplished through the ISAKMP/Oakley protocol (now updated to the IKE protocol) and the X.509 digital certificate system.

IPSec security issues

In order to erect a tunnel between two networks using IPSec (or any protocol, for that matter), each having a firewall on the Internet, you have to make sure both gateways have similar security policies. Different architectures could lead to one network being less secure than the other, and would draw attention to compromising the system there. Such a fault could lead to an attacker having access to the more secure network by sophisticated masquerading.

IPSec, if used with a bastion host, could also adversely affect the performance of the network. Bastion hosts have long been considered a substandard method for securing a network, as they restrict the traffic to a few points of failure. When you add the computationally expensive process of random number generation, key exchange, and strong payload encryption, a bastion host is burdened to the edge of its feasible limits. Further, it is likely that bastion hosts will handle these algorithms in software using a general-purpose microprocessor, whereas dedicated solutions positioned at an organization's gateway would use specialized hardware to accomplish the same task.

Other network security systems, such as PPTP, rely predominantly on securing higher-level communications. While these methods have met with some success in their arenas, they are still very focused solutions that require complex and in-depth knowledge of how to configure and maintain them. The flexibility and power derived by using TCP/IP can be extended to IPSec, and should prove to be a long-term and stable answer to the network security puzzle.

IPSec organizations

The Internet Engineering Task Force maintains the IPSec charter on their site, which is updated regularly. You can find it at *http://www.ietf.org/html.charters/ ipsec-charter.html*.

A large-scale practical example for pioneering work with the emerging IPSec standard can be seen in the vendors supporting the Automotive Network Exchange (ANX), a consortium of automakers. With more than 30 members participating in furthering the role of IPSec in equipment testing, interoperability, and functional requirements, great leaps of advancement were made. It is important to note that the work done at the IPSec technical roundtables on the ANX project contributed a great deal to the roll-out of the somewhat firm IPSec standard of the summer of 1998. More information can be found at *http://www.aiag.org*.

Another important consortium, the Internet Computer Security Association, is an independent organization that oversees the certification of security products, services, systems, and people. It is a member-oriented company that strives to build public confidence in the improved security of global computing systems. Developers, manufacturers, experts in cryptography and security, and users of computer systems make up the bulk of the ICSA. The ICSA has been active in the certification of IPSec products that have recently been brought to market. To learn more about the ICSA and to review their activities and charter, visit their web site at *http://www.icsa.net*.

ESP (Encapsulating Security Payload)

The fundamental unit of transmission on the Internet is the IP (Internet Protocol) packet, upon which most WAN and LAN communications rely. IPSec handles encryption right at the IP datagram level using a new protocol, the Encapsulating Security Protocol (ESP). ESP was designed to support almost any sort of symmetric encryption, such as DES or triple DES. Currently, ESP relies minimally upon 56-bit DES. ESP also supports some authentication, partially overlapping with the next IPSec protocol we will discuss: AH, the Authentication Header. Generally, ESP can be used inside another IP packet, so that ESP can be transported across regular IP communications channels. Instead of the normal TCP or UDP packet designation, the header information would declare the packet's payload to be ESP instead. Because it is encapsulated in this fashion, ESP can be transported across legacy networks, and is immediately backward compatible with the bulk of the hardware used to route networks today.

AH (Authentication Header)

Where ESP secures the data by encryption, the Authentication Header (AH) protocol of IPSec handles only the authentication, without confidentiality. The AH protocol can be used in conjunction with ESP, in tunnel mode, or as a stand-alone authenticator. The Authentication Header protocol handles securing the IP header information, where ESP is concerned with the payload. To support a base functionality, IPsec requires that implementations of AH contain HMAC-SHA and

HMAC-MD5 (HMAC is a symmetric authentication system supported by these two hashes).

Internet Key Exchange, ISAMKP/Oakley

In the parlance of the IPSec working documents produced by the IETF, a "Security Association" is any protected conversation between two (possibly hostile) parties. Having only ESP and AH does not complete the picture for an IPSec system. For secure communication, both parties must be able to negotiate keys for use while the communication is happening. Plus, both parties need to be able to decide which encryption and authentication algorithms to use. The Internet Key Exchange (IKE) protocol (formerly known as ISAKMP/Oakley) provides authentication of all peers, handles the security policies each can perform, and controls the exchange of keys.

Key generation and key rotation are important because the longer the life of the key, the larger the amount of data at risk, and the easier it becomes to intercept more ciphertext for analysis. This is the concept of *perfect forward secrecy*. By changing the keys often, it becomes difficult for a network snoop to get the big picture if they have to keep cracking keys. Further, the keys generated on the fly should *not* bear any resemblance to one another, and should *not* be generated from environmental variables that could easily be guessed (time of day, server load, etc). IKE uses the Diffie-Hellman key exchange protocol to handle this, and has proven to be adequate in its protection.

ISO X.509 v.3 (Digital Certificates)

Although not a security protocol in the same fashion as ESP and AH, the X.509 system is important because it provides a level of access control with a larger scope. Because the X.509 certificate systems are used with other Public Key Infrastructure devices and software, IPSec vendors have chosen to incorporate them into their equipment to handle authentication. Certificate management, as handled by a trusted third party, will play a big role in the future of the IPSec suite, and work is already being done by vendors to have their products communicate with the public CAs (Certificate Authorities) for authentication.

LDAP (Lightweight Directory Access Protocol)

Closely related to the X.509 system is the Lightweight Directory Access Protocol, or LDAP. LDAP is a smaller, and logically easier to implement, X.500 service that is supported on various VPN solutions to provide authentication and certificate management. Hardware products like the Bay Networks Extranet Switch use LDAP as well as some popular software solutions, such as Windows NT and Novell. It is becoming more common to use trusted third-party authentication systems (such as LDAP and the X.500 directory system) for remote access to a corporate network (or a VPN).

Radius

Where LDAP and the X.500 systems provide authentication and certificate management to users anywhere in the world, Radius is an authentication system used more for intra-organization lookups. The Radius system was developed as an open standard by Livingstone Enterprises, and is not currently sanctioned by the IETF, but is under consideration. Recently, Merit updated the Radius system to enhance its client/server capabilities and its vendor specific attributes, allowing manufacturers to tailor their products and services to specific markets. More VPN solutions currently support authentication using Radius than the other public certificate systems mentioned above, but a groundswell of support for the X.500 system is well underway.

PPTP (Point-to-Point Tunneling Protocol)

The Point-to-Point Tunneling Protocol (PPTP) is an extension of the standard PPP (Point-to-Point) Protocol. The tunneling services provided by PPTP are intended to ride on top of the IP layer, whereas the traditional PPP protocol underlies IP. PPP was ideally suited for modification because its functionality already mimics the behavior of what a VPN would need: a point-to-point tunnel. All that was missing was the security. PPTP, however, is more of a host-to-host secure communications channel, rather than a LAN-to-LAN one. Although it is quite possible to route traffic across a PPTP tunnel, the IPSec solutions are better geared for this type of application.

Methodologies for Compromising VPNs

In this section we vicariously take on the role of the people we are trying to thwart: those who want to inspect, intercept, and interfere with the transmission of your data.

Basic Firewalling

Services that you will likely offer to the Internet include mail (such as the POP, SMTP, and IMAP protocols), World Wide Web (HTTP and HTTPS protocols), and a host of other things including DNS, FTP, video or audio streaming, and network time. Our discussion of services plays directly into the first section, where we begin to explore one of the introductory yet powerful ways for protecting data (firewalls).

Although they are not tangible like data files that contain customer credit card numbers, services that you choose to offer your customers on the Internet play a huge role in defining the form the firewall takes and what types of data you think will assist the customer. Before even embarking on the creation of the firewall, you need to develop an overall data strategy. What do customers have access to? What do normal employees have access to? What can advanced security folks see and do? Once you have spent some time in detailing the blueprint for your network, you can begin to create the doors and windows that permit visitors.

Some popular services are sometimes dangerous to run, and come with security dilemmas that we can never seem to shake, but are so important that we would argue against removing them. The application that receives the most attention by security professionals is *sendmail*. The reasons for this are simple: the source code for the most popular implementation of sendmail (the Berkeley Version 8 software) is readily available and the running daemon is easily located on someone's network. Because of this, pay careful attention to the sendmail servers that are available to the public and how they are configured.

Our ultimate goal in setting up security barriers is to make a break-in too time-consuming, too difficult to complete, and once completed, too unrewarding to make it worth a cracker's time and effort. If you look like a terrible target, they will go elsewhere and leave you alone. Most computer crimes are much like everyday "real" crimes—they are crimes of convenience that could be avoided by erecting a minimal deterrent.

Cryptographic Assaults

It is probably unlikely that a cryptoanalyst will spend a great deal of time cracking private VPN traffic between two different sites. The compromise methodologies used to assault crypto schemes are sometimes complicated and time-consuming. Therefore, the following different attack mechanisms are illustrations of the tools used in analysis work. It is highly likely that interested individuals and organizations will develop applications to conduct these assaults. It is also reasonable to predict that such tools will be made widely available in the foreseeable future.

Ciphertext-only attack

The cryptoanalyst uses captured ciphertext, as much as can be obtained, to try to deduce the plaintext or reverse generate the keys (if possible). The purpose of this assault is ultimately to have keys to unlock new messages sent across the wire, with the sender and receiver oblivious to the fact that the eavesdropper can capture and read their messages. By using a faster key generation and exchange system, you can multiply the work of the cryptoanalyst by the number of keys used.

Known plaintext attack

The cryptoanalyst has access to the plaintext that produced certain ciphertext messages as well as the ciphertext itself. The goal is to either deduce the keys used to encrypt the data or develop an algorithm that produces similar results that can be used in reverse.

Chosen plaintext attack

Here, the cryptoanalyst has both the ciphertext and the plaintext as well as the ability to send his own plaintext through the algorithm to produce new ciphertext. This assault could also be used to insert correctly ciphered garbage into a communications stream, but since that provides such a small lever, the goal of the analyst would still be to recover the keys, so that he can either listen to communications as they happen, or intrude upon them by staging a man-in-the-middle attack.

Chosen ciphertext attack

Much like the chosen plaintext attack, it is assumed that the cryptoanalyst has somehow gotten a black box that does decryption based on an input of ciphertext. The attacker can pick and choose which ciphertext he wants to decrypt. Chosen ciphertext attacks can be used against public key systems such as RSA. For more technical detail on the weaknesses of RSA as an implemented protocol (not necessarily attacks upon the algorithms itself), consult Bruce Schneier's *Applied Cryptography* (John Wiley and Sons, Inc., 2nd Edition, 1996), probably one of the premier works done in the field.

Brute force attacks

A standard attack plan for a cipher cracker is to use what we call the "brute force" attack upon the algorithm. This assumes that the cracker has intercepted an encrypted message and knows the algorithm used to produce it, but doesn't know the key. Depending on the amount of time he is willing to invest in using a crowbar and whether he started with a key of all zero bits set, he should eventually find the key just by trying to decrypt the data with each successive key (adding the next large bit), and looking at the output. Some assumptions in cracking things this way are that he must be able to identify the output as cracked when it actually is. If the clear text were English text, then it shouldn't be too hard, but what if the input data was another crypted message? This would ensure that all brute force outputs would look like garbage, even in the event of a successful crack. Another assumption is that there is time enough to spend cycling through all possible keys. If the encryption algorithm is slow, it may take a second or so to calculate the cipher; if there are several billion combinations for the key, the amount of time needed to crack the code would be between 50 and 100 years. We are not that patient, and figure that no one else is either.

Password guessers and dictionary attacks

If you are not familiar with *Crack,* the most common of the tools available to the would-be break-in artist, establish a way to check your own passwords by using it. Although we covered the DES encryption algorithm in detail previously in this chapter, we will present a short discussion on password cracking. *Crack* is available from *http://www.10pht.com/.*

Most computers use the DES algorithm to protect the passwords on the authentication system. Unix systems, which account for the bulk of the Internet-based systems, are the largest installed base of DES authentication units.

Simply put, DES takes a user's clear text password, like the example password "MucH007", and converts it into a 13-character pile of seeming gibberish, such as "HnX2a4gLaMv3k." It is mathematically difficult to divine the original password from the encrypted one using brute force. So password-guessing programs don't try every possible string; they reduce the number of tries to a more feasible level by guessing what sorts of passwords people are likely to use. The *Crack* password-guessing program uses a dictionary of common words (in several languages), including a ton of proper nouns such as people's names and places, and tries them as the password. This is why you hear your system administrator trying to persuade you to use something uncommon or something unnatural as a password. Simple passwords are almost equivalent to having no password at all.

Social engineering

Don't think that all threats come from the online front. One of the most traditional cracks is simply to call a person and ask them questions. Or, send them a survey, ripe with personal queries, and a $20.00 bill, "for their trouble." You would be amazed at what people will tell you. This is how system attackers might get potential material for assisting them in piecing together password attempts. As we discussed earlier, a brute force hack of a password may take months (on a fairly significant machine), yet by reducing the total combinations to just "real" words found in a dictionary, in turn reducing the time spent on cracking that user to about 10 to 15 minutes, you can see where using personal information can drive guessing even complex passwords down to a trivial amount of time. Semi-public data such as phone numbers, birthdays, license plates, girlfriends, and favorites (movies, music, stores, etc.), can provide valuable resources to a password cracker. Social engineering can come in many forms, and is generally regarded as the easiest and most successful attack. Remember, even your 1024-bit RSA private key is protected by a passphrase or password that could be easily socially engineered.

Network Compromises and Attacks

Why would somebody want to hurt your site? If you have any public visibility, you could well attract unwanted attention from unsavory characters who are holding a grudge, nosy competition trying to ferret out new product information, or disgruntled employees out for a joyride.

Denial of service attacks

These types of attacks are usually hate- or vendetta-driven, because they have only one aim: to prevent you (or anyone else, for that matter) from using your own equipment. A couple of strategies of this nature are: flooding a network interface with traffic, making use of the whole network impossible, or sending specific "invalid" packets to a computer that cause it to crash several times an hour. A good analogy for this type of attack would be someone wasting your whole afternoon by repeatedly calling you and hanging up. Although there is little you can do in this instance, once an attack is isolated, a system administrator can use a firewall to block inbound requests that would normally cripple the machine or the network. Unfortunately, there is only experimental work being done right now that would allow a "scanning" process or router to dynamically block such attacks when it notices them and verifies that they are valid threats.

Address spoofing

TCP/IP, because of its widespread use, large-scale deployment, and ongoing worldwide development, is definitely the *lingua franca* of the Internet and will continue to be so. Enhancements to the lower levels of the protocol (such as IPSec) will not only support IP's use in a worldwide environment to deliver data, but will do so securely. The strengths derived from using the current IP implementation, unfortunately, make the protocol unsecure. Because of how packet routing works and how header information is constructed, it becomes very difficult to conclusively prove the path a packet takes from point A to point B, and difficult to guarantee that some packet originated from A to begin with. Because of this, attackers can masquerade or spoof their target's routers and systems into thinking packets originated from someplace they did not. By doing this, all manner of mischief can be wrought.

Session hijacking

By building a foundation of IP source spoofing in the above example, an attacker can effectively hijack an entire session between A and B. The parties need not be two individuals sending messages back and forth. More than likely, one of the parties involved will be a server of some sort, which the attacker will impersonate during the span of the communication. By posing as an organization's mail server or file server, he can collect a ton of private material and analyze it at his leisure.

Man-in-the-middle attack

Also built on the foundation of IP address spoofing, an attacker can not only stage a session hijack, but can also mimic A and complete the original requests made to B directly. Imagine that we are M, and are able to convince A we are B, and B we are A. Traffic sent to B from A could be caught by M, analyzed, modified, stored or merely witnessed, and then sent on to B, no one at all the wiser. Traffic returning from B to A could be treated in a similar fashion. The VPNs discussed in the book rely upon sophisticated techniques for combating the man-in-the-middle attack, sometimes relying upon per-packet or time-oriented authentication, or even the quick shifting of keys.

Replay attack

A replay attack is essentially what would happen if an attacker were to record a transmission from A to B, even if the attacker is unable to read the message, then replay the message at a later time. Sometimes attacks of this nature can work if used in concert with an IP spoofing assault or even a man-in-the-middle one. Some VPNs combat this threat by serializing the packets, some by encapsulating the IP header as well as the datagram, and some by using synchronized time-stamping. A combination of these techniques could also be used.

Detection and cleanup

Computer break-in incidents are difficult to detect and more difficult to prosecute. According to the Computer Emergency Response Team (CERT), a full 35% of all high-degree break-ins go completely undetected by the system administrators responsible for the equipment compromised; an even higher 85% of all incidents go unreported.

Sometimes it is only by accident that an administrator notices the tell-tale symptoms of a break-in. Strange things found in the temporary directory, strange processes running, applications found that were not distributed with the operating system, and users reporting that they are having trouble logging in or have "forgotten" their passwords somehow are clues. When attackers are careful to clean up after themselves, the odds that someone will notice decrease dramatically. If they are careless or just joyriders, detection is much easier and cleanup is simpler. The biggest gut-wrenching feeling occurs when the attacker seems not to have changed anything. If only a minimal clue to their penetration is left, you can be assured that you need to sanitize—and quickly.

For a whole host of security-related documents, including current advisories, check with CERT directly at *http://www.cert.org*.

In closing, always try to be quick to respond to any threat or apparent break-in as soon as you are notified or as soon as you discover it. The faster you are at taking care of things, the less impact there is overall. Even though you are sure to have a restricted budget and inadequate resources for your security efforts, try to follow through with all measures you can take to pursue the attackers. If they think you are too busy or uncaring, they will come back, with better tricks and harsher consequences.

Be attentive to what they were trying to do as well as what they did. If you can connect the dots, you may put yourself in front of them, and possibly even catch them. Don't just assume they will disappear or that they "didn't really do anything anyway." Just to reiterate: keep good backups, change user accounts and passwords regularly, and develop a registry for access and authentication levels that can be deployed organization-wide.

Patents and Legal Ramifications

Cryptographic routines are complex mathematical systems, and the people who have created them are experts who have spent a great deal of resources to create and protect their systems. As any good lawyer will tell you, intellectual property is just as tangible as real property, and in some cases easier to support in a court of law. Even using some technologies could constitute a legally binding agreement with the software's creators, so you need to take care when dealing with any and all such systems.

The U.S. government classifies all encryption routines as munitions, which is to say that they consider the mathematical formulas that protect data a dangerous technology. Cryptography, to the Feds, is the same as treason, illegal arms trading, smuggling, racketeering, and drug sales. The boys on the Hill do not take such matters lightly, either. You may ask yourself, "How could a little code hurt the giant U.S. government or its citizens?" To learn exactly why the government treats these technologies with such kid gloves, we have to look back at some historical elements. Remember the "enigma" box? It was a WWII German code box that scrambled military orders sent from the high command to the field. Along similar lines, the Japanese had developed a system involving a code box called "Purple." In times of war, code cracking and encryption take on a very important role, best described by the saying: "loose lips sink ships." The protection of even simple communication is of paramount importance to the government. If all the routines developed on U.S. soil were exported abroad with no restrictions and a war were to break out, it would be unclear to our military leaders if their communications were safe.

Products and services described in this book may be prohibited from being exported outside of the United States, or crippled in such a way as to make them freely exportable. Generally a reduction in the size of the key used to encrypt the data allows for a license to ship overseas. International organizations are already working on strong world-wide encryption technologies, and we are sure that the next 10 years will paint a new landscape of the data protection universe.

One typical legal protection that a cryptographic creator has is the patent. DES, contrary to popular belief, *is* patented, but it is distributed royalty-free, which is one of the reasons why it pops up almost everywhere. All public key (two-key) systems are patented as well, by either RSA Data Security Inc., or by the Public Key Partners (PKP) group (see Table 2-1). Obviously they make it their business to collect license fees and monitor for stray usages of their software.

Table 2-1. Cryptographic Patents

Encryption Routine	Patent Information
Hellman-Merkle	Patent #4,218,582, expired August 19, 1997. Supposedly covers all public key systems.
Rivest-Shamir-Adleman	Patent #4,405,829, expires September 2, 2000. Covers the RSA algorithm.
Hellman-Pohlig	Patent #4,424,414, expires January 3, 2001. Related to Diffie-Hellman (expired 1997).
Schnorr	Patent #4,995,082, expires February 19, 2008. The DSS Algorithm is based on this.
Kravitz	Patent #5,231,668, expires July 27, 2008. The actual DSS Algorithm.

3

Wide Area, Remote Access, and the VPN

Even though this book is about virtual private networks, we're prepared to admit that a VPN is not always the best networking solution. This chapter compares its costs and benefits, in very general terms, to two industry standard alternatives: a wide area network (in which you lease dedicated lines between sites) and remote access (in which users dial up banks of modems at a central site). Each solution has its merits and flaws, and likewise, each has its comparative cost points.

We do not offer an exhaustive price list, as this chapter would reach the size of an entire book (and the prices change weekly anyway). What we do cover, however, is each solution's pros and cons and some price breakpoints for general comparison. This will at least allow for an informed decision on where to begin researching your own WAN/RAS/VPN solution.

General WAN, RAS, and VPN Concepts

All three of these networking solutions provide the same result: connection of remote users to private network resources. Likewise, each has its own set of parameters that maintain three important networking concepts: security, scalability, and stability. Finally, all three have similar pieces that can be assigned a breakdown cost: telecommunication lines, networking hardware/software, and system administration. All six of these generic concepts will be used to compare the three networking solutions in the following sections.

A wide area network, or WAN, consists of two or more networks connected via dedicated and private telco lines. This could cover anything from two computers dialed in via a dedicated frame relay line (similar in concept to retail credit card clearing devices), to several large regional office networks connected to a central office over private ATM lines. Figure 3-1 depicts a simplified WAN, with its basic component parts: networks, gateway routers, and telco lines.

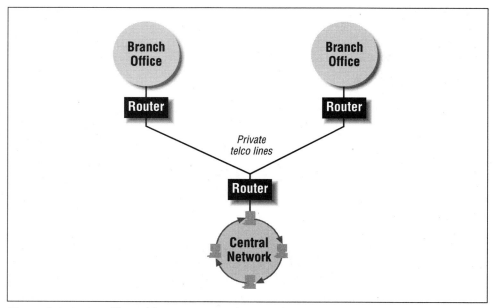

Figure 3-1. A typical leased line connection between two enterprise networks

Remote access services, or RAS, is composed of banks of incoming, on-demand telco lines for connecting remote users or networks. This could range from a terminal server with several modems to a RAS server with incoming PRI lines (PRIs are digital T1 lines channelized for 23 ISDN or modem connections). Figure 3-2 shows a simplified RAS solution, with its RAS server and incoming networks and users.

The virtual private network, our VPN, is somewhat more complex, as you may have gleaned from previous chapters. The VPN concept, of course, is to allow users or networks to access central private network resources securely via the Internet. There are three basic solutions that mirror both WAN and RAS implementations: the point-to-network, the network-to-network, and the integrated solution. The point-to-network solution is meant to replace RAS as a primary connection method for the typical end user. Instead of dialing in to a central RAS point, the user dials in to a regional Internet service provider and connects to the private network via some secure protocol (i.e., SSH, PPTP, L2TP, etc.). The network-to-network solution is similar except that the remote network connects to an ISP and sends its private communication to a central firewall or VPN server equipped with a secure protocol. The Cisco PIX firewall and the IPSec protocol fall into this scenario, though IPSec is also available for point-to-network connections. The integrated solution is generally VPN servers, firewall software, or dedicated hardware, or a combination of all three that allows both networks and end users to access

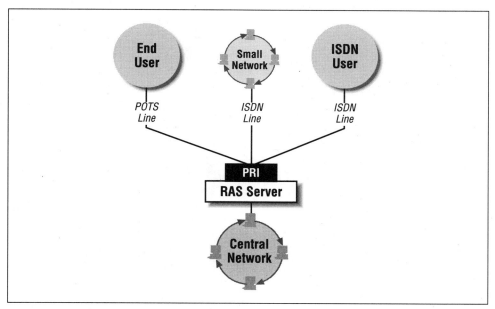

Figure 3-2. Dial-up connections

the private network. IPSec products such as Checkpoint Firewall-1 are considered integrated solutions. Figure 3-3 shows a generic integrated solution using an IPSec firewall for connecting networks and a PPTP server for incoming end user connections.

It is important to note that most WAN and RAS networks also have connections to the Internet. While the examples to follow do not assume an Internet connection, in today's networking world, converting from a WAN or RAS solution to a VPN would actually cut costs, as extraneous telco lines could be dropped and WAN/RAS-specific equipment and personnel could be used for other purposes. What is left is only to purchase and implement a VPN solution and increase bandwidth to the Internet.

VPN Versus WAN

This section illustrates how to use a VPN to solve WAN issues, and the various comparison points between the two. In sticking with our six generic criteria, we explore the small to medium VPN/WAN and the large VPN/WAN in turn, as each has its own specific issues.

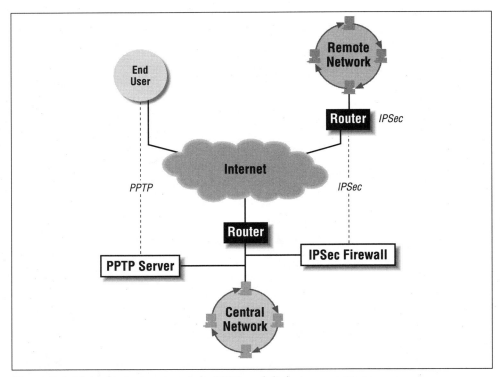

Figure 3-3. Virtual private network for WAN and dial-up connections

Small to Medium Solutions

While this is a broad topic, we will define a small to medium network as anything under 100 nodes (including the central network). Figure 3-4 compares a typical small to medium WAN to its VPN counterpart. Both scenarios include a small remote network that needs to connect to a central network resource.

Telco

The WAN connection could use an ISDN line if the remote network is within the local calling area of the main office. If the remote office is out of this area, a leased 56Kbps frame relay line would be the best bet. The big difference is that an ISDN line usually does not incur per-minute charges if the call is local, but would rack up long distance charges otherwise. However, some calling areas do incur per-minute charges for local ISDN calls. A frame relay line typically has a flat rate per-month charge, and is generally more expensive than an ISDN line, especially considering any mileage charges associated with the line.

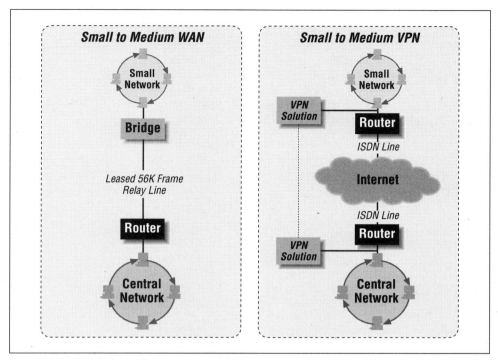

Figure 3-4. Leased-line solution versus virtual private network

ISDN offers more bandwidth (up to 128Kbps with a single basic rate ISDN line). Two 56Kbps leased lines would be needed to even get close to this level of bandwidth (112Kbps). The choice between the lines comes down to estimated usage and relevant charges associated with usage, as well as bandwidth needed to the remote site. Note that an ISDN or frame relay line is required on both ends of the connection. For networks with a hundred nodes or less, 128Kbps is adequate bandwidth in most cases.

A VPN could use either frame relay or ISDN, but the line would connect to a local Internet service provider. If both offices are in the same calling area, the same ISP should be used, reducing the odd nature of Internet routing (that is, ISPs across town routing traffic to each other across the country). If the remote office is outside the calling area of the central office, the ISP chosen from both sides should be connected to the same upstream Internet provider, if possible. This will significantly reduce Internet routing issues and increase the speed and reliability of the virtual private network. Both sides of the connection still require a line installed locally, be it ISDN or frame relay. Again, 128Kbps is adequate for a network of 100 nodes or less.

Hardware/software

VPNs and WANs require the same types of equipment at this level. ISDN or frame relay routers are available through such manufacturers as Cisco Systems, Farallon, Motorola, and Ascend Communications. Both sides of the connection require a router, which connects to the local ISP.

The WAN requires no extraneous software to complete the solution. Use the same networking protocol on each end and the network is functioning.

The VPN solution requires software of some kind to allow secure access to the central network. SSH, L2F, L2TP, and PPTP are solid solutions for small to medium network-to-network connections. Note that dedicated or specific hardware may be needed to support any of these VPN solutions. SSH is available for Unix servers, L2F and L2TP are supported on Cisco routers running IOS (including ISDN and frame relay routers), and PPTP is currently available on Windows NT 4.0 Server, as well as some ISDN routers. Also note that these software/hardware combinations are required on each end of the connection.

Administration

Expertise for a traditional WAN setup should be in a typical network administrator's skill set. Total set-up time for both sides of the WAN should not exceed 10 to 20 hours, which includes tracking down the best equipment, ordering lines, and configuring the connection. These types of connections do not usually require much recurring maintenance, as they tend to stay solid once properly configured. As much as 10 hours a month in maintenance time is standard, even if there are major connection or configuration problems.

The main failure point in this kind of connection is the telco provider, because they don't tend to communicate with their customers when lines are undergoing maintenance or fail completely. Another recurring issue is training end users in the use and general maintenance of the connection, as this scenario would not need a dedicated network administrator on both ends.

When implementing a virtual private network, the initial consideration for a network engineer is research and training. Most network administrators need to know how a VPN works and how it fits with the organization's networking needs. This book should get the process started, but an internal needs assessment should be done as well. Initial setup of a VPN will consume a significant amount of time, possibly as much as 20 to 40 hours, including research, training, pitching the solution upstairs, and actually implementing the network. Recurring maintenance shouldn't be significantly different from the WAN solution (presented earlier) with two exceptions: the ISP used and security of the VPN. Both issues are discussed at length later in this section. However, suffice it to say that the network administrator can add about 5 to 10 hours a month to the WAN maintenance estimate (a maximum of 30 hours total per month) for dealing with security and the Internet service provider.

Security, scalability, and stability

The WAN connection is arguably the most secure and stable solution for a network of any size. The connections are entirely private and are using proven, industry standard technology. Any questions concerning the stability of a WAN would affect any network, LAN, WAN, or VPN. Failures of equipment, protocols, systems, and server, for example, while not common, are a fact of life for any network. Where remote-to-central connections are concerned (WAN and VPN), the additional failure point is the telco provider. These are beyond the network administrator's control, for the most part, and the selection of a telco provider that communicates problems and planned downtimes to its customers is the best bet.

VPN's strength is not its stability, in a general sense. VPNs are a new technology, running on an inherently unreliable technology (the Internet). When dealing with Internet routing issues, communication between various platforms, encryption processes and the like, you can expect a less robust system. But as the world moves more to an interconnected society and as real standards emerge (protocols, hardware, etc.), VPNs will have a stabler base on which to operate.

The real differences between the VPN and the WAN come to light when scalability is considered. Moving from our simple small/medium to a large WAN requires a serious investment in equipment, workforce, and telco lines, especially when adding multiple networks across a nationwide organization. The main cost difference would be line charges for the upgrade. If the central office had to upgrade to a T1 (with all the equipment necessary for this), the remote sites would likewise need at least a fractional T1 with the equipment necessary to make this work. With the VPN, initially only the central network would need an upgrade in bandwidth and equipment, even to accept connections from multiple networks. Then, boosting the VPN server's capacity becomes minuscule when compared to the equipment and line upgrades on the WAN solution.

Large Solutions

Large WAN or VPN scenarios can encompass many different configurations, from multiple large interconnected networks to a central network connecting many smaller networks. For simplicity's sake, we present the two scenarios in Figure 3-5.

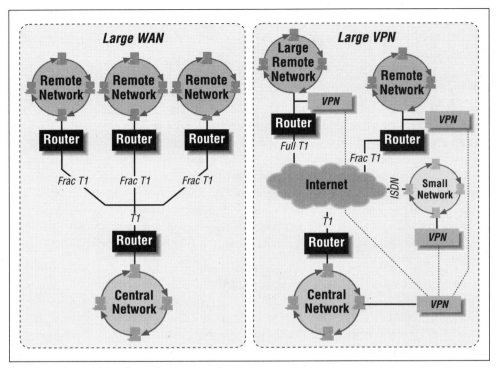

Figure 3-5. Telephone lines for WAN and VPN connections

Telco

A large WAN needs substantial bandwidth. To connect multiple medium-to-large networks to a large corporate network, nothing less than a fractional T1 at each site suffices. At the central network, we suggest multiple incoming T1s, a single T3, or an ATM connection, depending on incoming bandwidth requirements. Telco costs related to these connections include initial setup fees, local loop charges (for the line from the local telco central offices to the various sites), and recurring transit fees for the lines. Costs can be significantly reduced by choosing frame relay connections, but if guaranteed bandwidth is required, frame relay is not the best choice. Frame relay networks compete in the "frame cloud" for bandwidth, and most connections are not guaranteed to achieve their full speed end to end. For more reliable bandwidth, the more expensive option is a leased point-to-point connection. The hardware described later in this section supports either frame relay or point-to-point connections.

A VPN has similar bandwidth needs. Both the central network and the various satellite networks need high-speed connections to the Internet simply to support their outgoing traffic. However, these connections are typically to a local Internet service provider, thus reducing the local loop and possibly the recurring line costs.

Try to keep options for easy upgrades available. A scalable fractional T1, T3, or ATM connection is best, depending on the size and activity of the network in question. The real strength of the VPN, however, is the variety of connection options available to the satellite offices. Note in Figure 3-5 that the three remote networks connect to the Internet via ISDN, fractional T1, and full T1. This is a clear advantage over a WAN, where only specific types of connections are available, depending on the solution chosen for the entire network (i.e., fractional point-to-point T1s, multiple incoming ISDNs, etc.).

Hardware/software

With high-speed network connections comes high-end access equipment, and with that comes high cost in both initial investment and ongoing support. Though routers, hubs, and the like are not often prone to failure, they do have a short life cycle as far as technology goes. An IP router stays on the market about two years before the next revisions make it obsolete. Multiple remote network connections over leased high-speed data lines require high-end IP routers. For example, Cisco's 2500 series routers and Bay Networks' Access Router series could support multiple fractional or full T1 connections over frame relay or point-to-point. For higher bandwidth connections, such as fractional or full T3 or ATM, Cisco's 7500 series routers or various carrier class switches from Cascade, Ascend, or Cisco are common. The central network's equipment costs could run in the tens to hundreds of thousands of dollars. For the satellite offices, the cost would be at most a few thousand dollars. Of course, bandwidth needs of the various networks, hardware vendors, and other issues affect these estimates.

For a VPN, connection equipment is again dictated by connection method and speed. The model could look very much like the previous WAN solution, depending on the Internet connections at the various sites and the central network. The VPN diverges in two areas: servers and ISP connection equipment. Depending on the software chosen, the organization is limited to three platforms.

If PPTP is implemented on the ISP side of the connection, the organization is limited to Windows NT, Windows 95/98, Linux, and Macintosh for software clients. If PPTP is implemented on the organization side, both client and server software must be acquired. The server software is supported only by Windows NT 4.0, either the Server or the Workstation version, or the Linux version of PPTP, which is far from stable. Clients are limited to Windows NT, Windows 95/98, Linux, and Macintosh, as above.

If the AltaVista Tunnel is used, the server software is available for Digital Unix or Windows NT. Clients are available only for Windows NT, Windows 95/98, or Macintosh. If the organization currently runs its operations on platforms other than these, a switchover may involve more cost and hassle than the benefits of the VPN are worth.

The final choice is an integrated solution such as the Cisco PIX firewall or one of the many IPSec products, of which a well-known example is CheckPoint Firewall-1. An integrated solution avoids client platform limitations entirely.

Administration

The main issues here are related to the scale of the operation. Every satellite network will need one or two full-time network administrators to support the initial WAN implementation, the ongoing operations, and the users. Ordering and coordinating lines and equipment, configuring the network, troubleshooting it, stabilizing it, and documenting changes could take 40 hours or more each month per site, including the central network. Ongoing administration, support, reporting, and other duties should require 160 to 200 hours per month during normal operation. In the event of a problem, such as failed connections or equipment, this hourly estimate is much higher.

For a virtual private network connection, the biggest benefit could also be the biggest hindrance: the ISP. Most ISPs that service connections of this scale are competent and knowledgeable about engineering the connection. These ISPs will assist, support, and in most cases actually include the setup of the connection as part of their services. This will reduce the hourly cost of the setup for the network administrators, and may not increase the monetary costs significantly. For this reason, selection of a good ISP should be a number one priority when considering using a virtual private network.

Additionally, as we noted in the preceding section, you should choose the same ISP for the central network and all its satellites, if possible, or ISPs connected to the same backbone (e.g., Savvis, BBN Planet, etc.). This will reduce the network routing problems that affect the speed of the virtual network between the sites and may take the network down completely on occasion. Also, if you use PPTP, the organization should consider selecting an ISP that supports this protocol on their equipment. This could significantly reduce the workload of the network administrator, as there will be no PPTP servers to support; user support is essentially outsourced to the ISP's support staff.

An estimated time commitment for a connection on this scale is about half that of the WAN connection (about 20 to 40 hours). The majority of the network administrators' time initially will be evaluating and selecting an Internet service provider for the multiple sites. Ongoing administration and support of the virtual private network should not exceed 100 to 150 hours a month, taking into account that the ISP is doing much of the user-end support. If the ISP proves to be incompetent or their connections faulty, your site administrators can expect double the normal hours a month to support and maintain the VPN.

Security, scalability, and stability

Again, on this larger scale, VPN's real advantage is scalability, which translates directly into price. While not having the security of a WAN, a VPN is much more flexible in its connections and grows with the expanding network. While the WAN maintains its stability to some degree, the large WAN is basically a model of the Internet, with some of the routing and protocol issues inherent with that medium, though on a smaller and more controllable scale. The security of the large WAN is still unmatched, as lines are private and all resources controlled by the organization; however, the larger VPN solutions, such as the Cisco PIX firewall and Checkpoint Firewall-1, are the cutting edge of Internet security, using the most trusted encryption methodologies.

VPN Versus RAS

In this section, we explore VPNs as a replacement for RAS services. While RAS is an industry standard remote connection method for thousands of individual users, it is, by its nature, extremely expensive, somewhat unstable, and generally just not fun to deal with from an administrative perspective. Most users connect through long distance calls, which racks up huge bills for even small RAS services. And the modem-as-network-device has never been stable enough to count on for critical services. Incoming lines, modems, and other such equipment become a network manager's nightmare. The VPN, with all its weaknesses, has the strength to supplant RAS as the connection method of choice for individual remote users.

Small to Medium Solutions

Small networks are generally less volatile and more likely to use a RAS solution for incoming remote users. Typically these users are in a local calling area and use RAS in emergencies or to occasionally work from home. A VPN for a small network would probably even be counterproductive, with the overhead of ISP problems, Internet idiosyncrasies, and general VPN issues. Approaching the medium size network, the VPN has real superiority. Not only does a VPN allow individuals to connect to the organization's private LAN, it also (as seen in the "VPN Versus WAN" section) allows other networks to connect. Thus, as the organization expands, so does the networking solution, without a huge reinvestment of resources.

Figure 3-6 shows a medium RAS scenario and its VPN solution. This section covers these two situations in more depth.

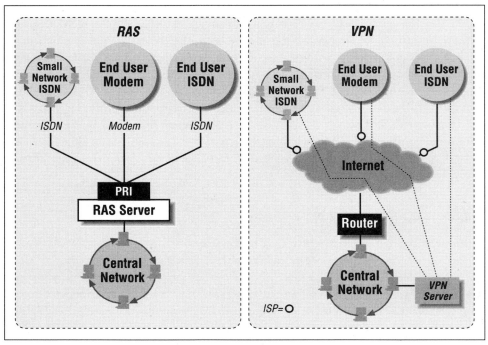

Figure 3-6. Dial-up scenario—RAS solution versus virtual private network

Telco

For the medium RAS solution, we chose a single PRI for incoming ISDN or modem calls. An ISDN PRI supports up to 23 incoming calls on a single line (T1). Costs associated with a PRI are initial installation, recurring monthly charges, and any long distance charges incurred either on the actual phone bill or on a long distance credit card used by the remote users that the company reimburses. Since few carriers guarantee a digital connection end-to-end for ISDN data calls outside a local calling area, the organization that needs high-speed digital connections will have more interest in the VPN solution. Of course, each remote user will need his or her own ISDN or analog line as well.

Telco issues with a virtual private network hinge mostly on the ISP chosen for each of the connecting users. Each site or person that wishes to connect will need some sort of dial-up access line (analog or digital) to connect to the ISP. The central corporate network will need a dedicated digital connection such as ISDN to an ISP. Alternatively, the firm could maintain a dynamic (on-demand) connection to the ISP, where the ISP initiates the call to the corporate site when traffic destined for the corporate network is detected. For the corporate network here, we've chosen a fractional T1 at 256Kbps. This line will support up to 300 or so VPN users, not including other Internet traffic.

The VPN, like any Internet service, is only as fast as the slowest connection between the user and the server. The main consideration when choosing an ISP for the virtual private network is its capacity and ability to support the number of users to which your organization expects to need connections. Again, it is important to evaluate the ISP based on your company's needs, and not some abstract set of criteria. If it is critical that users access the corporate network, an ISP with a low user to dial-up line ratio must be chosen. Currently, the industry standard is 12 users to 1 modem, but peak times and network down percentages are as varied as the number of ISPs out there. An ISP whose primary business focus is corporate Internet access would have its peak times from 8 a.m. to 5 p.m. on weekdays, whereas one specializing in regular home users would see peaks on the weekends and from 6 p.m. to midnight weekdays. Also, with roving VPN users, look for an ISP with a strong national presence or 800 dial-up access.

Hardware/software

For an incoming PRI, remote access requires an RAS hub. Most can take more than one PRI, making their price scalable as the organization grows. ISDN routers or terminal adapters, or analog modems, are required for end users to connect.

With a virtual private network, the organization needs access equipment for the remote connections and the central office. The central office would most likely connect via a fractional T1 to an ISP, and therefore need an IP router, such as the Cisco 1000 or 2500 series router. The remote connections would use either ISDN terminal adapters or analog modems to connect to their ISPs. For the central network side, a VPN server of some kind would be required (AltaVista Tunnel Telecommuter, PPTP, etc.), or if L2TP or L2F are used, the respective protocol should be initiated on the Cisco router. Additionally, if a software-based VPN is used, such as the AltaVista Tunnel, this software must be purchased. Since Cisco routers have L2F and L2TP by default, and Windows NT 4.0 has PPTP by default, these are probably the best solutions for the medium-size network.

Administration

With remote access, a network administrator faces several challenges to keep the system running and to provide support to its users. Modem connections are buggy at best, experiencing regular problems with modem compatibility (i.e., getting two modems to talk to one another), the quality of phone lines, and general end user problems. The setup described in this scenario will have intermittent problems and some outages should be expected. The network administrator should expect to spend 30 to 50 hours a month on end user support, general maintenance of the remote access system, and general administration of the remote access server.

With a VPN, the two primary concerns of the administrator are security and dealing with the ISP. We've covered most of the ISP issues in the previous "Telco" section. Security is a bigger problem.

In order to maintain the integrity of the private network, the network administrator will have to monitor the VPN systems logs, error reports, and other documentation very closely. Users must be trained extensively in security issues, such as password and digital key integrity and confidential information procedures. The main anxiety for the systems administrator is that the entire Internet's host of criminals looking for a challenge will have a shot at your private network. These people will try to break in to your system, but common sense and precautions will keep your private network from being an easy target. The network administrator can expect to spend 20 to 40 hours a month dealing with ISP, security, and Internet issues.

Security, scalability, and stability

Like WAN solutions, the VPN is by far more economical than RAS with regard to scalability, but scalability translates directly into economy. As the network expands, an RAS service could devour more than half of the network department's budget and time, while a VPN's cost can be kept at a more manageable level.

And, while not entirely stable, a VPN is at least as stable as RAS. Users still dial in to a central point, but the burden of maintenance and support is on the ISP, not the organization's network administrator. While your local administrator may be as knowledgeable, those running an ISP are focused almost entirely on their RAS services. The network administrator in an organization has a plethora of issues to address daily. The VPN lightens this load, somewhat.

The complete security of a RAS service is not as assured as a WAN, though it probably equals that of a VPN. Anyone with a modem and a password can hit the organization's RAS services. Attacks on private RAS pools are as old as the profession of hacking itself. With VPNs you have the security of encrypted traffic, including passwords, usernames, and, in many cases, IP addresses and communication ports (via firewalls). While the Internet is the staging ground for most network attacks today, a VPN will keep a medium-sized network as safe as it can be.

Large Solutions

A large network is a prime candidate for replacement of RAS with a virtual private network. Figure 3-7 compares the two solutions. With a large RAS solution, many times there are small- to medium-sized remote sites connecting to the central network, in addition to roaming and static end users. Sales personnel calling from remote customer sites in other countries, developers telecommuting from home, and many other scenarios make a RAS pool a living nightmare for a network administrator. With the VPN, not only are costly long distance charges avoided, but the flexibility and scalability allow for efficient evaluation of upgrade and end user needs.

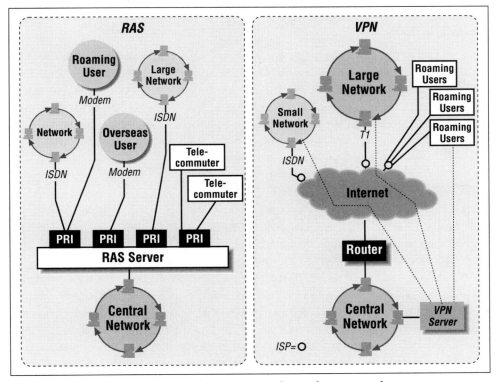

Figure 3-7. Leased-RAS versus virtual private network on a large network

Telco

A remote access site of this size requires at least a 1-to-5 ratio of lines to users. The example network on which we've based this section has about 450 users of the system and 180 incoming lines. Several of these lines are dedicated ISDN connections for nearby branch offices, and are connected 24 hours a day. The remaining lines are carried on PRI ISDN lines, which allows for 23 analog and/or digital connections simultaneously per PRI. The only other addition to the telecommunications puzzle piece is an 800 access line for roving users. Though this is an expensive route, an 800 number is still cheaper than a long distance call for traveling users of the system.

With the VPN, the minimum connection to an ISP is a fractional T3 line. The T3 is connected to a large national Internet service provider, such as BBN Planet or Sprint. Connecting through such a large ISP may be more costly, but it will save the system administrator headaches when there is a problem. National ISPs tend to have better support and some sort of notification system when problems are anticipated or emergencies arise. Another benefit of staying with a national ISP is the availability of service for all users and remote sites and the strength of their national backbone.

Most national ISPs also offer other Internet services such as modem or ISDN dial-up. This allows the organization to standardize on an Internet carrier, and thus have a single point of contact. For the remote offices, an ISDN connection to the ISP is required, though it need not be a dedicated connection unless the site's network is large or has an around-the-clock need for a constant connection to the main office or the Internet. The individual users have a choice of either modem or ISDN dial-ups, as the individual need requires.

Hardware/software

With an incoming T1 PRI line, the central office needs a robust remote access hub. Such hubs, like the Total Control Access Hub by U.S. Robotics or the 4004 by Ascend Communications, are designed to handle incoming lines like these. This type of equipment also offers the network administrator the convenience of administration tools such as SNMP monitoring of network usage, as well as capacity and user account management options lacking in a home-grown or smaller solution. Modems and ISDN adapters are built in and upgradable, removing the hassle of maintaining racks of modems, ISDN TAs, or routers. In addition, access hubs can handle multiple incoming T1s, making upgrading incoming capacity easier and more affordable. However, hubs and their accoutrements are expensive to purchase, set up, and maintain.

Other equipment you'll want for such a setup includes an SNMP workstation or server and an accounts management server (which could be on the same computer). Accounting for users via logs, databases, and other data will assist the administrator greatly in tracking usage, troubleshooting problems, and generally keeping all the users, sites, and networks in order.

The central office in the VPN scenario looks very similar to the one in the large network among our earlier WAN solutions. The central office needs a T3 class Internet Protocol (IP) router, such as a Cisco 7500, with CSU/DSU and appropriate software. Each connecting site needs appropriate hardware to connect to their ISP.

Administration

A large remote access network is a general nightmare for a system administrator—just ask any Internet service provider. With multiple and varied connection types, user profiles, and unplanned incidents, you'll need a full-time staff dedicated just to administering the remote access network. The remote access staff should be responsible for supporting users, managing accounts and the capacity of the network, and coordinating communications, upgrades, and maintenance. Remote networks certainly require a network administrator who maintains the dial-up or dedicated connection to the central office and acts as a liaison between the end users on that network and the support staff at the central office. This is a full-time job for up to ten people.

With the VPN, most of the network administrator's support functions are reduced because the ISP maintains this role. A small administration staff should be able to support a VPN of up to 300 users. The network administrator's main job is to monitor and maintain the central office's connection to its ISP. The ISP should do the rest. Of course, account management and security are still the big issues for the administrator, and approximately 30 to 50 hours a month should be earmarked for this task.

Security, scalability, and stability

Again, the scalability of the VPN is tantamount to that of the large RAS solution. By upgrading a few servers, routers, and/or firewalls, and connectivity to the various sites, you can expand the VPN. With RAS, you are facing downtime to install new hardware, time to pull in more incoming lines, and just general headaches when it doesn't all come together as planned. As put forth at the beginning of this section, the VPN is next in line to supplant RAS at every level, except maybe the small network scenario, for its scalability alone.

With an expanding RAS service come more opportunities for attack. A password left in some hotel room by an inattentive travelling user could cause havoc at the central network. The VPN is a self-contained security solution that makes RAS entirely obsolete. While RAS and VPNs may be approximately the same in stability, the economy, security, and diversion of work away from the network administration staff make the VPN an obvious solution for the large network.

4

In this chapter:
• *Differences Between PPTP, L2F, and L2TP*
• *How PPTP Works*
• *Features of PPTP*

Implementing Layer 2 Connections

This chapter will discuss some of the major tunneling protocols used by VPN vendors. These protocols are the Point-to-Point Tunneling Protocol (PPTP), Layer 2 Forwarding (L2F), and the Layer 2 Tunneling Protocol (L2TP).

Tunneling protocols essentially make square pegs fit into round holes. Imagine you have a round pipe and you want to send a cube through it. The cube is just going to get stuck, or isn't going to fit at all. The way to get around this is to encapsulate the cube within a sphere, then send it through the pipe. In other words, you take something that your transport medium can't work with and package it within something it can. All computer networking works this way, in one fashion or another.

All of these tunneling protocols operate by tunneling Layer 2 of the OSI Reference Model for communications protocols, also known as the Data Link Layer, over IP. It is at this layer that protocols such as PPP operate. As you may know, PPP is commonly used to transport IP and other protocols over serial and digital connections. Typically PPP connections are made between a client and a remote host, such as a remote access server. Likewise, PPTP, L2F, and L2TP are all used to tunnel PPP connections over the Internet so that they may be terminated on a remote host. In this case, the tunnel essentially acts in place of the line. Because they use existing PPP infrastructure, these protocols gain the advantages of the PPP protocol, including dynamic address assignment from a pool or from DHCP, user-based authentication, and compression.

The Point-to-Point Tunneling Protocol was jointly developed by engineers from Ascend Communications, U.S. Robotics, 3Com Corporation, Microsoft Corporation, and ECI Telematics to provide a virtual private network between remote access users and network servers. In this chapter, we will discuss the functionality of PPTP and how it might fit into certain virtual private network scenarios. In

Chapter 5, *Configuring and Testing Layer 2 Connections*, we'll take the knowledge we gain here and apply it to setting up a VPN using PPTP.

The companies that created PPTP banded together to form the PPTP Forum. At the same time that the PPTP Forum was formalizing their specification, Cisco was independently developing the Layer 2 Forwarding protocol. Working with the Internet Engineering Task Force, the PPTP Forum and Cisco banded together to create the Internet draft specification for the Level 2 Tunneling Protocol, a new core protocol that combines the best features of PPTP and L2F, while maintaining some backward compatibility. As of this writing, L2TP was on draft version 11 (due to expire in November 1998), but an RFC number was expected to be assigned soon.

Differences Between PPTP, L2F, and L2TP

Both PPTP and L2F allow you to use any authentication method you would normally use with PPP, including PAP and CHAP—essentially whatever authentication protocols both the client and server support. For encryption, PPTP uses the RC4 cipher with either 40-bit or 128-bit keys. L2F, on the other hand, supports 40-bit or 56-bit DES encryption with the 11.2 versions of Cisco's IOS. IOS version 11.3(3)T and later supports IPSec, which can also be used to encrypt an L2F connection.

L2TP combines the best features of PPTP and L2F and allows for either client-initiated or remote access switch-initiated L2TP connections. You can use L2TP in any situation where you might use PPTP or L2F. It can still use the same authentication protocols as the others, including PAP, CHAP, and MS-CHAP. IPSec is the recommended encryption mechanism for L2TP. Although that L2TP was reputed to "replace" PPTP, Microsoft has chosen to continue providing PPTP in Windows NT 5.0 for those who do not wish to maintain the public key infrastructure required for IPSec.

PPTP is available on currently shipping versions of Windows NT Server 4.0 and Windows NT Workstation 4.0 as part of Remote Access Services (RAS)—NT's dial-up networking software. Microsoft's PPTP support for Windows 95 is included in their Dial-Up Networking Upgrade Version 1.3. Microsoft has also released LAN-to-LAN PPTP connections for Windows NT in their "Routing and Remote Access" software (codenamed "Stronghold"), as part of the Windows NT Option Pack. PPTP support is included in Windows 98. Microsoft Windows NT 5.0 will also support PPTP connections.

A Macintosh PPTP client is available from Network TeleSystems (*http:// www.nts.com*). Called TunnelBuilder, it offers full PPTP support, including NT domain login and data encryption. Network TeleSystems (NTS) also has a version of TunnelBuilder for Windows 95, Windows 98, Windows for Workgroups, and Windows 3.1. Since Microsoft doesn't plan on supporting PPTP on down-level versions of Windows, this allows users with legacy systems to run PPTP. The NTS Windows clients support L2TP. In addition, Linux is now capable of supporting PPTP.

There are also a number of hardware devices that support PPTP out of the box. These devices are known variously as remote access servers, remote hubs, terminal servers, and remote access switches. In this chapter, we will refer to them simply as remote access switches, because that term is prevalent in the industry and best describes what they do. There are a number of remote access switches that support PPTP, among them Ascend's MAX line, the 3Com/U.S. Robotics Total Control line, and ECI Telematics' Nevada. These are typical brands used in ISP points-of-presence and corporate networks to terminate modem and ISDN calls. PPTP is included as part of all of these products free of charge—no additional activation fees are required. There are also some hardware devices that act as PPTP servers, but do not operate as a standard remote access switch. Examples of these are the Bay Networks Extranet Switch and the NTS TunnelMaster.

L2F is supported by Cisco in their IOS software for their routers. Other vendors, such as Nortel and Shiva, also support L2F. L2TP is supported in Cisco IOS 11.3(5)AA and later. In addition, many other hardware devices support it. Microsoft will include L2TP support in Windows NT 5.0. Because PPTP, L2F, and L2TP operate similarly, we will concentrate on PPTP and L2TP.

How PPTP Works

As a tunneling protocol, PPTP encapsulates network protocol datagrams within an IP envelope. After the packet is encapsulated, any router or machine that encounters it from that point on will treat it as an IP packet. The benefit of IP encapsulation is that it allows many different protocols to be routed across an IP-only medium, such as the Internet.

The first thing to understand about PPTP is that it revolves around Microsoft RAS for Windows NT. RAS allows a network administrator to set up a Windows NT server with a modem bank as a dial-in point for remote users. Authentication for the RAS users takes place on the NT server, and a network session is set up using the PPP protocol. Through the PPP connection, all of the protocols allowed by RAS can be transported: TCP/IP, NetBEUI, and IPX/SPX. To the RAS users it appears as though they're directly connected to the corporate LAN; they notice no difference between RAS through direct dial-in and RAS over the Internet.

PPTP was designed to allow users to connect to a RAS server from any point on the Internet and still have the same authentication, encryption, and corporate LAN access they'd have from dialing directly into it. Instead of dialing into a modem connected to the RAS server, the end users dial into their ISPs and use PPTP to set up a "call" to the server over the Internet. PPTP and RAS use authentication and encryption methods to create a virtual private network.

There are two common scenarios for this type of VPN: in the first, a remote user is dialing into an ISP with a PPTP-enabled remote access switch that connects to the RAS server; in the second, the user is connecting to an ISP that doesn't offer PPTP, and must initiate the PPTP connection on their client machine.

Dialing into an ISP That Supports PPTP

Dialing into an ISP that supports PPTP requires three things:

- The network with which you want to establish a VPN must have a PPTP-enabled Window NT 4.0 RAS server. By "PPTP-enabled" we mean that the PPTP protocol is installed and there are VPN dial-up ports set up in RAS. The server must also be accessible from the Internet.

- Your ISP must use a remote access switch that supports PPTP, such as the Ascend MAX 4000 series or a U.S. Robotics Total Control Enterprise Network Hub. (Together, these two products make up a significant portion of the ISP dial-up hardware market.)

- Your ISP has to actually offer the PPTP service to users, and must enable it for your account.

To offer a typical scenario, a central corporate office in Denver has set up a Windows NT 4.0 server running PPTP and RAS. A sales manager named Sara N. is at a conference in Atlanta, and wants to dial into the corporate network to check her email and copy a presentation from her desktop machine. Her remote system is a Windows 95 laptop computer with a 28.8Kbps modem. She's obviously out of the local dialing area of her office, but has an account through a national ISP that supports PPTP through their U.S. Robotics remote access switches. The ISP was told the IP address of the RAS server at Sara N.'s corporate office, and has added it to her user profile. The IP address is 2.1.1.60.

When the sales manager dials into her PPTP-enabled ISP, the following events occur:

1. Sara N. initiates a call into her ISP's POP using Microsoft's Dial-Up Networking. She logs in with her username, "saran." Doing so starts a PPTP session between the ISP's remote access switch and the corporate office's NT server, whose IP address is specified in Sara N.'s user profile as 2.1.1.60.

2. Sara N.'s PPP session is tunneled through the PPTP stream, and the NT RAS server authenticates her username and password and starts her PPP session.

Essentially, this all takes place just as if she were dialing into the RAS server via a directly connected modem.

3. The PPTP session can then tunnel the protocols that dial-up users are allowed to use. In Sara N.'s case, TCP/IP is one of those protocols, and the NT RAS server assigns her machine the internal corporate IP address of 2.1.1.129.

Looking at Figure 4-1, you can follow these events and see where the client's original Point-to-Point Protocol (PPP) session is encapsulated by the PPTP tunnel. This figure is a simplified version of what the actual topology looks like—routers at the ISP and corporate LAN, for instance, have been removed.

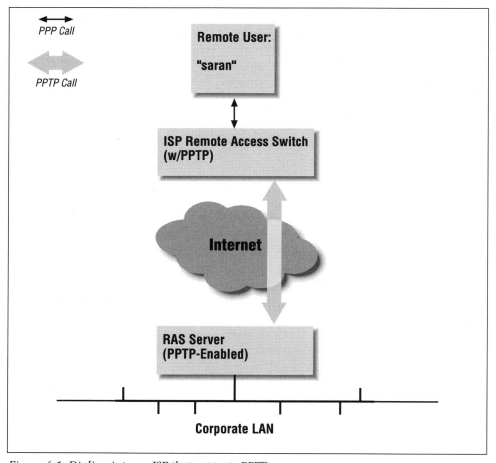

Figure 4-1. Dialing into an ISP that supports PPTP

Once the PPTP is completed and the sales manager is authenticated, she has access to the corporate network as if she were on the LAN. She can then check her email and access files on her desktop machine using file sharing.

Dialing into an ISP That Doesn't Support PPTP

In order for an ISP to support PPTP, they must be using one of the remote access switches we mentioned at the beginning of this chapter. Not every ISP uses those brands of remote access switches, and some don't use these devices at all. Instead they might use modems connected to a multiport serial card in a Unix system, or some other terminal server device. Others might have the appropriate hardware, but choose not to implement PPTP because they don't want to be forced to do technical support for tunneled connections. Whatever the reason, there's a chance that your ISP may not offer PPTP; however, that doesn't mean that you can't use it.

This scenario requires two things: first, you again need to have a Windows NT 4.0 RAS server with PPTP installed on your network, and it must be accessible from the Internet; second, your Windows NT Workstation, Windows 95, or Windows 98 client machine must have the PPTP protocol and Dial-Up Networking installed.

We'll use Sara N. for this example as well. This time, however, she's dialing into an ISP that doesn't support PPTP. In addition, she's running Windows NT 4.0 Workstation on her laptop computer. The sequence of events for a tunneling session with a non-PPTP-enabled provider is as follows:

1. Sara dials into her ISP using a dial-up networking profile for her account and establishes a standard PPP connection.

2. After the PPP connection has been made, Sara uses Dial-Up Networking again to "dial" into the PPTP RAS server at the corporate office. In this dial-up profile, however, she puts the IP address of the RAS server, 2.1.1.60, in the phone number field, and selects the dial device to be a VPN port set up through Dial-Up Networking (we'll explain in Chapter 5 how to set this up).

3. A PPTP connection is made through Sara's PPP connection over the Internet and to the RAS server. The RAS server then logs her into the corporate network using the username and password she supplied. The RAS server assigns her the internal IP address of 2.1.1.129, and she is then granted access to the corporate network.

Figure 4-2 shows how the second PPTP call is encapsulated through the initial PPP connection to the ISP.

Again, once the PPTP connection is made, Sara N. will have access to the corporate LAN just as if she were connected to it via a network card or dial-up RAS connection.

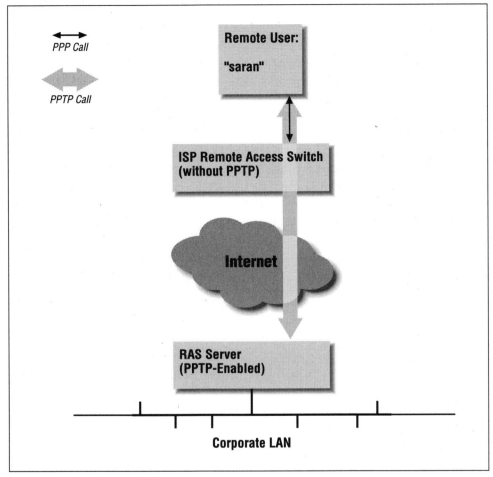

Figure 4-2. Connecting to a corporate RAS server via an ISP that doesn't support PPTP

Where PPTP Fits into Our Scenario

In Figure 4-3 we have a representation of a corporate office network with a T1 connection to the Internet. The router that connects to the Internet is also a packet-filtration firewall. User Sara N. wants to check her corporate email, and is dialing into her ISP, which is using a PPTP-enabled remote access switch. After she connects to the switch, it starts a PPTP call to the RAS server specified in her user profile. In this figure, a lightly shaded line extends the PPTP session back to the client, rather than just to the remote access switch. Sara uses this line when she has to dial into an ISP that doesn't support PPTP, and initiates the PPTP session on her workstation with a second RAS call.

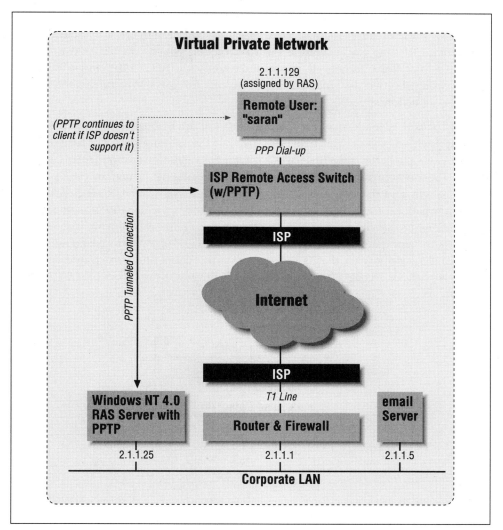

Figure 4-3. A full diagram of a PPTP connection over the Internet

On the corporate router and firewall, the TCP/IP port on which PPTP creates a socket (1723) must be open to both inbound and outbound traffic. If the rest of the network is protected by a firewall that disallows inbound and outbound Internet traffic, then a single point of entry to the LAN is established, which is protected by the user-based authentication.

Dissecting a PPTP Packet

The PPTP encapsulation technique is based on another Internet standard called the Generic Routing Encapsulation (GRE) protocol, which can be used to tunnel protocols over the Internet. (If you're interested, see RFCs 1701 and 1702.) The PPTP version, known as GREv2, adds extensions for specific features such as Call ID and connection speed.

A PPTP packet is made up of a delivery header, an IP header, a GREv2 header, and the payload packet. The delivery header is the framing protocol for whatever medium the packet is traveling over, whether it's Ethernet, frame relay, or PPP. The IP header contains information essential to the IP datagram, such as the packet length and the source and destination addresses. The GREv2 header contains information on the type of packet encapsulated, as well as PPTP-specific data that pertains to the connection between the client and server. Finally, the payload packet is the encapsulated datagram itself. In the case of PPP, this datagram is the original PPP session data that is sent between the client and server, and within it can be IP, IPX, or NetBEUI packets. Figure 4-4 illustrates the layers of PPTP encapsulation.

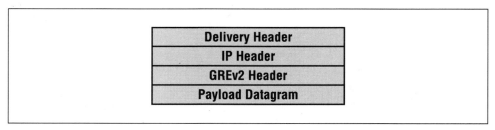

Figure 4-4. The four layers of a PPTP packet being transported across the Internet

The encapsulation process

The encapsulation process for a user dialing into an ISP that supports PPTP is as follows:

1. The user dials into the ISP's remote access switch using PPP. Between the client and the remote access switch flow PPP packets that are surrounded by the PPP protocol-specific frames being delivered.

2. At the switch, the media-specific frames are stripped away, and the call triggers the remote access switch to open up a PPTP tunneling session over the Internet between itself and the PPTP-enabled NT RAS server specified in the user's profile. The remote access switch encapsulates the PPP payload packet within a GREv2 header, then an IP header. Finally, the packet gets a delivery header before going out of the switch. Throughout the packet's journey, the

delivery header may change depending on the type of media through which the packet is being sent. For instance, it may go from Ethernet, to frame relay, to Ethernet again, to PPP over ISDN, and to Ethernet yet again before finally reaching its destination at the RAS server.

3. The RAS server treats the incoming PPTP connection as an incoming call, just as if it were coming in over a modem. It strips off the delivery header, the IP header, and the GREv2 header from the payload packet. It then handles the PPP connection as it normally would if the user were coming in over a modem connection. The RAS server validates the PPP client using whatever authentication method is required on the RAS server: Microsoft encrypted authentication, encrypted authentication, or any authentication type (including clear text).

4. Before packets from the client reach the LAN, PPP framing is removed from the enclosed IP, NetBEUI, or IPX datagrams. Figure 4-5 is a diagram of those protocol layers that are active during each portion of the connection for dialing into ISPs that support PPTP.

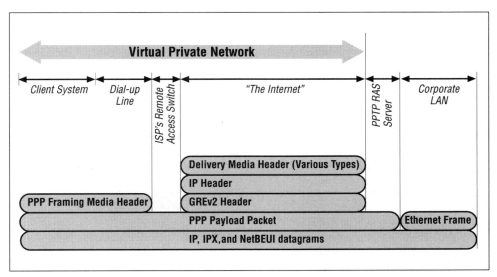

Figure 4-5. Active protocol layers during a PPTP connection

In a situation where the RAS user is dialing into an ISP that doesn't support PPTP, much of the process is the same. The only change would be in step 2. Instead of the remote access switch starting the PPTP session with the RAS server, the client makes a PPTP connection to the RAS server using Dial-Up Networking (as we said earlier). The PPTP packets are therefore sent through the standard PPP connection the client is making with the ISP's remote access switch. At that point in the connection, the client's PPP datagram is encapsulated by PPTP which is, in turn, encapsulated again by PPP. At the remote access switch, the first layer of PPP is stripped off, and the delivery header, IP header, GREv2 header, and payload packet remain.

Although this outlines how a PPTP call is initially placed, communication between the client and server proceed in the same order of encapsulation. The main difference is that authentication no longer needs to take place.

PPTP Security

Like most security systems, PPTP has two components: authentication to prevent improper connections, and encryption for data sent once the connection is made.

RAS authentication methods

PPTP uses Windows NT RAS authentication. The choices for the different authentication types the RAS server can accept are located in the RAS properties under "Encryption Settings." This setting lets you specify the level of authentication that the RAS server will perform against the client's login attempt. This section discusses the options you have: standard encrypted authentication, Microsoft-enhanced encrypted authentication, and allowing any type of authentication. Your choice will determine how secure your VPN will be.

Accept encrypted authentication. Encrypted authentication in RAS is actually the Internet authentication standard known as CHAP (Challenge Handshake Authentication Protocol). CHAP is described in RFC 1994 as an extension to PPP in which clear-text passwords are not passed between the client and server. Instead, both the client and server have an agreed-upon password, called a "secret," that is never sent over the link unencrypted. Here's how CHAP authentication occurs:

1. The server "challenges" the client to identify itself when the client tries to connect.

2. The client sends the secret through a one-way hashing algorithm, RSA's MD5. The algorithm uses mathematical formulas and random factors to come up with a hash value. "One-way" means that the hash value cannot be reversed into the original elements, and the use of random elements means that someone sniffing the connection will be less likely to see the same value twice. The hash value is sent across the connection to the server.

3. The server compares the value the server sent to its own calculation of the hash value. If the two values match, the connection is authenticated. If not, the connection is terminated.

Another benefit of CHAP is that this authentication process can take place several times during the course of a connection. This limits the probability of being bumped off and having an impostor "hijack" your connection.

In the case of PPTP, the secret is the password the user uses to log into the NT domain, which is also known by the RAS server (either directly or through NT domain services).

Accept Microsoft encrypted authentication. Microsoft encrypted authentication is also known as MS-CHAP. MS-CHAP performs RSA's MD4 hash, as well as the DES hashing technique. Windows 95/98 and Windows NT RAS clients use the MD4 hash, which doesn't require clear-text passwords on the client or server. DES allows for backward compatibility with older RAS clients such as Windows for Workgroups 3.11 and RAS 1.1a. Otherwise, MS-CHAP operates the same way as CHAP. The main drawback of MS-CHAP is that not every platform has a PPP client that supports it. If your remote users are all on Windows systems, however, it's the best protocol to use. In addition, you must use it to get the added benefit of data stream encryption over PPTP. We'll explain why in the section on data encryption.

Accept any authentication, including clear text. Accepting any authentication, including clear text, means that the RAS server will accept MS-CHAP, CHAP, or the Password Authentication Protocol (PAP). PAP has long been a common way to authenticate a PPP connection. In fact, most ISPs use PAP authentication for their PPP dial-up connections. Its main drawback is that it sends the password over the connection in clear text, meaning that someone monitoring the connection between the client and server may be able to see the login exchange, then log in later as that person. PAP is an unsuitable authentication method for a VPN, since secure authentication over a public network is a VPN's primary goal. It's therefore suggested that you require CHAP or MS-CHAP authentication on your PPTP server. If your remote users are on varied platforms, you may find that not every client on every platform supports CHAP or MS-CHAP authentication. If you can't find a CHAP implementation at all for a particular operating system, you may be forced to accept clear text passwords.

Data encryption

In the RAS properties for Windows NT, you'll find a checkbox to require data encryption for the RAS connection. This option will make all data going across the connection stream unreadable to an interceptor. The box can be checked only if the option to require Microsoft encrypted authentication is also selected, meaning that you can use it only if you're also using MS-CHAP. The reason for this is that the value generated by the MD4 hash is used by the RAS client and server to derive a session key for encryption. The encryption algorithm used is RSA's RC4, with a 40-bit session key.

As we said in Chapter 2, *Basic VPN Technologies*, U.S. export laws prevent the distribution of ciphers that can use session keys of greater than 40 bits. On the other hand, keys of 40 bits are often considered too vulnerable for transmitting secure data over the Internet. In order to meet the demand for better encryption methods, Microsoft has included a 128-bit "strong" encryption module in a U.S.-only version of their Service Pack 3 for Windows NT 4.0.

Features of PPTP

There are several factors in PPTP's favor. Among these are availability, easy implementation, multiprotocol tunneling, and the ability to use corporate and unregistered IP addresses.

Availability

Because PPTP is included with Windows NT Server, Workstation, and Windows 98, it is readily available to users of these platforms. No additional software need be purchased. Microsoft is giving away the PPTP upgrade for Windows 95/98 as well. In addition, it is included free of charge in many different brands of remote access switches, including Ascend, 3Com, and ECI Telematics equipment. Because it has become part of the package of a leading network operating system and numerous remote access switches, PPTP enjoys a huge product-placement advantage. An administrator for a Windows NT network can start experimenting with a VPN right away, without spending any extra money.

Easy Implementation

On Windows NT systems, PPTP is installed as a network protocol, just like IPX/ SPX, TCP/IP, or NetBEUI. In RAS, instead of using a modem as the RAS device, you use a VPN port with the name RASPPTPM. Many Windows NT administrators will already be familiar with how to set up network protocols and RAS, so using PPTP shouldn't be difficult for them. Likewise, on Windows 95 systems, PPTP is installed as a new version of the Dial-Up Adapter that's already a familiar part of Windows 95 Dial-Up Networking. On Windows 98, the VPN Adapter can also be installed and used like a modem for VPN connections.

On remote access switches that support PPTP, enabling PPTP is typically straightforward. For users who wish to dial in using PPTP, you simply add the IP address of their PPTP server to their profiles. ISPs that use authentication and accounting software such as Merit Network's RADIUS server will also find PPTP as easy to implement in a user profile as PPP. We'll go into detail about how to set up PPTP on both RAS and remote access switches in Chapter 5.

Multiprotocol Tunneling

The ability to tunnel multiple protocols is one of PPTP's greatest advantages. Some tunneling software allows you to tunnel only IP packets. PPTP, however, can tunnel all of the protocols currently supported by RAS. Users connecting to a RAS server through a VPN will have access to the full range of protocols and servers they would normally have on their LAN. For Windows NT and Windows 95/98 users, this means that their usual username and password, and all access privileges associated with their profile, will pertain to the dial-up user. They will be able to browse the network and access file servers and network printers, as always, through their Network Neighborhood.

Ability to Use Corporate and Unregistered IP Addresses

When VPN users make PPTP connections with the RAS server, they can be assigned IP addresses by that server. The address can be part of the corporation's range of IP addresses (2.1.1.129 is part of the 2.1.1.0/24 CIDR address range in our earlier examples), thus making the RAS user's system appear to be on the corporate IP network.

Sometimes corporations don't use what are known as "registered" IP addresses on their internal networks. If a block of addresses is registered, it means that it was obtained by an address registry (such as the InterNIC) that assures that the addresses are unique on the Internet. The Internet Assigned Numbers Authority (IANA) has set aside blocks of unregistered IP addresses for use on private internets, or Intranets. These addresses can be used on IP networks that don't have Internet access or that have access through a router that uses Network Address Translation (or NAT, which we'll discuss more later). A listing of these unregistered blocks of addresses can be found in RFC 1918.

If a company is using an unregistered range of addresses, a RAS client using PPTP can obtain one of these addresses and have access to the corporate IP network. If the user were simply dialing into an ISP and attempting to access the network without PPTP, a hole in the corporate firewall would have to be opened up for that user. If the user obtains a dynamic IP address whenever they dial into their ISP, this would be nearly impossible.

5

Configuring and Testing Layer 2 Connections

In Chapter 4, *Implementing Layer 2 Connections*, you were introduced to the Point-to-Point Tunneling Protocol, which can be used to create a secure connection between remote users and a network. Out of the box, PPTP is primarily an extension of Windows NT Remote Access Services that helps establish a VPN between an Internet user and a destination network using the RAS server as a gateway. Microsoft's Routing and Remote Access addendum to Windows NT Server allows for LAN-to-LAN PPTP connections. This chapter mostly contains hands-on material for those of you wanting to set up your own PPTP connections. The first procedure we'll discuss is how to configure PPTP on your NT server. Rather than going into detail about setting up RAS, we'll assume that you've done it before, and only cover the places where RAS and PPTP intersect in detail. (If you have no RAS experience, the NT Help files can help you out, and there are several good books available on the subject.) When configuring RAS, you'll specify the number of ports you want to make available for VPN dial-up access. Although most administrators set their RAS servers up for dial-in only, you can also allow outgoing PPTP connections from the server.

RAS also lets you specify which protocols the NT server will route to dial-up users. Limiting the protocols will give you some control over which servers dial-up users can access. For example, allowing only IP will let users get to a TCP/IP email server, but prevent them from connecting to a shared drive on a Novell server using IPX. Likewise, if your internal servers don't use IP at all, you can disable IP while enabling the other protocols. The section "Choosing the protocols to tunnel" will point out where you can set this.

The RAS server also supports PPTP filtering, which lets you restrict who can connect to the system's LAN adapter. In order to connect, the user must pass through NT domain authentication. On multi-homed NT servers (servers with two network adapters), you can use PPTP filtering to restrict access to either local networks or the Internet. Used in combination with IP address filtering and fixed IP addresses, you can use the RAS server as a powerful firewall. If you prefer flexibility, however, NT also supports dynamic IP address assignment via the Dynamic Host Configuration Protocol (DHCP). We'll delve into how to configure both types of filtering and DHCP in this chapter.

As we said in Chapter 4, some ISPs support PPTP on their access equipment, while others don't. In this chapter, we'll show you how to handle either possibility. We'll also show you how to set up two popular routers for PPTP. ISPs can use PPTP support to make VPN connectivity easier for their customers, while network administrators can use it to offload some of the call processing on their RAS servers.

At the end of this chapter, we'll go over a list of tests to perform and monitors to check if your PPTP connection doesn't work the first time. We'll also discuss how PPTP interacts with some other network security products.

Installing and Configuring PPTP on a Windows NT RAS Server

Installing and configuring PPTP on Windows NT 4.0 is as straightforward as installing any other Windows NT component. There are three basic steps involved: installing the protocol, setting up RAS, and configuring users for dial-up access.

Installing PPTP

The PPTP protocol does not automatically come installed on a Windows NT 4.0 server. It's up to the administrator to add it to the list of network protocols active on the system, and you'll need your NT 4.0 CD-ROM disk or the NT installation hierarchy (e.g., "\I386" for Intel and clone processors) accessible from some other location. The steps for installing the PPTP protocol are pretty straightforward:

1. Under the Start menu on the control bar, select Settings, then Control Panel.

2. When the Control Panel window comes up, double-click on the Network icon.

3. In the Network dialog box, click on the Protocols tab.

4. In the Network Protocols list in the dialog box, you'll see the protocols currently installed on your system. Unless you've installed PPTP on the system before, it shouldn't be one of them. Click on the Add button at the bottom of the list.

5. The Select Network Protocol dialog box will appear, displaying a list of protocols available. Scroll down the list using the scroll bar until you see the Point Tunneling Protocol. Select this item and click the OK button.

6. Another dialog box will appear, entitled PPTP Configuration. Here you must select the Number of Virtual Private Networks you wish to support (i.e., the number of simultaneous PPTP connections that are allowed to the RAS server). It's a good way to keep the machine from getting bogged down by too many users. The range is from 1 to 256. For our example, we'll choose 8 from the selection box and click OK. The installation program will then scan the NT 4.0 CD-ROM disk for the needed files, or ask you for the location of those files.

Setting Up RAS

After the PPTP protocol itself is installed, the process automatically continues with RAS configuration. You'll get a pop-up Setup Message stating that RAS setup will be invoked. Click the OK button on this message to continue. Here are the steps to set up RAS for virtual private networking:

1. The Remote Access Setup dialog will come up, listing the current RAS ports and devices. If you already have a modem configured for RAS, it will appear in this box. To configure RAS to use PPTP devices, click the Add button.

2. The Add RAS Device dialog box will then appear. Use the pull-down selection list to select a RAS-capable device. In addition to your system's serial ports, you should see a list of VPN devices under the Ports heading. Each device will be numbered from 1 to the maximum number of VPN ports you configured when installing the PPTP protocol. In our case, we'll see one device for each of the eight ports we configured (see Figure 5-1). While RAS was kind enough to automatically include these ports for us, it allows us to select only one at a time from the list. Once you've selected the port to add, click the OK button. You'll then have to click the Add button again from the Remote Access Setup to start the procedure again.

3. The new VPN ports are configured for dial-in only. If you wish to set up the ports for dial-out as well (which we cover later in the section "Configuring

PPTP for Dial-up Networking on a Windows NT Client"), click on the Configure button in the Remote Access Setup dialog box.

4. Also from the Remote Access Setup dialog box, you can click the Network button to be brought to the Network Configuration dialog box for a selected VPN port. We'll discuss the options it presents in the following sections. As you'll see, since there's no way to force a particular user to dial into a specific VPN port, you might as well set all of them to the same values. Experienced RAS administrators will recognize this dialog box as the very same one used to configure a regular dial-up RAS connection.

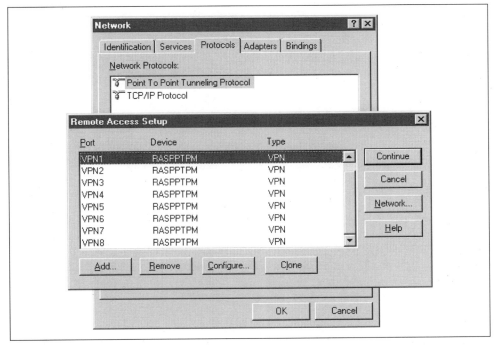

Figure 5-1. Setting up a PPTP RAS device

Choosing the protocols to tunnel

From the Network Configuration dialog box, one of the things you'll be able to select is which protocols to allow over a particular VPN port (see Figure 5-2). The choices are IP, IPX, and NetBEUI. For our example, we want to enable IP so Sara N. can get to the Internet mail server, and enable NetBEUI so she can attach to the shared drive of her desktop machine, but disable the unused IPX protocol.

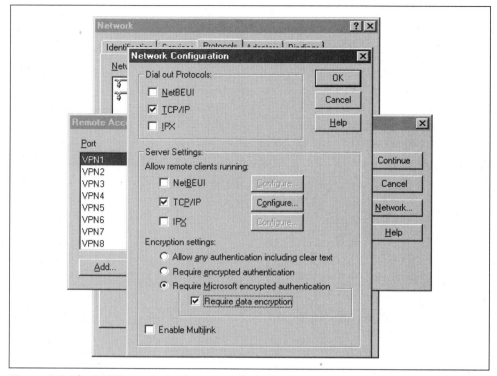

Figure 5-2. The RAS Network Configuration dialog box

From the same dialog box, you can also limit the user to the RAS server, rather than give access to the entire network. For our scenario, Sara N. will have access to the entire network. We don't recommend limiting access for several reasons:

- First of all, it's uninteresting. One of the exciting things about VPNs is that they give users secure remote access as if they were directly connected to the LAN. Limiting them to the RAS server means that you're limiting what they're allowed to do on the network to the services the RAS server is performing.

- If you're limiting remote user access to the RAS server itself, this probably means that you're running other services on the RAS server, such as email or printing services, or that you're using the RAS server as an application server. Unless you have four or fewer clients on your network, we don't recommend using the RAS server for anything but RAS. Otherwise, it can get bogged down by acting as both a router and a server.

- A PPTP RAS server, by its very nature, needs to be at least partially accessible from the Internet. Thus, it will also be open to attacks from the Net. If you're running critical applications on or from the RAS server and it proves vulnerable to one of these attacks and crashes, your application will go down with it.

Choosing your authentication method

In Chapter 4, we went over the authentication methods available in RAS: authentication with encryption (CHAP), authentication with Microsoft-enhanced encryption (MS-CHAP), and clear text (PAP). You can either require CHAP or MS-CHAP, or allow both encryption methods plus PAP. You make your choice in the Network Configuration dialog box.

If it's available to all of your clients (e.g., if they're all Windows clients or you're using TunnelBuilder on your Macs), we suggest that you use MS-CHAP. Using it will give you the benefit of being able to turn on data encryption, so that the PPTP connection will be truly secure. Using the other methods is certainly possible if you don't have MS-CHAP–capable clients, but you run the risk of sending unencrypted data over the Internet, and unencrypted passwords (in the case of PAP).

IP address negotiation using DHCP

The Dynamic Host Configuration Protocol (DHCP) is an ideal way to configure incoming PPTP clients with a dynamic IP address. Windows NT 4.0 comes with a DHCP server service that must be installed through the Network Control Panel.* Follow the instructions for installing RAS, but install the Microsoft DHCP Server service instead. Once the service is installed, a DHCP Manager program will also be installed under the Start menu in Administrative Tools.

To configure DHCP, follow these steps:

1. Under the Start → Programs → Administrative Tools listing, open the DHCP Manager. The DHCP Manager dialog box will appear (see Figure 5-3).

2. Under the DHCP Servers column, select the "Local Machine." Then go to the Scope menu item and select Create.

3. The Create Scope dialog box shown in Figure 5-3 will appear. Enter the Start Address and End Address for your assignments. In our case, we'll choose 2.1.1.129 for the starting address and 2.1.1.136 for the ending address.

4. Enter the Subnet Mask for the range. Since these addresses are part of the 2.1.1.0 range, we'll enter 255.255.255.0.

5. At this point, we'll leave the Exclusion Range addresses blank. We don't want to exclude any addresses from this range.

6. We'll enter the Name of the scope as "Dial-Up Address Range," then click OK. When a dialog asks you if you want to activate the scope, click Yes.

---

* DHCP will not work on a Windows NT 4.0 RAS server that has two network cards with PPTP filtering enabled on one of them. Microsoft found the problem and issued a fix in Windows NT 4.0 Service Pack 2. We recommend having Service Pack 3 (or later) installed if you want to use DHCP with RAS. See other problems between DHCP and PPTP filtering in the "Filtering caveats" section later in this chapter.

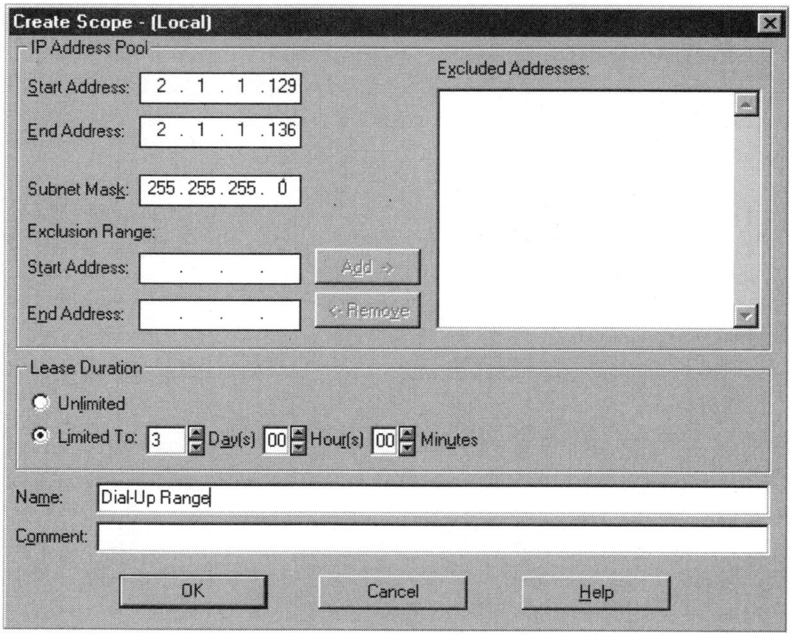

Figure 5-3. The Windows NT DHCP Manager

If you have several RAS servers, you'll probably want to use the DHCP Relay Agent NT service, also installed through the Network Control Panel. Using this service, the RAS server will forward a connecting client's request for an IP address to a DHCP server specified in the DHCP Relay Agent properties. This allows you to assign IP addresses from a single, central pool for every RAS server on your network, even across different LANs.

PPTP Filtering

We discussed what PPTP filtering does at the beginning of this chapter. To set up PPTP filtering, open the Network Control Panel, click on the Protocols tab and choose TCP/ IP, then click the Properties button. Finally, click the Advanced button on the TCP/ IP setup dialog box. At the bottom of the Advanced IP Addressing box is the Enable PPTP Filtering checkbox.

Outbound authentication using PPTP filtering

On multihomed hosts, PPTP filtering can also be used as a type of outbound firewall by enabling it on the network adapter connected to the LAN. Users on the internal network would dial the PPTP server as if they were coming over a PPP link, using the RAS server's IP address as the phone number. They would then be forced to authenticate at the RAS server in order to tunnel out to the Internet using the server's routing capabilities. This allows a network administrator to limit Internet access, monitor who's accessing the Internet and for how long, and limit the number of simultaneous Internet connections.

Filtering caveats

Enabling PPTP filtering on a Windows NT 4.0 system with only one network card can make other NT network services you might be running (such as the DHCP server service and the FTP server service) inaccessible to non-PPTP clients; the adapter will require PPTP authentication on any request it gets. There is a way to allow packets to reach the RAS server itself, without going to the network beyond. To do so you must install the Windows NT 4.0 Service Pack 3 or later version and add a particular entry to the Windows NT Registry.

 Editing the Windows NT Registry can be very dangerous. Invalid data entry could corrupt the Registry and cause numerous—possibly irreversible—system problems. You may be forced to reinstall Windows NT. As always, make sure you have a recent backup of your system.

Run the Registry Editor by selecting the Run option under the Start menu and entering REGEDIT.EXE in the filename field. The parameter to add is under the following Registry key:

    HKEY_LOCAL_MACHINE\SYSTEM\Services\RASPPTPE\Parameters\
    Configuration

Add a new Registry entry with the data type REG_DWORD. Call the entry "Allow-PacketsForLocalMachine" and give it a value of 1, then enter the changes and close the Registry Editor. You'll have to reboot for the change to take effect.

As we've said before, however, we don't recommend that you run services that can cause security breaches (anonymous FTP) or disrupt the workings of your internal network (DHCP) on your RAS server.

Filtering by IP Address

Another type of security allows you to specify the IP addresses from which the RAS server will allow PPTP connections. In order to implement this, your remote users will need to have fixed IP addresses assigned by their ISPs, and you'll need to know these addresses. Used in combination with PPTP filtering, this can make the RAS server secure from both unauthenticated connections and connections from unauthorized hosts. Unfortunately, this can't be done simply from a graphical user interface, so you must go back into the Windows NT 4.0 Registry.

Run the Registry Editor again and go to the following Registry key:

> HKEY_LOCAL_MACHINE\SYSTEM\Services\RASPPTPE\Parameters\
> Configuration

Under this key, you'll need to create a new entry of data type REG_DWORD. The new entry should be called "AuthenticateIncomingCalls." Make it a decimal value and give it a value of 1. Under the same key, create a new entry of data type REG_MULTI_SZ. Give this entry the name of "PeerClientIPAddresses." This is where you'll want to enter the valid IP addresses of the hosts you wish to be able to connect to the RAS server using PPTP. They should all be separated by single blank spaces.

Configuring Users for Dial-up Access

A dial-up user under Windows NT RAS is essentially set up the same way as a regular Windows NT domain user:

1. Use the User Manager for Domains, found under the Administrative Tools menu, to add or modify the user.

2. When editing the User Properties, click the Dialin button on the lower left-hand side of the dialog box.

3. The Dialin Information dialog box will appear (see Figure 5-4). For a PPTP user, check "Grant dialin permission to user," and set the Call Back radio button to No Call Back.

4. Click OK to exit both the Dialin Information and User Properties dialog boxes.

Configuring PPTP for Dial-up Networking on a Windows NT Client

To dial into an ISP that supports PPTP using a Windows NT client, you simply configure dial-up networking as you normally would—with the addition of setting authentication and encryption options. In this section, we'll focus on setting up an NT client to use the PPTP protocol when you're connecting to a provider that

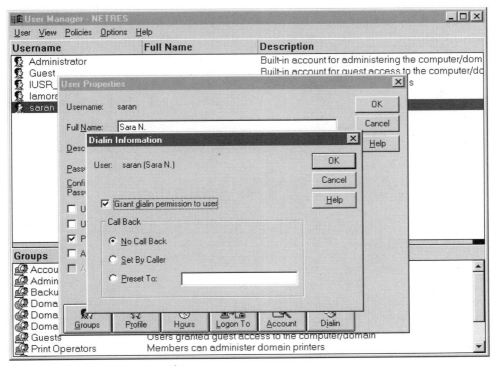

Figure 5-4. Configuring a user for remote access

doesn't support it. Below we've listed the steps for setting up a PPTP connection. We'll assume that you've already configured Dial-Up Networking to call your ISP and set up a PPP connection.

1. Set up the PPTP protocol the same way you set it up for the RAS server in items 1 through 6 in the "Installing PPTP" section.

2. RAS configuration is also similar to the way it was done in the "Setting Up RAS" section. This time, for item 3, click the Configure button in the Remote Access Setup dialog box. From there, select the Dial Out box, since we want to be able to dial out from the client rather than dial in.

3. From the start menu under Programs → Accessories, select Dial-Up Networking.

   When the Dial-Up Networking dialog box appears, click the New button and enter the name you want to call your VPN connection on the Phonebook Entry dialog box. For our scenario, we'll use "Central Office VPN." In the Phone Number field, enter the IP address of the PPTP RAS server to which you're connecting. For our example, it's 2.1.1.60. In the Dial Using field, select one of the VPN ports you created while installing PPTP and RAS. They will have the name RASPPTPPM (VPN*n*), where *n* is the number of the port. (See Figure 5-5.)

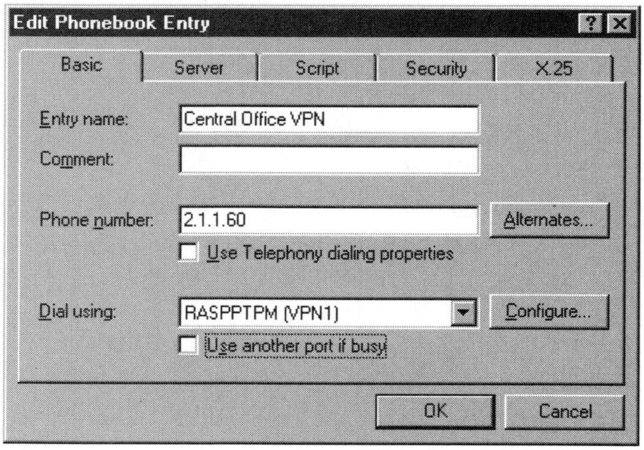

Figure 5-5. Configuring dial-up networking over a PPTP device

4. You can also specify which authentication method to require, and whether or not to require data encryption on the client. From the same Edit Phonebook Entry dialog box, click on the Security tab and you will see the same security choices you had on the server (see Figure 5-6). For the most secure VPN, make the selection to Accept only Microsoft encrypted authentication and check the "Require data encryption" checkbox. Whether you're dialing into an ISP that supports PPTP or not, you'll want to use MS-CHAP and encryption if your client allows it.

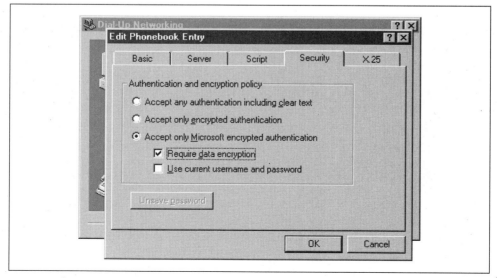

Figure 5-6. Setting the dial-up networking security options

Configuring PPTP for Dial-up Networking on a Windows 95 or 98 Client

As we've said, Windows 95 doesn't come with PPTP already installed. To use it, you'll have to obtain Dial-Up Networking Update 1.3 from Microsoft's web site. Since updates and service packs change from time to time, you should check the Microsoft web site to see what level of software you might need. The installation of the Dial-Up Networking (DUN) update is very simple. There aren't any parameters to enter, and Microsoft includes a useful help document. Because of this, we're not going to go over the step-by-step setup instructions for installation. As we've also said, Windows 98 comes with VPN access as a standard part of the OS.

To configure PPTP for Windows 95 or 98, you must configure two dial-up networking profiles: one to connect to the ISP and one to connect to the PPTP server. Because many people are familiar with configuring DUN to connect to their ISP, we'll skip over that step. If you've never done it before, you can find information on how to set up a DUN entry in the document Microsoft included with the DUN update.

In order to set up your VPN DUN profile, follow these steps:

1. Go to the Start menu, and select Programs → Accessories → Dial-Up Networking.

2. When the Dial-Up Networking window appears, click Make New Connection.

3. The Make New Connection wizard will appear. Type in what you want to call the connection profile in the "Name of the computer you are dialing" entry field. We'll call ours "Central Office VPN" again (see Figure 5-7). In the Select a device pull-down menu, choose the Microsoft VPN Adapter.

4. You'll then see a dialog box asking you to type in the host name or IP address of the VPN server to which you wish to connect. For our example, we'll use 2.1.1.60 (see Figure 5-8).

5. Click Next, then Finish. An icon for your connection profile will appear in the Dial-Up Networking window.

6. Select the profile icon, then click on it with the right mouse button. Select Properties from the pop-up menu. A dialog box will appear, showing you the information you entered earlier for the VPN connection (see Figure 5-9). Click on the Server Types tab.

7. In the Server Type dialog box (Figure 5-10), under Advanced options, check "Log on to network" if the network you're connecting to requires you to log on, such as in a Windows NT or Novell NetWare network. "Enable software compression" can remain checked. "Require encrypted password" doesn't need to be checked—it's better to let the answering end determine this.

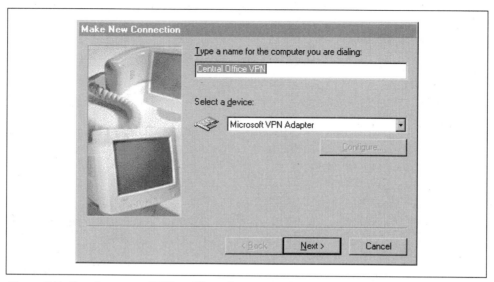

Figure 5-7. Creating a new VPN profile in the DUN Make New Connection wizard

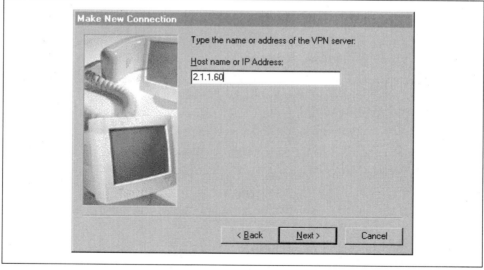

Figure 5-8. Entering the IP address of the VPN server

8. Under the allowed network protocols section, check the protocols you'll be using on the remote network. If necessary, you can click on the TCP/IP Settings button to input a static IP address, gateway address, and DNS server. Click OK to save your changes.

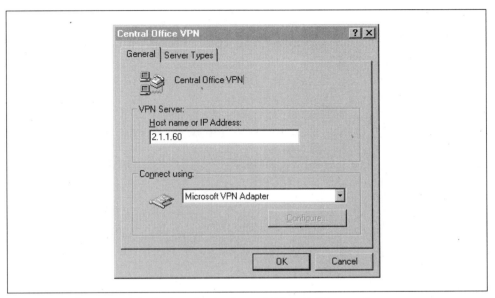

Figure 5-9. The General dialog box for the Central Office VPN properties

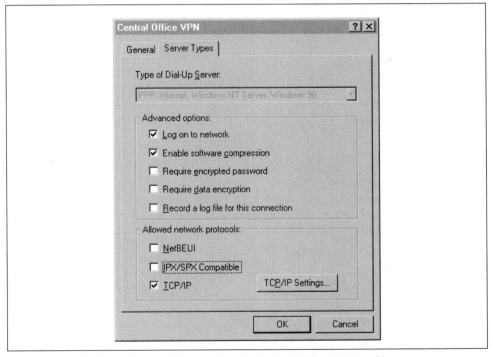

Figure 5-10. The Server Types dialog box for the Central Office VPN profile

Enabling PPTP on Remote Access Switches

This section is intended for ISPs or network administrators who wish to configure PPTP on their remote access switches. ISPs may want to do this as a value-added service for their clients. Network administrators may want to set up their own remote access switches in order to offload some of the communications overhead involved in remote access from the RAS server, or to increase capacity. For instance, an Ascend MAX 4004 can handle 48 analog modem calls, while actually hanging that many modems off an NT server would cripple it. Here, we'll look at two common remote access switches: the U.S. Robotics Total Control Enterprise Network Hub and the Ascend MAX 4004.

Configuring PPTP on a 3Com/U.S. Robotics Total Control Enterprise Network Hub

PPTP is available on 3Com/U.S. Robotics's Total Control Enterprise Network Hub, beginning with Release 3.2 of their NETServer card firmware. The typical hub has one NETServer card, one ISDN PRI card with two ports (giving you a total of 23 64-Kbps channels), plus a total of 48 digital modems. There are three options for implementing PPTP on the U.S. Robotics switch: configuring global PPTP parameters, configuring a port for PPTP, or configuring a specific user for PPTP.

Setting up global PPTP parameters

You can set up the hub's NETServer card with up to eight global PPTP RAS hosts. The NETServer card will use these hosts if a port or user has been set up for PPTP, but no specific RAS servers are specified. The first host in the list will be tried first, followed by the subsequent ones if the first host is not available. We recommend using the global parameters if the hub is providing dial-up services for a single NT domain, as in the case of a corporate network. It's not the ideal solution for an ISP, where you'll have many users from many different companies, each with a unique RAS server.

Here are the steps for setting up the global parameters:

1. Log into the NETServer card as "!root" (the administrator account), using either Telnet or the serial interface.

2. Use the following command to set up the PPTP hosts:

   ```
   set pptphost number hostname | ipaddress
   ```

   where *number* is the optional listing number (1 through 8) of the PPTP host. If no number is specified, the default of 1 is used. You can either specify the *hostname* of the RAS server, which is its fully qualified domain name, or the *ipaddress* of the server. We recommend using the IP address rather than the hostname, in case the hostname can't be resolved.

3. Use the Save All command to commit the changes to the hub's memory.

Setting up a port for PPTP

The NETServer card has numerous communications ports available—one for each dial-up device it supports. These are labeled "S0" through "S64." You may want to set PPTP on a specific port if you have certain channels nailed up, such as in the case of a leased line. Here are the steps to set this up:

1. At the command prompt, type in the following command to set up a port with PPTP:

   ```
   set port network hardwired
   ```

   Where *port* is the port number (i.e., S1, S24, S48, etc.) or "all" for the change to apply to all ports.

2. Enter the following to enable the PPTP protocol on the previous port:

   ```
   set port protocol pptp
   ```

3. The following command assigns a PPTP host to the specified port:

   ```
   set port pptphost number hostname | ipaddress
   ```

   If this command is omitted, the global PPTP hosts will be used.

4. Finally, reset the port with the following command to make the changes take effect:

   ```
   reset port
   ```

5. Use the Save All command to save the changes to the hub's memory.

Setting up a user for PPTP

Configuring a remote access switch with PPTP on a per-user basis is the ideal method for an ISP wishing to provide the service. This configuration will allow each individual user to connect via a different PPTP host. As with ports, each user can have a sequence of seven RAS hosts with which to attempt connections.

The following are the steps for setting up a user for PPTP on the hub:

1. Add a PPTP user with the following command:

   ```
   add netuser username password clear-text password protocol pptp
   ```

   username is the eight-character login name of the user, **password** is the optional password parameter, and **clear-text password** is the user's chosen eight-character password entered in clear text.* In the case of our example, we would enter:

```
add netuser saran password cat^FLAM protocol pptp
```

You can add the RAS hosts with which the user should attempt to authenticate. If this option is omitted, the global PPTP hosts will be used. This command is similar to assigning PPTP hosts to ports, except that the netuser parameter is used:

```
set netuser username pptphost number hostname | ipaddress
```

For our example, we would use:

```
set netuser saran pptphost 1 2.1.1.60
```

2. Enter the Save All command to enter the changes into the hub's memory. The Show Netuser command on "saran" will give you the following output:

```
Command> show netuser saran
    Username: saran              Type: Dial-in Network User
    Protocol: PPTP           Options:
 PPTP hosts: 2.1.1.60
            2.1.1.33
```

Configuring PPTP on an Ascend MAX 4004

On the Ascend MAX 4000 line, PPTP was first released on the firmware revision 4.6Bi12. The typical Ascend MAX 4004 configuration supports four T1 or PRI lines and 48 digital modems. Unlike the U.S. Robotics switch, the only way to specify PPTP servers is on a per-line basis, where each line is a WAN interface. On a MAX 1800, these will be BRI ISDN lines, while on a MAX 4004, they'll be T1 or PRI lines. This can be a serious limitation for ISPs that want to provide PPTP services to clients from various companies, all of whom will have different RAS servers. We expect Ascend to change this in the future to support these ISPs. For a company providing dial-up services to a single NT domain, however, this should pose no problem. Note that the MAX forwards all authentication on a PPTP-configured line to the RAS server, so a PPTP user won't have to be entered in a configuration profile or RADIUS profile on a MAX.

Here are the steps for configuring PPTP on the Ascend MAX 4004:

1. From the main Edit menu, select Ethernet → Mod Config → PPTP options.

2. Under the PPTP options menu, turn PPTP on by changing the PPTP Enable option to Yes with the Enter key.

---

* The password is said to be in clear text because anyone staring over your shoulder can see what password you're entering with this command. It doesn't mean that the password is stored in clear text or delivered in clear text at login time.

Enter a PPTP host for at least one of the Route line parameters. If you only want a certain line to handle PPTP calls, just enter an IP address for that line. The other lines, left as the default of 0.0.0.0, will handle calls normally. However, if you enable PPTP and leave all lines at 0.0.0.0, the MAX will treat all calls as PPTP calls and the MAX will no longer accept any incoming calls—it will stop routing and be functionally disabled. For our example, all four of our PRI lines will use the same PPTP host of 1.1.1.60 (see Figure 5-11).

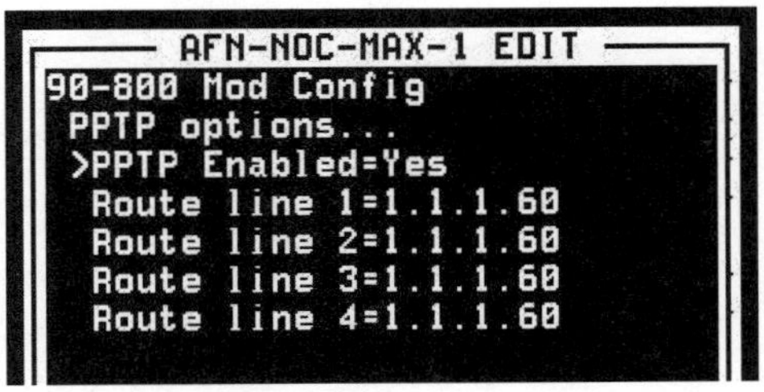

```
┌──────── AFN-NOC-MAX-1 EDIT ────────┐
│90-800 Mod Config                   │
│ PPTP options...                    │
│ >PPTP Enabled=Yes                  │
│  Route line 1=1.1.1.60             │
│  Route line 2=1.1.1.60             │
│  Route line 3=1.1.1.60             │
│  Route line 4=1.1.1.60             │
└────────────────────────────────────┘
```

Figure 5-11. The PPTP line configuration screen on an Ascend MAX 4004

3. Press the Escape key and select to accept the changes and exit in order to save the new PPTP information to the MAX's nonvolatile RAM.

Making the Calls

When calling into an ISP that supports PPTP, all of the VPN work is done for you by the ISP on their remote access switch. You just have to configure your client as if you're dialing directly into your RAS server; the ISP's switch will pass all the authentication information to that RAS server.

When dialing into an ISP that doesn't support PPTP, you'll need to initiate a PPP call to the ISP using the Dial-Up Networking dialog box. Once the call has been connected, leave your PPP session up, select the PPTP entry you made (in our case, it's called Central Office VPN), and click the Dial button. This will initiate the PPTP call to the corporate RAS server over your PPP Internet connection.

Troubleshooting Problems

What do you do if your system doesn't connect? Is the trouble with your remote user's ISP, the Central Office's ISP, with the Internet itself, or with the configuration on the RAS client or server? Because of all the factors involved, problems with VPN connections are some of the most difficult to track down.

Login problems

For dial-up RAS users, the most common problem in getting connected is working with the modem. In that case, all troubleshooting can be done on the client side. Authentication problems (bad usernames or passwords, or incorrect authentication type) follow shortly thereafter, and often require that someone look through the logs or watch the connection attempt at the destination RAS server. Windows NT's Event Viewer and Dial-Up Networking Monitor help you isolate such login problems.

The Event Viewer

The Event Viewer is the common logging system on all Windows NT machines. It can be found from the Start menu under Programs → Administrative Tools. Let's say that Sara N. is having trouble dialing in—she seems to be having negotiation problems and isn't sure why. When you bring up the Event Viewer, look at the Source column for any RemoteAccess messages that occurred at the approximate time she was attempting to dial in. In the left-hand column, there are icons that distinguish informational messages (an "i" encircled in blue), from warning messages (an exclamation mark encircled in yellow), and from error messages (a red STOP sign). You see a red STOP sign with the Source of RemoteAccess at the time Sara N. was attempting to dial in. Double-clicking on it will reveal the full error message (see Figure 5-12). The error appears to stem from a DHCP negotiation problem. The next logical step would be to make sure Sara N. is set up to obtain an IP address using DHCP, and to ensure that your DHCP server is configured correctly.

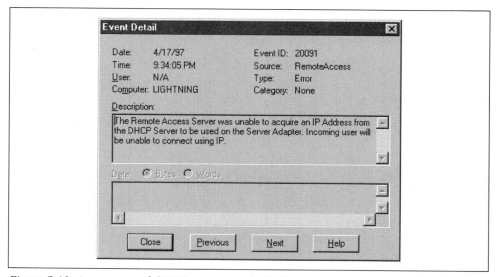

Figure 5-12. An unsuccessful VPN connection in the Event Viewer

The Event Viewer can also be used to obtain useful information about successful logins, including username, port number, time connected, port speed, and bytes sent and received. Figure 5-13 shows some of the successful connection information reported by the Event Viewer.

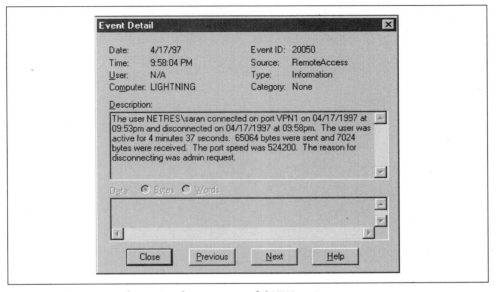

Figure 5-13. Logout information from a successful VPN session

The Dial-Up Networking Monitor

The Dial-Up Networking Monitor is found from the Start menu under Programs → Administrative Tools. It can be used to watch the status of an incoming or connected call. Not only can you watch for authentication problems, you can also see if any packets are being sent or received, and look for any connectivity errors in the Device errors section. (See Figure 5-14 for the information displayed.)

Connectivity Testing

If your PPTP client is having trouble dialing in, one of the first things to check is connectivity. This includes the PPP connectivity between your client and your ISP, and between your dial-up ISP and the ISP to which the RAS server is connected. Note that connectivity testing will work only for connections where you're dialing into an ISP that doesn't support PPTP. That's because in the cases where you're dialing into a provider that does support PPTP, you're not really "connected" until you're authenticated by the RAS server. If that much can happen, there's nothing wrong with the connectivity.

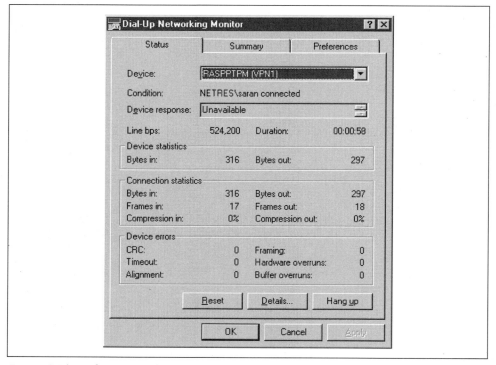

Figure 5-14. Dial-Up Networking Monitor

ping and traceroute

The best way to test connectivity is to run the *ping* command from the Start → Run
menu item. After you've connected to the ISP, you can attempt to ping the RAS
server with the following command:

```
PING IP address of RAS server
```

In our case, you would attempt to ping 2.1.1.60. If you get a successful return,
your connectivity is okay. If you don't, you should try to ping something else on
the Internet for which you know the IP address or hostname—an excellent test
would be your ISP's DNS servers. If you can ping something else on the other side
of your connection, but you can't ping your RAS server, the problem could be one
of the following:

- You've been disconnected. Sometimes it happens that a modem will discon-
  nect you, but Dial-Up Networking will still report you as connected. If you
  have an external modem, you might be able to check the carrier detect to see
  if you're actually connected.

- Your PPP link is incorrectly configured. Double-check the PPP and TCP/IP
  information given to you by your ISP against what you have in your TCP/IP

properties. Unless you have a fixed IP address, your IP address and gateway should be assigned by the ISP's PPP server. Also, make sure you have your ISP's correct DNS servers listed.

- Congestion or backbone routing problems on the greater Internet are preventing you from reaching the corporate network (a common occurrence!). A good test would be to attempt to ping your corporate Internet gateway router's IP address. If you can reach it across the Internet, then you can probably assume the RAS server is configured incorrectly or not connected.

Another good tool for testing connectivity is Traceroute. Traceroute is familiar to Unix users as the *traceroute* program, which traces the path of packets sent from the starting host to the destination host, listing the "hops" (other gateway routers) along the way. On Windows 95/98 and Windows NT systems, Traceroute is named TRACERT. The only problem you might have with using Traceroute is that it sends UDP packets on an invalid (and high) port, and some ISPs or companies block incoming UDP packets for security reasons. If Traceroute doesn't trace past a certain ISP's router and onto their internal network, it doesn't necessarily mean that the network or machine is down.

Using PPTP with Other Security Measures

What we've covered so far are the basic steps for setting up a VPN using PPTP. The viability of VPNs is directly affected by security measures implemented on the destination LAN. PPTP is a protocol like any other, and must be allowed to pass through (or bypass) a firewall or proxy server in order to work successfully.

How to Allow PPTP Through Firewalls

Like most IP-based tunneling protocols, PPTP operates on a specific IP port—in this case, TCP port 1723. On your firewall or filter, you'll want to allow IP access to and from that port for your RAS server. If your firewall also filters by protocol, you'll need to allow GRE (IP protocol 47) to pass through. It's a good idea to block every other port off on your RAS server, especially the nefarious NetBIOS name service, datagram, and session ports of 137, 138, and 139. These ports can be used to browse the NetBIOS names and shares of the machines on your network.

Fixed IP addresses

Since remote PPTP users will be dialing in through ISPs, they may not always have the same IP address. This eliminates the possibility of host-based filtering and means that a PPTP VPN will rely strictly on its user-based authentication system. A fixed IP address, where a user will be assigned the same IP address every time they dial in, is a way around this problem. Some ISPs offer a fixed IP address as an account add-on for a nominal monthly fee. If available, this is a great way to enhance security by allowing only hosts with one of those IP addresses to pass through port 1723 of the firewall and connect to the RAS server.

How PPTP Can Bypass a Proxy Server

A proxy server acts as a "go-between" for your internal hosts and hosts you'll need access to on the Internet. Typically, a proxy server will be the only machine on a network, outside of an Internet server such as SMTP mail, that's allowed to pass through a firewall. An administrator can control who has access to what Internet services outside of the firewall. Although they seem like a perfect match, PPTP will not work with some proxy servers (one exception to this is Microsoft Proxy Server 2.0). At this time, PPTP clients and servers don't know how to interoperate with the sockets services on proxy servers. This means that you can't have your PPTP server sitting behind a proxy server on your network. The clients won't be able to get through. If you're running a proxy server, you'll still need to keep your RAS server open to the firewall. In such a case, both the RAS server and the proxy server may need to be multi-homed between your router and your local network. Multi-homed servers are connected via two network cards to two separate LAN segments. For these situations, you'll want to turn on IP Forwarding (routing) in the TCP/IP Properties for each network card.

6

Implementing the AltaVista Tunnel 98

The AltaVista Tunnel is a product from Digital Equipment Corporation (now Compaq) that supports moderately heavy use over a virtual private network connection.

As virtual private networks mature, the AltaVista Tunnel continues to evolve, increasing security and adding features and functionality. Now reincarnated as the Altavista Tunnel 98, this client-server package is still a solid solution to a company's VPN needs. In this chapter we introduce some of the advantages, drawbacks, and key concepts to the functionality of the AltaVista solution. Though this is not the only virtual private networking solution, it is one that seems to be taking the lead in this still maturing field.

The AltaVista Tunnel 98 is available in two versions: the Extranet Server and the Telecommuter Client. The Extranet server manages connections on the office side, while remote users dial in using Telecommuter Client. The Extranet server itself can also act as a tunnel client, allowing an entire LAN to access a tunnel to a remote LAN.

The server keeps a file on each user, defining each user with a username, group name, password, and half of a digital key for the purposes of encryption. Each user's client software is configured to issue this information to the server upon initiating a connection.

The server secures traffic for the tunnel network with a combination of encryption and conventional authorization using usernames and passwords. This authorization scheme allows remote connections to the tunnel network from any point on the Internet. Each user belongs to one or more groups, and each group gains access to certain systems protected behind the server. The server manages the user group's name and password files, and each group's individual encryption keys. This system gives the enterprise a secure and fairly versatile solution to implementing a virtual private network, without a great expense in administrative time and headaches.

While the AltaVista Tunnel Extranet Edition can be used on a computer running other network services, it is advised that this server be managed as a highly trusted system, as the AltaVista Tunnel software handles key generation and management, and authorizes remote tunnel clients. In other words, you should isolate it physically and remove non-essential software.

The Telecommuter Client manages each virtual private network connection that the user has access to, allowing for multiple group configurations, keys, and routing information. The tunnel session from the end user side of the connection is transparent to the user's Internet service provider, as the remote tunnel server handles all virtual IP assignments and routing information. The virtual IP address is assigned from a defined range in the Extranet server's configuration. These IP addresses are assigned to connecting users for the purpose of routing tunnel traffic. The end user's PC then connects to the private network as if it were a node on the local network. The tunnel session is secure, and transparent to the end user.

The AltaVista Tunnel Extranet server is available for Windows NT (4.0 SP3 or later), or Digital Unix. The AltaVista Tunnel Telecommuter Client is available for Windows NT (4.0 SP3 or later), MacOS v.8.0, or the Windows 95/98 operating systems.

Demo copies of the AltaVista Tunnel Extranet Server or Telecommuter Client may be obtained at *http://altavista.software.digital.com:80/tunnel/index.htm.*

Advantages of the AltaVista Tunnel System

The AltaVista Tunnel system has three advantages of note: accessibility, security, and general flexibility.

Accessibility

Other virtual private network solutions are geared toward providing secure network-to-network access over the Internet. This setup requires fixed IP addresses on both sides, and specific firewall configurations for tunnel traffic on both sides. While the AltaVista Tunnel can provide a LAN-to-LAN virtual private network, its main difference from other solutions resides in its independence from fixed IP addresses, and its user-based verification system. With the use of unique group names, passwords, and encryption keys, the AltaVista Tunnel lets a user log in from a variety of locations, free to use a different IP address each time. This allows the individual user to "roam" from one Internet access point to another, maintaining access to the corporate LAN.

User groups make configuration easier. For instance, you could assign all salespeople to one group, letting them share a single password, and limit their access to particular machines on your corporate network that are owned by the sales organization. User-group authentication, rather than IP authentication, is the functional widget that allows roaming access.

The inbound Extranet server is configured with tunnel groups that have specific group usernames, passwords, and individual tunnel keys. These groups, once verified, are routed from a range of dynamically assigned virtual IP addresses to ranges of physical IP addresses on the local network. This allows certain groups of users from the Internet access to specific machines or groups of machines on the local net. The authentication and encryption information is shared by all users authorized to access each specific tunnel. Each user configures an AltaVista Tunnel Telecommuter client with the appropriate username, password, and session key, and connects to the corporate private LAN.

Security

The Tunnel is quite state-of-the-art as far as encryption and authentication go.

Three-part encryption technique

The AltaVista Tunnel initially employs RSA's 1024-bit public key exchange technology to provide authentication between tunnel participants. After the initial authentication, the tunnel switches to RSA's RC4 128-bit secret key encryption, which seals all data into secured cryptographic packets for transport to the receiving tunnel client. The receiving tunnel client then decrypts these sealed packets into a readable form. Tunneling data remains encrypted until it is received by the Extranet Server, ensuring data security even within the trusted network. Data integrity of the encrypted packets is transparently checked using RSA's MD5 checksum algorithm, verifying that the data has not been tampered with via transport. Finally, AltaVista Tunnel exchanges new encryption keys among tunnel clients from 30 minutes to 1,440 minutes (1 day) during the tunnel session, depending on the configuration parameters set on the server. This re-keying operation happens automatically and is transparent to the various users on the tunnel.

The international version of AltaVista Tunnel uses a 56-bit RC4 key, as U.S. export laws prohibit the export of higher forms of encryption technology. By necessity, 56-bit keys are less secure and can be cracked by a determined snooper. The tunnel recognizes and compensates for the differences between domestic and international keys, which allows users to log in to the virtual private network from one country to another. The AV Tunnel 98 also supports 40-bit encryption keys if required.

Support for an emerging security standard

RSA has recently begun development of the Secure Wide Area Network (S/WAN) standard, which is based on IPSec. Though AltaVista's security methods were developed by AltaVista, they are committed to supporting the emerging standard once it has been finalized. They will likewise continue to support their proprietary security methods as well. No announcements for IPSec support were apparent for AV Tunnel 98.

Support for Security Dynamics SecureID

You can get even more secure authentication by using the AltaVista Tunnel 98's support for Security Dynamics SecureID authentication tokens. By generating random access codes every 60 seconds, SecureID tokens provide a further line of defense against persons trying to gain unauthorized access to the secure private LAN. The Extranet server actually acts as a client for the ACE/SERVER, the guts of the SecureID system. More information about Secure Dynamics authentication solutions is available at *http://www.securitydynamics.com*.

Flexibility

The AltaVista Tunnel 98 works with many types of conventional firewalls. The LAN's firewall is configured as a generic relay, which automatically forwards all traffic addressed to the tunnel port on the firewall to a unique port on the tunnel server. The unique tunnel port and the generic relay configuration not only hide the physical IP address of the tunnel server, but also log all attempts to connect to the tunnel network at both the firewall and the tunnel server. Other firewall configuration options for IP tunnels may be found in Chapter 9, *The Cisco PIX Firewall*.

AltaVista Tunnel Limitations

While it includes a full-featured tunnel setup, the AltaVista Tunnel still has a few limitations that may render it inappropriate for some enterprises needing a virtual private network.

Platform Limitations

Given its limited support of platforms, AltaVista Tunnel is definitely not the answer for the enterprise with a mix of operating systems. AltaVista has released a Telecommuter client package for the MacOS, though there is no mention of this release on their tunnel web site. However, a demo copy of the Mac Telecommuter Client software is available for download at the AltaVista Tunnel 98 site listed at the beginning of this chapter. No versions have been announced for flavors of Unix other than Digital Unix, and AltaVista has gone so far as to drop support for both BSD/OS and FreeBSD in this revision of their software.

Security Drawbacks of User Authentication

Though the security features are one of the most powerful aspects of the AltaVista Tunnel, user-based authentication still poses some security concerns. In order to provide the flexibility to log in from anywhere, the product removes one of the most common types of authentication normally used by VPNs: checking the incoming IP address. Network administrators, already burdened with users losing or compromising passwords to the system, must stress extra care in protecting generated keys, tunnel user group names, and passwords; these are the only factors by which AltaVista Tunnel verifies its connections. As stated, the AltaVista Tunnel Extranet server should be closely managed as a highly trusted system, because compromising a tunnel key negates the purpose of the virtual private network in the first place.

How the AltaVista Tunnel Works

Each AltaVista Tunnel network consists of two sides, the inbound and outbound, both connected to the Internet in some fashion. The inbound side is the private network, which consists of some number of hosts and an AltaVista Extranet server. The outbound side can be either a single computer or another LAN. In the first case, the user would run the AltaVista Telecommuter client, and in the second, the remote LAN would have an Extranet server of its own to manage inbound or outbound tunnel traffic by hosts on its network. The Extranet server on the inbound side always manages authentication, dynamic IP assignment, and the routing of tunnel traffic for incoming connections.

A simple VPN might consist of three individual users connected to the Internet via three separate ISPs. Each user is running a Telecommuter client, and has access to the tunnel group through the remote LAN's Extranet server. Users have unique physical IP addresses on their respective ISPs' networks.

The tunnel server and hosts on the remote LAN are likewise assigned physical IP addresses. On the tunnel server, a range of virtual IP addresses is available for assignment to incoming tunnel connections. Each tunnel receives two virtual IP addresses: one for the client end and one for the server end.

Tunnel traffic destined for the virtual private network is first routed, via the tunnel client software, from the client's physical IP address to its virtual IP address. This virtual IP address points to the tunnel server's virtual IP address for that connection, which, in turn, is routed to an internal host on the local network's physical IP range. In this way, the remote clients act as if they were nodes on the local network.

When a remote user initiates a tunnel session with the tunnel server, an encrypted connection request is sent, which, once relayed through the firewall, is authenticated against the tunnel server's list of authorized clients. Once the request is granted, the tunnel server issues a response encrypted with the client's public key. The client decrypts this message using its own private key, and then the two exchange parts of a session key. These parts are combined to form a secret session key, which is regenerated every 30 to 1,440 minutes of the connection.

The AltaVista Tunnel 98 software on both ends is installed as a separate network protocol, and is routed to a piece of software called a pseudo-adapter. The virtual IP address assigned for the tunnel connection is attached to this pseudo-adapter through which all tunnel traffic is routed. Since it uses a separate, albeit virtual, network adapter, the AltaVista Tunnel does not interfere with other network traffic on the client machine. Thus, with a functioning tunnel session, the client may browse the Web, download mail, and perform whatever operations are needed on the tunnel network, without interrupting either the tunnel connection or any other network connections the client's machine may have opened. This scenario can be duplicated with all three of the tunnel clients in the previous example simultaneously.

System Considerations

We have discussed the platform limitations for both the Telecommuter Client and the Extranet server. Examples in the "VPNs and AltaVista" section later in this chapter were tested with these system and networking setups.

Extranet server

Platform:

- Pentium 233 running Windows NT 4.0 with 64 MB of RAM, 2 GB hard drive, 100 Mb/s Ethernet connection.
- Pentium 166 running FreeBSD with 128 MB of RAM, 2 GB hard drive, 10 Mb/s Ethernet connection.

Connectivity:

- The LAN for each Extranet server is connected to the Internet via multiple T1s.

Telecommuter client

Platform:

- Mix of Pentium 233s and 166s running Windows 95 or Windows NT Workstation 4.0 with 32 to 128 MB of RAM, 1 to 5 GB hard drives, and 10 Mb/s Ethernet to 28.8Kbps modem connections.

Connectivity:

- The AltaVista Extranet server takes about 3 MB of disk space and runs at about 3000 KB of memory sitting idle. The Telecommuter Client takes approximately 2 MB of space and runs at about 500 to 700 KB of memory idle or connecting.

- The Extranet edition allows for incoming and outgoing tunnel connections; thus, it can be used as a client as well. This would be useful in a LAN-to-LAN virtual private network configuration, where the tunnel traffic would need to be two-way.

Planning

Before configuration, assign users to groups based on how they share access to hosts on your internal network.

The Guts

Let's look at the structure for information provided by the AltaVista Tunnel.

AltaVista Tunnel Extranet server

The tunnel server consists of three integral parts that allow it to function as a router for tunnel sessions:

Routing tables
> The routing table maps a range of local physical IP addresses to hosts on the local network that will receive tunnel traffic. A defined route may be set as a default route for all tunnel groups, or dynamically assigned as needed to one or many groups. A default route for all tunnel groups would allow those groups to access the same hosts on the enterprise LAN or WAN, whereas a dynamically assigned configuration would allow certain groups to access specific ranges of IP addresses on the network. The routing table on the tunnel server consists of three parts:
> — *Subnet:* This is the subnet of the network addresses on the local network that are part of the tunnel. Traffic destined for these IP addresses will use the tunnel network.

— *Netmask*: This is the Netmask corresponding to the assigned subnet.

— *Description*: A unique designation assigned to this route.

Dynamic IP tables

Each dynamic range of IP addresses can be routed to the physical IP addresses listed in the tunnel server's routing table. The dynamic IP addresses are virtual. The server assigns one IP address to the client requesting a tunnel session, and a second to the server's "end" of the tunnel session. The server end of the tunnel session is then routed to the physical IP range configured in the routing table. Each tunnel group has its own range of dynamic virtual IP addresses, and each of these ranges may be routed to the same or different physical IP addresses, as needed. Each dynamic IP address range has five definable parameters:

— *Range name*: This name is arbitrary and assigned by the system administrator for defining the IP range in a manageable way.

— *Range description*: A brief description of the IP range (i.e., "IPs for the Sales Tunnel"). This is useful when managing many dynamic IP ranges on the same server.

— *First IP*: This is the lowest IP address in the dynamic IP range, and thus the first usable IP address within the range.

— *Total tunnels*: This value is the total number of tunnel sessions available at any given time. The total number of IP addresses that can be dynamically assigned is twice that of the Total Tunnels setting (one IP address per "end" of the tunnel).

— *NetMask*: The network mask that corresponds to the total group of usable IP addresses in the dynamic range.

Authentication tables

Each tunnel group is assigned a specific username, password, and session key. The tunnel client is configured with this authentication information, and transmits it to the server for verification before tunnel traffic can commence. The Extranet server generates the authentication key, user group name, and password as exportable files (described in the next section) for installation into the Telecommuter Client clients that require access. These files should be treated as confidential information, and should be closely managed.

The three parameters presented here are configured for each tunnel group. Configuration of the local firewall is also required for successfully routing tunnel traffic. See the "VPNs and AltaVista" section below for details.

Security procedures

When you create a tunnel group, the AltaVista Tunnel Extranet server requires you to manually enter a unique username and password. Once the group is configured, the tunnel server creates a unique 1024-bit RSA authentication key for that particular group. Both of these authentication pieces may be extracted into separate ETA and key files. The ETA file contains the user group name and password, and is by default named *groupname.eta*. The key file is typically named *groupname.key*. These authorization files are needed by remote clients for connecting to and authorizing tunnel sessions to the tunnel server. Once extracted, these files should be distributed to all authorized remote clients. These security files should be handled as highly confidential information, as anyone with this file will be allowed access to the virtual private network. Distribution by floppy disk or private FTP site are semi-secure ways of distribution, but all transfers should be logged by the system administrator to maintain the integrity of the security system.

AltaVista Tunnel Telecommuter Client

The tunnel client software contains a single configuration for each tunnel group to which the client has access. Thus, the user could be a sales forecaster for a manufacturing company, and have access to the Sales group for historical sales data and the Manufacturing group for factory throughput. The following parameters are specific to each group:

Username
> This is the unique tunnel group name as it appears in the tunnel server's authentication tables. This parameter is part of the extractable ETA file from the Extranet server, or it may be entered manually.

Server key ID
> The server key also comes from the tunnel server's authentication tables. Each group has a specific key, which allows the client access to the tunnel group. A copy of this key is provided in the extractable key file from the Extranet server.

Tunnel server
> This is the domain name or IP address of the tunnel server on the Internet and the port for which tunnel traffic is handled (default 3265).

First firewall
> The first firewall is not typically used for single remote PCs, as the traffic is transparent until received by the remote firewall. This first firewall is typically the end user's ISP, through which outbound tunnel traffic passes transparently. On the Extranet server acting as an outbound tunnel client, the first firewall parameter lists the address and port (default 3265) of the local firewall between the LAN and the Internet.

Second firewall

> This is the physical address and tunnel port for the private network being accessed. Ultimately, it is the first destination for tunnel traffic, and it is relayed from the tunnel port on the firewall to the tunnel port on the Extranet server for verification.

VPNs and AltaVista

AltaVista's flexibility allows an enterprise to accept several tunnel sessions to the virtual private LAN, either from a remote LAN or from remote single machine connections. The configurations here are each subtly different, because the Single Connection-to-LAN and LAN-to-LAN/LAN-to-WAN implementations of the AltaVista Tunnel are different. The LAN-to-LAN/LAN-to-WAN tunnel configurations are for an enterprise that requires two-way tunnel traffic between its two networks where an Extranet server is required on each end of the connection. This scenario is actually meant to replace traditional private leased line connections by using secure tunneling sessions over the Internet. The Single Connection-to-LAN scenario allows multiple end users to access the private network over the Internet, in a secure fashion, without being tied to a fixed IP address or a single access provider

In the following sections we show a sample configuration illustrating each scenario.

Implementing a LAN-to-LAN Tunnel

This configuration features a firewall on each side.

Sample configuration

In the LAN-to-LAN tunnel configuration shown in Figure 6-1, LAN 1 is a corporate office connected to the Internet via a full T1 and protected with a firewall. There are four machines on the LAN: the AltaVista Extranet server, Finance, Human Resources, and Research & Development. LAN 2 is a remote sales office running a second AltaVista Extranet server and three host machines. LAN 2 is connected to the Internet via 128Kbps ISDN and is protected by a firewall. This configuration is set up to illustrate the ability of the AltaVista Tunnel server to act as either an outbound or inbound tunnel router. In this example, LAN 1 is the inbound tunnel group and LAN 2 is the outbound tunnel group.

Tunnel server configuration

Since LAN 1 is the inbound tunnel network, it's configured to accept tunnel traffic from LAN 2. The tunnel connection is dedicated, meaning it begins automatically and stays up constantly.

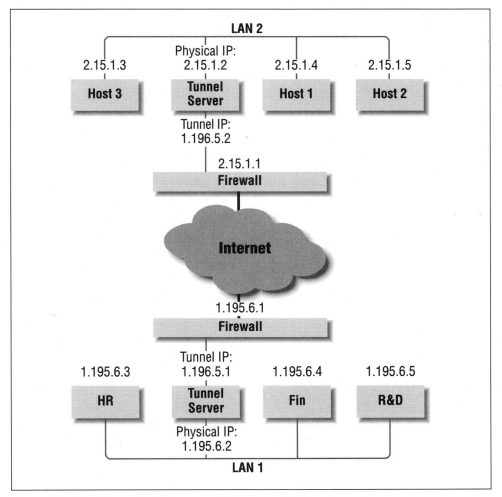

Figure 6-1. Two Enterprise LANs connected over an AltaVista Tunnel

Routing table

The inbound tunnel server routes all incoming tunnel traffic to its local net-work address range (1.195.6.*). Its routing table is set up like this:

— *Subnet*: 1.195.6.*

— *Netmask*: 255.255.255.0

— *Description*: Local Tunnel Clients

Dynamic IP tables

The tunnel server, in this case, assigns 1.196.5.1 to the tunnel pseudo-adapter on its end, and 1.196.5.2 to the pseudo-adapter on LAN 2's tunnel server. A dynamic range may be set up for multiple remote LAN or single PC connections to this tunnel. The Dynamic IP tables are configured like this:

— *Range name*: Sales Tunnel.

— *Range description*: Regional Sales Office Tunnels.

— *First IP*: 1.196.5.1.

— *Total tunnels*: The total number of tunnels for this tunnel group is set to one. There is a range of two dynamic IP addresses. The LAN 1 tunnel server assigns a virtual IP address to itself and the other LAN's tunnel server in the LAN-to-LAN tunnel connection.

— *NetMask*: 255.255.255.252 for the two IP virtual networks.

Authentication table

The group username is LAN 2. The password is WHO$there. These two parameters have been extracted into an ETA file called *lan2.eta* and distributed via secure FTP session to the tunnel server on LAN 2. The key file has been created by the tunnel server on LAN 1 and is specific to this tunnel group. The key file has also been extracted and distributed via secure FTP session to the tunnel server on LAN 2. By default this key file is named *lan2.key*.

LAN 2 controls the outbound tunnel session, and is acting as a tunnel client for its local network. The tunnel connection itself has a single virtual IP address (1.196.5.2), assigned by the tunnel server on LAN 1. The tunnel server on LAN 2 routes all tunnel traffic from its local network to that virtual IP address. The outbound tunnel has been set up to connect in automatic mode, meaning that whenever the tunnel server is up, so is the tunnel connection. The ETA and key files from LAN 1 have been installed, and the outbound tunnel session is configured as below:

Tunnel name

The name for this tunnel is Sales, as from LAN 1 earlier.

Tunnel description

This is also the same as the LAN 1 tunnel description: Regional Sales Office Tunnels.

Network addresses

This outbound tunnel is set up as a static route tunnel, because the virtual IP address assigned to the tunnel comes from the tunnel server on LAN 1. The local IP address for LAN 2's pseudo-adapter is 1.196.5.2. The remote IP address for LAN 1's pseudo-adapter is 1.196.5.1.

Routing tables

On the LAN 2 end, the tunnel server must route traffic from its local hosts to the tunnel's virtual IP address. This is set up as a default route coming from the network 2.15.1.*, with a netmask of 255.255.255.0.

Hostname

    The remote host's physical IP address is 1.195.6.2 and the default tunnel traffic port is 3265.

First firewall

    This is defined according to the view from LAN 2, the outbound direction of the tunnel. The firewall on LAN 2 is the first encountered by tunnel traffic, so this field is set to 2.15.1.1, with a default tunnel traffic port of 3265.

Second firewall

    This is the LAN 1 firewall address on its Internet interface, 1.195.6.1. The default tunnel traffic port is, again, 3265.

Server key ID

    The server key ID for this tunnel session is *lan2.key*. This key is part of the extracted key file from the tunnel server on LAN 1.

Firewall configuration

The firewall on each respective network is configured to route all traffic bound for the tunnel to the tunnel server on their network. With the inbound network (LAN 1), this is all traffic received on the default tunnel port 3265. With the outbound network, any traffic received that is destined for the tunnel network is routed to the tunnel server.

- LAN 1—This firewall is part of the inbound network, and relays all tunnel traffic to the LAN 1 tunnel server. Thus, incoming tunnel traffic received on port 3265 and destined for the network 1.196.5.* is relayed to 1.195.6.2 (the physical IP address of the tunnel server).

- LAN 2—The LAN 2 firewall receives traffic for the tunnel from its local hosts, as they are default routed to 2.15.1.1. All traffic bound for the tunnel network (1.196.5.*) is relayed to the LAN 2 tunnel server's physical IP address: 2.15.1.2.

Host configuration

Each host on both networks is set up to default route all tunnel traffic to its respective firewall. As seen in the previous firewall configuration, this traffic, if bound for the tunnel, is routed from the firewall to the tunnel server's physical IP address.

- LAN 1—The three hosts on this network (Finance, Human Resources, and Research & Development) route traffic to the firewall first (1.195.6.1), which then relays tunnel traffic to the tunnel server.

- LAN 2—The two host machines on LAN 2 have 2.15.1.1 as the default route for all network traffic.

Routing over the VPN

With the preceding configuration, traffic on the virtual private network progresses much like a leased line connection between two LANs. For instance, a host on LAN 2 wishes to open a tunnel session to the Finance server on LAN 1. The traffic bound for the tunnel network (1.196.5.*) is routed directly to the firewall (2.15.1.1), via a static route ·configured on the Host 1 machine. The firewall on LAN 2 relays all traffic for the tunnel network back to the tunnel server on LAN 2 (2.15.1.2), using a default route. The tunnel server on LAN 2 routes all traffic bound for the tunnel onto its pseudo-adapter end of the tunnel (1.196.5.2) and across the Internet. This virtual IP address is its default interface for all tunnel traffic. LAN 1's firewall receives traffic at port 3265. All traffic to this port is relayed to the tunnel server's virtual IP on its local network (1.196.5.1) at port 3265.

After the initial security verification process, the tunnel server regenerates a session key every 30 minutes and tunnel traffic commences, oblivious to this process.

The traffic from the host on LAN 2 is then routed to the LAN 1 tunnel server's virtual IP to its physical IP, and on to the Finance server. The host machine on LAN 2 now functions as a node on LAN 1's network, and is able to access any files and services on the Finance server to which the user would normally have access.

Implementing Single Connections-to-LAN Tunnels

Sample configuration

Figure 6-2 sets up a typical PC tunnel connection to a remote network over the Internet. The PCs are Windows 95 machines connecting to the Internet via a 64-Kbps ISDN. They are running the AltaVista Tunnel Telecommuter Client. The corporate LAN connects to the Internet over a fractional T1 (256 Kbps), and is running an AltaVista Tunnel Extranet server, which provides tunnel connections to two hosts (Host 1 and 2). Though there are other hosts on the corporate LAN, these are the only ones available to the tunnel.

Tunnel server configuration

Routing table

The routing table is set up to route all tunnel sessions to the local LAN's physical network: 1.195.6.*. All dynamic IP addresses are routed to this network for tunnel traffic.

— *SubNet*: 1.195.6.*

— *NetMask*: 255.255.255.0

— *Description*: Local Hosts

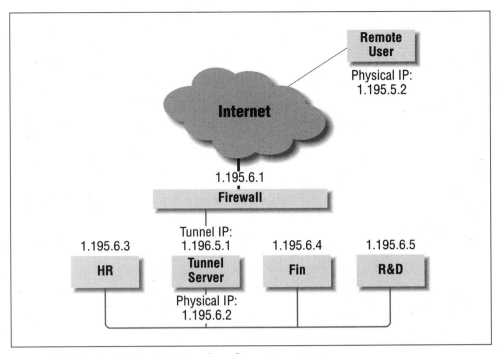

Figure 6-2. A typical PC-to-LAN tunnel configuration

Dynamic IP table

The dynamic IP range starts at 1.196.5.1 and comprises a Class C network (255 addresses). The tunnel server on the corporate LAN is set up to connect multiple single PC tunnel connections, and routes all tunnel traffic to its physical network from the routing parameters above.

— *Range name*: Sales Tunnel.

— *Range description*: Remote Tunnel Clients.

— *First IP*: 1.196.5.1.

— *Total tunnels*: The total number of tunnels for this tunnel group is set to 128. As each tunnel session is assigned two IP addresses, this makes the total IP address range equal to 256 IP addresses.

— *NetMask*: 255.255.255.0 for the 256 IP virtual network.

Authentication table

The group name for this tunnel is Sales. The password is Bubba. These two parameters have been extracted into an ETA file called *sales.eta* and distributed via floppy disk to the various tunnel clients. The key file has been created by the tunnel server on the corporate LAN and is specific to this tunnel group. The key file has also been extracted and distributed via floppy disk. By default, this key file is named *sales.key*.

Firewall configuration

The local firewall is configured to relay all external tunnel requests (those reaching 1.195.6.1 on port 3265) to the tunnel server at its physical IP address: 1.195.6.2, port 3265.

Local host configuration

The host machines on the corporate LAN have a default route to 1.195.6.2, the tunnel server's physical IP address. Any traffic destined for the tunnel takes the tunnel server's virtual IP "end" of the tunnel; all other traffic bound for outside the local network passes to the firewall and out to the Internet.

Remote PC configuration

The remote PC's Telecommuter Client Tunnel client is configured to route all tunnel traffic to the dynamic IP address assigned by the remote tunnel server. Within the tunnel client software, the tunnel group is defined like this:

Username
> The name of this tunnel group is Sales. There is also a password (Bubba), which must be manually entered when a tunnel session is opened.

Server key ID
> The local key file is *sales.key*. It is stored with the ETA file obtained from the remote tunnel server (in this case via floppy disk).

Tunnel server
> The tunnel server's physical IP address is 1.195.6.2, with a tunnel traffic port of 3265.

> *First Firewall*
>> Unused in this case.

> *Second Firewall*
>> The IP address to the remote LAN's firewall is 1.195.6.1, with a tunnel traffic port of 3265.

Tracing the packets

The remote PC begins by opening a tunnel request to the tunnel server. The PC is connected to the Internet via an ISP and has initiated the tunnel connection with its AltaVista Tunnel Telecommuter client. The request passes through the end user's ISP transparently, destined for the remote firewall's IP interface on the Internet (1.195.6.1) on the tunnel port of 3265. The remote firewall is set up to relay all traffic received on this port to the tunnel server's physical IP address (1.195.6.2). The tunnel server checks the authentication information against its Authentication tables, and encrypts a reply using the remote client's private key. This reply is sent back to the remote client, which decrypts the reply with its private key. The two sides then exchange parts of the session key (*sales.key*), which is combined to form a secret session key. The tunnel server assigns the virtual IP address of 1.196.5.2 to the remote client's pseudo-adapter. This will act as the client's end of the tunnel, and all traffic destined for the remote network will be routed to this address. The tunnel server takes 1.196.5.1 as its pseudo-adapter interface to this tunnel session, and any traffic received at this IP address is routed to its local network (1.195.6.*). The remote client now interacts with nodes on the local network as if it were physically connected to that network. Thus, on a Windows NT network, the user can log into the domain and browse the Network Neighborhood, or in a Unix environment, protocols and services normally restricted from outside the network are now possible (i.e., FTP to some secured server, access to the corporate intranet web pages, etc.).

When the second remote PC connects to the tunnel server, the new tunnel is assigned a second pair of IP addresses from the tunnel server's dynamic range. In this case, the second remote client is assigned 1.196.5.4, and the tunnel server takes 1.196.5.3 as its end of this tunnel session. The remote client routes all tunnel traffic to its pseudo-adapter interface to the tunnel, and the tunnel server routes all incoming traffic to its local network range for that tunnel (as previously stated).

In both cases, the secret session key is regenerated by the tunnel server every 30 to 1,440 minutes and redistributed to the remote clients transparently.

Implementing PC-to-WAN Tunnels

In this situation, the user connects directly to the Internet without a firewall.

Sample configuration

In the PC-to-WAN tunnel scenario shown in Figure 6-3, the corporate WAN is comprised of two subnets connected to a router, which routes traffic between them. Each subnet is comprised of several host machines, and one of the subnets has an AltaVista Tunnel Extranet server. The WAN is connected to the Internet through a T1 connection, and protected with a standard firewall. The remote users are all client computers running the AltaVista Tunnel Telecommuter Client, and are connected to the Internet through separate Internet service providers.

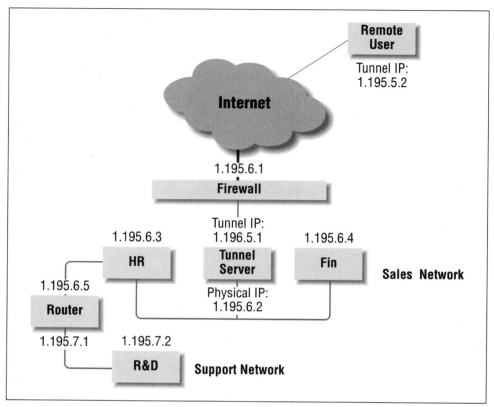

Figure 6-3. A generic PC-to-WAN tunnel connection

Tunnel server configuration

Routing table

The tunnel server actually has two separate routing tables with which to direct traffic between the two subnets. Both routing tables are set as default routes for the dynamic tunnel IP addresses (see Table 6-1). Any traffic bound for the second (support) subnet is relayed to the WAN router's interface for routing.

Table 6-1. Routing Tables for Figure 6-3

	Routing Table 1	Routing Table 2
Subnet	1.195.6.*	1.195.7.*
Netmask	255.255.255.0	255.255.255.0
Description	Sales Subnet	Support Subnet

Dynamic IP table

The dynamic IP range starts at 1.196.5.1 and comprises a Class C network (255 addresses). The tunnel server on the corporate LAN is set up to connect multiple single PC tunnel connections, and routes all tunnel traffic to its two physical subnets from the routing parameters.

— *Range name*: Sales Tunnel.

— *Range description*: Remote Tunnel Clients.

— *First IP*: 1.196.5.1.

— *Total tunnels*: The total number of tunnels for this tunnel group is set to 128. As each tunnel session is assigned two IP addresses, this makes the total IP address range equal to 256 IP addresses.

— *NetMask*: 255.255.255.0 for the 256 IP virtual network.

Authentication table

The group name for this tunnel is Sales/Support. The password in this case is WHO$listenen. These two parameters have been extracted into an ETA file called *salsup.eta* and distributed via floppy disk to the various tunnel clients. The key file has been created by the tunnel server on the corporate LAN and is specific to this tunnel group. The key file has also been extracted and distributed via floppy disk. By default, this key file is named *salsup.key*.

WAN router configuration

The WAN router's function in this scenario is to route network traffic between the two subnets (Sales and Support). All hosts on the two subnets have default routes to the router, which routes traffic either between the two networks or out onto the Internet. The WAN router is likewise configured to route tunnel traffic from the virtual network (1.196.5.*) to the tunnel server at 1.195.6.2 on port 3265.

Firewall configuration

The local firewall is configured to relay all external tunnel traffic (those reaching 1.195.6.1 on port 3265) to the WAN router at 1.195.6.5. The WAN router then routes the traffic to the tunnel server (as in the previous WAN router section).

Network host configurations

All hosts on both the 1.195.6.* subnet and the 1.195.7.* subnet are configured with default routes pointing to the WAN router.

Remote client configurations

The remote PC clients are configured similarly to the methods presented earlier in the "Implementing Single Connections-to-LAN Tunnels" section. The only differences are the names of the ETA and key files. In this case, each PC will have *salsup.eta* and *salsup.key* files installed for the Sales/Support tunnel user group.

Tracing the packets

The remote PC begins by opening a tunnel request to the tunnel server. The PC is connected to the Internet via an ISP and has initiated the tunnel connection with its AltaVista Tunnel Telecommuter client. The request passes through the end user's ISP transparently, destined for the remote firewall's IP interface on the Internet (1.195.6.1) on the tunnel port of 3265. The remote firewall is set up to relay all traffic received on this port to the WAN router's interface for its subnet (1.195.6.5). The WAN router then routes this traffic to the tunnel server's physical IP address, at 1.195.6.2 on port 3265. The tunnel server checks the authentication information against its Authentication tables, and encrypts a reply using the remote client's private key. This reply is sent back to the remote client, which decrypts the reply with its private key. The two sides then exchange parts of the session key (*salsup.key*), which is combined to form a secret session key. The tunnel server assigns the virtual IP address of 1.196.5.2 to the remote client's pseudo-adapter. This will act as the client's end of the tunnel, and all traffic destined for the remote network will be routed to this address. The tunnel server takes 1.196.5.1 as its pseudo-adapter interface to this tunnel session, and any traffic received at this IP address is routed to the WAN router for further routing to one or the other subnets. The remote client now interacts with nodes on the WAN as if it were physically connected to that network.

When the second remote PC connects to the tunnel server, the new tunnel is assigned a second pair of IP addresses from the tunnel server's dynamic range. In this case, the second remote client is assigned 1.196.5.4, and the tunnel server takes 1.196.5.3 as its end of this tunnel session. The remote client routes all tunnel traffic to its pseudo-adapter interface to the tunnel, and the tunnel server routes all incoming traffic to its local network range for the tunnel that is directed at the WAN router.

In both cases, the secret session key is regenerated by the tunnel server every 30 to 1,440 minutes and redistributed to the remote clients transparently.

7

Configuring and Testing the AltaVista Tunnel

Getting Busy

We've given you theoretical background on the AltaVista Tunnel, and now it's time to get down to business: configuring it for your enterprise. In this chapter, we lay out step by step how to install, configure, test, and troubleshoot the AltaVista Tunnel Extranet server and Telecommuter client. Note that though this package is available for Unix, we only cover in depth the Windows NT/95/98 installation and configuration. AltaVista is kind enough to have provided a comprehensive installation and configuration guide for its Unix flavors. This documentation is available from *http://altavista.software.digital.com/tunnel*.

We do, however, cover installation requirements and considerations for all platforms available to the AltaVista client.

Installing the AltaVista Tunnel

The installation of the AltaVista Tunnel on all platforms is assisted by a GUI installation program, which makes all the necessary updates to the system and installs the networking pseudo-adapters and icons. This process is fairly generic across platforms, but there are specific installation requirements for each platform. Review the next section carefully before running out and purchasing the software.

The AltaVista Tunnel Extranet server for Unix is available in one version: Digital Unix. Table 7-1 shows the installation requirements for this operating system. Confirm that your system matches these attributes before installation.

Table 7-1. Requirements for AltaVista Tunnel on Unix Systems

Requirements	Digital Unix
Hardware	All Alpha System
OS	Version 3.2c or later
Memory	32 MB
Hard disk space	25 MB
Root privileges	Yes

The AltaVista Tunnel for the Windows operating system is available as an Extranet server or a Telecommuter client (see Table 7-2).

Table 7-2. Requirements for AltaVista Tunnel on Windows Systems

Requirements	Extranet Server	Telecommuter
Processor and RAM	See below	Intel 80486 or higher with 8 MB of RAM
OS	NT 4.0 SP 3 or higher	NT 4.0 or higher or Windows 95
Hard disk space	15 MB	5 MB
Administrator access	Yes	N/A

The processor and memory requirements for the Extranet server are dependent on the number of tunnels needed for the virtual private network. Table 7-3 breaks down the minimum requirements.

Table 7-3. Requirements for AltaVista Tunnel on Windows for Extranets

Tunnels	Processor	RAM
50	Intel Pentium 90	48 MB
100	Intel Pentium 133	64 MB
200	Intel Pentium 200 or Digital Alpha Processor	64 MB

Preparing to Install

During the installation process, the AltaVista Tunnel edits the registry file on Windows NT machines, or the License database on Digital Unix. For all platforms, it installs a networking pseudo-adapter onto the operating system. In order to safeguard your computer against corruption, you should perform a backup of the entire system. Ensure that you have Administrator privileges on the NT server or root access on the Unix platforms before installing.

Installing the AltaVista Tunnel Extranet Server for Windows NT

The Windows NT version of the AltaVista Tunnel Extranet server is distributed either as a ZIP file available for purchase from the AltaVista web site, or on CD-ROM. In NT 4.0, exit all other applications before installing.

The installation procedure provides default settings that are compatible with most systems, but you may need to tweak these settings. Unless otherwise specified, all files are installed into the default directory: *C:\AltaVista\Tunnel*. The installation program installs the following components to the following locations:

- AltaVista Tunnel Service (*itnd*)—to the Services Control Panel
- AltaVista Tunnel pseudo-adapter—to the Network Control Panel
- TunMan AltaVista Management Program (*tunman.exe*)—to the AltaVista Folder
- Etunnel Help File (*etunnel.hlp*)—to the AltaVista Folder
- Tunnel Database File (*tunnel.dat*)—to the *\AltaVista\Tunnel\Data* directory
- The master encryption key (*master.key*)—to the *\AltaVista\Tunnel\Data\Keys* directory

---

 The *tunnel.dat* and *master.key* files should not be moved from their installed directories. If they are moved, you must manually edit the Registry or the AltaVista Tunnel Extranet server will not function.

The AltaVista Tunnel sets IP routing (IP forwarding) to be enabled and sets all tunnel ports to 3265. Though the tunnel ports can be configured manually via the Registry, disabling IP routing will likely disable the Tunnel server.

Windows NT 4.0

Once again, follow these steps to achieve your VPN:

1. Log in to the Windows server as an Administrator or equivalent.
2. Either insert the AltaVista Tunnel CD-ROM or use WINZIP or PKUNZIP to extract the Tunnel server archive into a temporary directory.
3. Open the Control Panel, then the Network control panel.
4. Select the Services tab.
5. Click the Add button.

6. The system will build network services options. When it's done, click the Have Disk button.

7. Type the path to the installation files. The path must be to a directory with the *oem-setup.inf* file.

8. From the Select OEM Option dialog box, select the AltaVista Tunnel.

9. The installation wizard will take over. Just follow the directions. Don't be afraid. You will be asked to provide a password for this server.

10. When you've finished, the Network control panel will reappear, with the AltaVista Tunnel as a service. Click Close.

11. The system will prompt you to reboot.

Installing the AltaVista Tunnel Telecommuter Client for Windows

The Telecommuter Tunnel is distributed on 3.5-inch disks and via the Internet as a *.ZIP* file. Once the installation files are obtained, run the *setup.exe* file and follow the directions as they appear. All Tunnel files will be installed to this default path: *C:\AltaVista\Tunnel\Program*. You will be given the option to change this path at the time of installation.

When installing on Windows NT, you must first open the Networking control panel, open the Services dialog screen, and select Add. Type in the path to the directory and drive where the installation files reside, and click OK. A dialog box will appear with the AltaVista Tunnel as an installation option. Clicking on this option initiates the installation process.

The following files are available in the Program folder:

etunnel.exe
> This starts the AltaVista Telecommuter Tunnel client.

krm.exe
> The Keyring Manager is a database of encryption keys available to the client.

etunnel.hlp
> This is a comprehensive help file for configuring and using the Tunnel client.

Installing the AltaVista Tunnel Telecommuter Client for MacOS

The minimum requirements for the Telecommuter Client for MacOS are as follows: a PowerPC processor, MacOS version 7.5 or later, Open Transport 1.1.1 or later, 16 MB of memory, and 1 MB of free disk space.

The client is distributed either on floppy disk or via AltaVista's download site in binhex format. Once the media is decompressed, double-click on the AltaVista Tunnel Install icon. In the installation window, drag the Tunnel icon to the System Startup disk. You will be prompted to restart by the installer.

To start the tunnel application, simply double-click on the AltaVista Tunnel Setup icon in the AlstaVista Tunnel folder on your System Startup disk. Configuration of the AltaVista tunnel client is covered in the "Configuring the AltaVista Telecommuter Client" section, later in this chapter.

Configuring the AltaVista Tunnel Extranet and Telecommuter Server

The configuration of the AltaVista Tunnel Extranet and Telecommuter servers are fairly generic across platforms. Both servers install identically. Most references in this section apply specifically to the Windows NT configuration. Any quirks in the Unix configuration are noted.

The first step is to decide which physical servers or computers on the local network will be allowed tunnel traffic. Next, create a group of dynamic IP addresses. There should be twice as many IPs as tunnels to connect to the tunnel server. A pair of IP addresses will be assigned to each "end" of the connecting tunnel, one for the server's interface and one to the end user's. Note that Windows NT versions of the Extranet/Telecommuter server are capable of connecting only a certain number of tunnels, so be sure to check the number of tunnels needed. Once these items are taken care of, the administrator must decide which tunnel groups are needed. As explained in Chapter 6, *Implementing the AltaVista Tunnel 98*, the administrator is able to configure the tunnel server for several different groups. Each group would have different users and connection attributes. Users can belong to one or more groups, depending on their needs and duties. For example, the network administration staff should belong to all groups for testing and troubleshooting purposes.

Adding Routes and Dynamic Addresses

These tasks make your network configuration known to the AltaVista Tunnel.

Initial configuration

After the tunnel groups are planned out, you're ready to begin configuration. When you launch the Tunnel Manager for the first time, you will be prompted to enter the routed network and dynamic range for the tunnel server. First, the

network available to the tunnel groups is added to the server. In Figure 7-1, the
following variables are required:

Subnet

This is the subnet of the network addresses on the local network that are part
of the tunnel. Traffic destined for these IP addresses will use the tunnel network. Should this route contain the entire local network, a zero as the last IP
address position is required. For instance: 205.196.222.0.

Netmask

This is the Netmask corresponding to the assigned subnet.

When choosing IP addresses for a dynamic range, do not use
addresses already in use on your network. The best policy is to use
a subnet of your corporate network. Thus, if your corporate network is 1.196.0.0, the subnet 1.196.5.0 might be reserved for tunnel
IP usage.

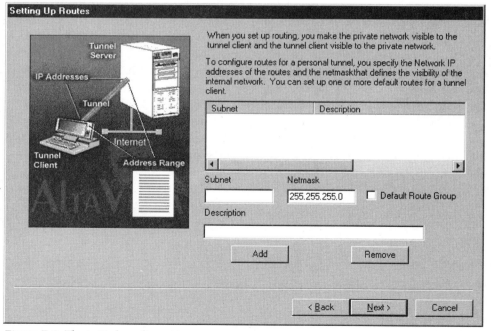

Figure 7-1. The initial configuration screen

The Description is not required for the configuration to work, but for administration purposes it may be helpful.

Be sure to set routes to all computers that need to be accessed from the tunnel connections. You may add as many routes as needed and you may select one of these routing groups as a default route. This allows for easier configuration of tunnel groups later. (See "Adding Tunnel Groups" later in this chapter.)

Once the route is added, add your dynamic address ranges. Figure 7-2 shows the configuration screen. The Range Name and Description are optional, but they are useful for keeping track of several dynamic address groups. The First IP entry is (as you probably guessed) for the first IP in the range of dynamic addresses. The Total Tunnels slide bar allows you to select the total number of tunnels allowed by the server for that IP group; the Netmask entry is the network mask for the corresponding IP group. Once this ordeal is finished, you are ready to start adding tunnel groups.

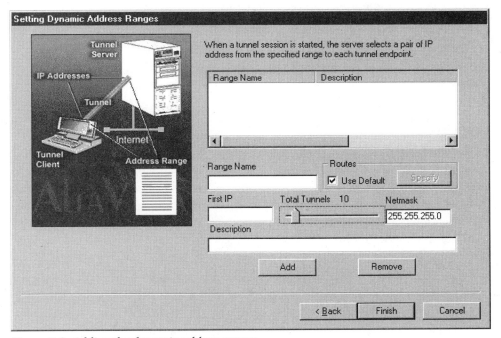

Figure 7-2. Adding the dynamic address ranges

Managing routes and dynamic IPs

From the main "tunman" window, select the Tunnels menu and the Configure menu option. This will yield a configuration screen, as shown in Figure 7-2. The sequence of dialogs lets you set up routes and dynamic addresses. Information required for both routes and dynamic addresses is the same as those stated earlier in the "Initial configuration" section.

Adding DNS and WINS Servers

Domain Name System (DNS) maps TCP/IP host names to IP addresses, while WINS servers map NetBIOS names to IP addresses. Both of these name resolution methods are supported by the AltaVista Tunnel.

To configure DNS and WINS properties, open the AltaVista Tunnel Configure window and select the Name Server tab. Both DNS and WINS have fields for primary and secondary resolution servers. Enter the Internet hostnames of the respective servers in these fields. Then click OK to accept the changes.

It is important to note that incoming tunnels must have access to internal DNS and WINS servers if these servers are private (i.e., not normally accessible to the public Internet). Thus, these servers' addresses must be made available to all incoming tunnels via the tunnel group configuration.

Adding Tunnel Groups

Grouping users together by function makes administration much easier. The groups you choose here don't need to have any relationship to group membership on one of your systems or networks.

Group configuration

You can also add tunnel groups. Selecting the Add button sends you through a series of configuration screens. The first screen, shown in Figure 7-3, allows you to select the type of tunnel you wish to configure: incoming, outgoing, or both. The Extranet server acts as a tunnel server and/or a tunnel client. In this case, we are selecting an incoming tunnel. After clicking Next, you are asked to provide a password for this tunnel group. The connecting clients require this password, as well as the key file that is subsequently generated.

The next screen asks for the Tunnel Name and Description. The Tunnel Name is required, and is likewise needed by the connecting clients. Also, from this screen, you select whether the dynamic IP range you configured for your tunnels is to be dynamically or statically assigned. The client connecting to the group can have either a virtual IP address assigned to it randomly or a fixed IP address every time it connects. Clicking Next sends you to the Dynamic IP address screen. This allows you to choose which range to use for this tunnel group. If you have only one dynamic range, it will be selected automatically. Next is the Specify Routes to Internal Network screen. Here you select which routing group is allowed to the tunnel group. You can select either the Default Route (if you've defined one) or a Specific Route. Selecting Specific Route will allow you to choose another routing group from your routing tables.

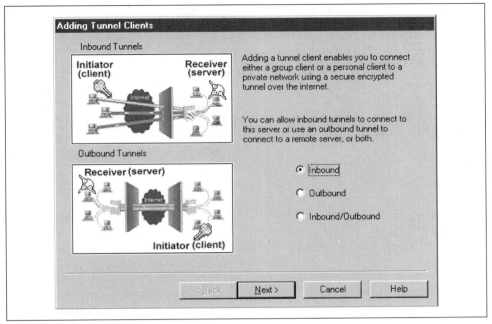

Figure 7-3. Adding a tunnel group (first screen)

The last screen is the Server Definition window. The hostname and port number are configurable as needed. By default, the name of the host where the server software resides is automatically entered into the hostname field. Also by default, the port number is 3265.

You have to enter the interceding firewall IP addresses, if applicable. The firewalls should be specified from the client end to the server end. Thus, the First Firewall field is the IP address of the firewall that the client first encounters when attempting to reach the tunnel server. The Second Firewall field is the firewall on the local network. By default, the port number for the AltaVista Tunnel is 3265. Ensure that this port number is not in use by any other service before entering it.

Figure 7-4 shows the properties of a sample tunnel group. Once a tunnel group is configured, this information can be viewed by selecting the tunnel group entry in the AltaVista Configure window and the Tunnels tab, then clicking on the Properties button. This screen gives a full view of the tunnel group, including the name of the group, the name of the dynamic IP address range and routing groups, the tunnel server (endpoint) name, and firewall addresses. Information can be modified on this screen by clicking the Modify Wizard button, or more simply by changing the information in the appropriate fields and clicking the Update button.

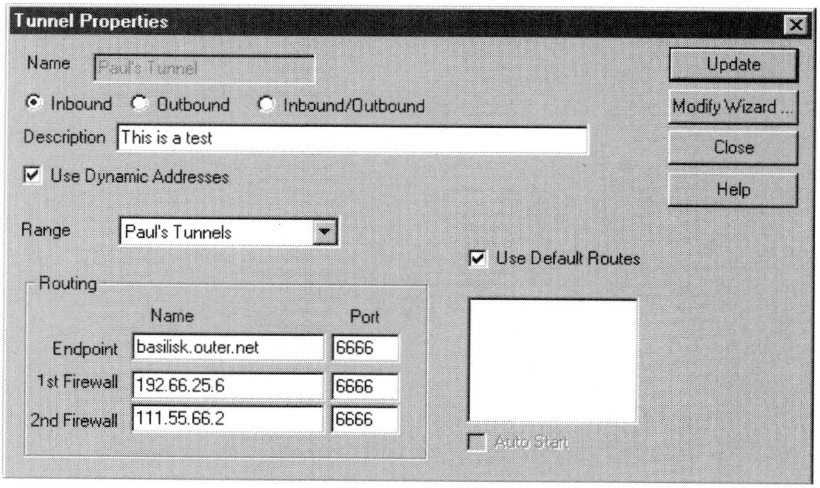

Figure 7-4. The Tunnel Properties screen

Tunnel client information

Once the tunnel group is configured, you need to extract information for the end users. This information is required for them to connect to the tunnel:

.key file
> The public key for this tunnel group. This key is exchanged by the client and server for encryption purposes.

.eta file
> The connection information file, including Tunnel Group name and password.

The *.key* and *.eta* files are created when you complete the tunnel group configuration. If you are in doubt, when the configuration process completes, click on the Key Management tab in the AltaVista Configure window. An entry should be present with the tunnel group name and a long string of numbers and letters, which is the key. The key file is created in the *\AltaVista\tunnel\data\key* directory. If you want to make copies for backups or for other users, extract the files by clicking on the Extract button on the Tunnels tab in the AltaVista Configure window. Though only the *.eta* file is named when extracting the files, the *.key* file is also copied. These files may be extracted onto a floppy disk or other writable media, and distributed to end users as needed.

Tools for Tunnel Management

Other than a handy configuration front end, the tunman application contains management and logging tools for those of you who don't get enough of this stuff with other network services. Figure 7-5 shows the main tunman window, with connected tunnels. From this GUI, you can keep tabs on existing connections, view a log of past and present tunnel connections, and view the status of the tunnel server, all at a glance. The interface is intuitive, and you should play with it at your leisure to find what information is useful to your network department. For the most part, the logs and such are particularly useful when troubleshooting connection problems, or when tracking attempted security breaches. Other than that, they could be used to prove to your manager that you are actually keeping logs of this stuff, or to liven up network operations meetings.

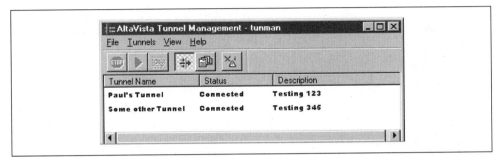

Figure 7-5. Main tunman window

Changing Port Settings

The AltaVista Tunnel allows the system administrator to change the TCP port settings for tunnel communication. As noted earlier, the default port is 3265. If for some reason another port is required, the sysadmin must edit the Services file in the *drivers**etc* directory of the server's system directory. Under Windows NT the path is:

```
\system32\etc
```

Use Notepad, or some text editor, to edit the Services file. Find the line below and change 3265 to the desired port:

```
altav-tunnel              3265/tcp
```

After saving the file, restart the tunnel service.

Rekey Interval and Minimum Encryption Settings

The AltaVista Tunnel has a default setting of 30 minutes for the rekey interval. Thus, every 30 minutes, the encryption key used by two tunnel endpoints expires and a new one is generated and exchanged. This setting can be modified by editing the registry on Windows NT.

The Rekey Time registry entry is at:

> HKEY_LOCAL_MACHINE\SOFTWARE\DigitalEquipmentCorporation\
> AltaVista Tunnel\CurrentVersion

This entry has a range of 30 to 1,440 minutes (24 hours).

The minimum encryption applied to tunnel communication is dynamic, based on the highest level supported by both ends of the tunnel. The tunnel server may be able to support 128-bit encryption while the client may be limited to 40-bit. In this case, the tunnel would have 40-bit encryption applied to it. However, a base minimum can be set on the server via the Windows NT registry. Edit the Minimum Encryption DWORD value to the desired setting located at:

> HKEY_LOCAL_MACHINE\SOFTWARE\DigitalEquipmentCorporation\
> AltaVista Tunnel\CurrentVersion

Note that connecting PCs may not be able to support whatever minimum setting you apply, thus disabling the tunnel for those PCs.

Configuring Unix-to-Windows NT Tunnel Connections

Tunnel connections between Unix and Windows NT are possible, but only with V.1.0 of the Unix Extranet server software. The Windows NT tunnel server must be the outbound side of the tunnel, meaning that the Windows NT server initiates the connection to the Unix server. Configuration on both ends is the same as on homogenous networks, with only a few exceptions.

On the Digital Unix side, be sure to enable IP forwarding (in startup files) with this set of commands:

```
iprsetup -s
rcmgr set ROUTER yes
```

On the Windows NT side, be sure that the tunnel is set as an outbound tunnel.

Configuring the AltaVista Telecommuter Client

Configuration of the Tunnel client is straightforward for all four platforms (Windows 95/98/NT and MacOS), but make sure you have the following information from the administrator:

Username

> This is the name of the tunnel group on the Tunnel server to which you have access privileges. This name is case-sensitive and must exactly match what the tunnel administrator has set up on the tunnel server.

Server key ID

> The group name for the encryption key.

Tunnel server

> The IP address and tunnel port number.

First Firewall

> Should there be an intervening firewall from your connection point to the Internet, the IP address and tunnel port number are required. Intervening firewalls that keep traffic from leaving the network are rare, but check with your Internet service provider or network administrator to be sure.

Second Firewall

> The IP address and tunnel port number are needed to allow your tunnel traffic to pass through to the remote private network. The network administrator of the remote private network generally supplies this information.

Key file

> The *.eta* encryption key file is generated and distributed by the network administrator on the remote private network. This file will allow access to the private network to anyone who obtains it and should be treated as extremely confidential information. Loss or theft of this file should be reported to the tunnel network administrator immediately.

This information should be obtained for every tunnel network to which you have access. Once the information is available, you can configure and test your tunnel network client.

Troubleshooting Problems

Problems with network services, especially those related to the Internet, are sometimes difficult to pinpoint. The AltaVista Tunnel is no exception. In addition to the common Internet problems, such as throughput issues, Internet or transit provider network problems, and end user education, you must add encryption and verification issues, virtual address resolution, and a host of other specifics which must be exactly right for the tunnel to function. Of course, common sense troubleshooting is still the name of the game. When you encounter a problem connecting the tunnel, do not forget to check the client and server machines' configuration and the Internet connection on both ends. Sometimes, as anyone who's solved a computer problem knows, it's the simplest problems that are overlooked. Confirm that both ends have an Internet connection and that the tunnel client and server are running on the respective machines.

Once you've determined that both ends have Internet connectivity, there are four main areas where a problem may reside: the tunnel server configuration, the tunnel client configuration, the local network, or the Internet gateway configuration on the tunnel server's network.

Tunnel Server and Client Configuration Checks

The tunnel server usually will experience the most problems, especially if this server is running other network services such as a mail server or web server. Should a client or group of clients fail to connect to the tunnel, first check the tunnel server software configuration. The problem areas are incorrect dynamic address ranges, mistyped tunnel name information, or improper key extraction. To check the validity of the dynamic address ranges, simply ensure that the list of Ranges on the Dynamic Address tab (in the Configuration option under the Tunnels menu) matches those available to the server. The available dynamic address range is a field in the tunnel properties window. Next, verify that the tunnel name matches what the end user has typed. Tunnel names are case-sensitive, so you'll need to have the user spell out exactly what is typed. If you've ever had to troubleshoot a username/password problem, this is old hat. Last, re-extract the key files and distribute them to the end user.

Additionally, IP forwarding must be enabled on the tunnel server, or the tunnel will not function, period. On Digital Unix, type the following commands:

```
iprsetup -s
rcmgr set ROUTER yes
```

Note that these commands are case-sensitive. You must have root access to execute the commands.

With Windows NT, IP forwarding is enabled from the TCP/IP Protocol Properties in the Networking control panel. Simply click the checkbox labeled Enable IP Forwarding.

If all these areas are correct, the difficulty may be an end user problem. Users fall into two camps for the most part: "I don't know anything about this" or "I know enough about this to be a real pain in the...." Of course, your job as network administrator is to guide both camps with a gentle, knowledgeable hand. Have them again repeat the exact configuration, taking each field separately and slowly. IP addresses are often miskeyed, as are server names and passwords. Ensure that if there is an interposing firewall, the user has port 3265 in the firewall port field. Additionally, check that the AltaVista Tunnel pseudo-adapter is installed in the Networking control panel. In our testing, we experienced a scenario where the user didn't reboot the machine after installing the tunnel client software. This is, of course, imperative. If all looks clean, then there could be configuration problems on the local network or the Internet gateway.

Local Network and Internet Gateway Configuration Checks

The easiest way to begin checking the local network and Internet gateway configuration is to have the user attempt to telnet to the tunnel server's network firewall at port 3265. To do this, have the user go to the Start Menu on Windows 95, choose the Run menu option, and type:

```
telnet your_firewall 3265
```

The user should be able to connect to the firewall at that port. However, the firewall will display an error message when keystrokes are entered. The firewall will immediately issue a "connection failed" message if this port is not enabled. This port will obviously have to be enabled for tunnel traffic to commence. Also, this port should be set up as a generic relay. This will forward all traffic for port 3265 to the tunnel server's pseudo-adapter. If the user can connect to the tunnel, but subsequently gets disconnected, this is symptomatic of a misconfigured firewall port.

If the tunnel client can connect to and authorize the tunnel server, but cannot reach other machines on the internal network, there could be two problems: either IP forwarding is not enabled on the tunnel server, or the tunnel is in an infinite loop. Such a loop can occur between the virtual IP address and physical IP address of the tunnel server. The loop indicates a misconfiguration in the Routing tab of the tunnel server configuration.

To diagnose which problem exists, have the user ping the tunnel server's pseudo-adapter address. To do this, the user must open a DOS window and type:

```
ping virtual_IP
```

where *virtual_IP* is the pseudo-adapter address. If this ping is successful, ping the tunnel server's real IP address. If this ping fails, the tunnel is in an infinite loop. If the first ping fails and the second is successful, the IP forwarding is not properly enabled on the tunnel server. If both pings fail, the client machine cannot reach the server at all. This could be a firewall or router issue on the server side of the connection and should be investigated further.

If all these tests pass, and IP forwarding is properly enabled on the server, the user should attempt to traceroute to a machine on the local network. The command in Windows 95 is:

```
tracert other_machine
```

or, from a Unix command line:

```
traceroute other_machine
```

where *other_machine* refers to the domain name of the internal machine to which we want to trace traffic. If this is successful, it shows that the client machine is sending packets through the server's tunnel pseudo-adapter and to the internal machine on the server's network. If it fails, routing is misconfigured on the tunnel server. Recheck the routes on the Routing tab in the Tunnel → Configuration menu.

Next, do the same procedure from the machine internal to the tunnel server's network. Trace back to the client's unique domain name. If this checks out, and there is still a problem, it resides in some other application or service. If this test fails, routing for the internal network is improperly configured. Refer to the examples in Chapter 6 for internal network configuration scenarios.

To support these tests, you may also check the tunnel server's Read/Write counters in the Tunnel Manager application. These counters will tell you how many bytes were read and written to the tunnel by a particular tunnel client.

It may take some time to educate both system administrators and end users to this new twist in the Internet troubleshooting process, but with the points presented here and simple networking common sense, you should have your AltaVista Tunnel up in no time.

8

Creating a VPN with the Unix Secure Shell

Unix has long been *the* development platform for the Internet. Everything from the TCP/IP suite to HTTP was developed on Unix first. Much of the development for private LAN-to-LAN connections, including IPSec and IPv6, is taking place on Unix platforms.

In addition, the Linux operating system has become an important Internet server and development platform. Linux, a Unix-like OS, is freely available over the Internet, or can be purchased on CD for a modest price from a number of sources. Linus Torvalds created Linux as a non-commercial alternative to the other flavors of Unix available on Intel-based platforms. Linux became popular thanks to ISPs, web presence providers, and universities choosing it to deliver Internet services. Although originally shunned by large businesses because of a perceived lack of support, it has since garnered applications support from companies such as Corel and Netscape. In 1998, it was estimated that as many as seven million people worldwide use the OS. Linux's proliferation has meant that more and more networks are running a Unix OS variant, often as a web server, router, or proxy server.

The Secure Shell (SSH) is a replacement for insecure methods of accessing a remote Unix host. It's meant to replace the common Unix tools *rsh, rcp,* and *rlogin,* and can also replace telnet in many cases. Its open-ended versatility means that it can also accomplish things like forwarding secure X11 connections and copying files remotely (using a companion tool called *scp*). In addition, it can be used to tunnel a PPP connection to create a secure virtual private network. If you're willing to spend the time and effort, you'll find that this type of connection can be just as secure and efficient as many of the more expensive solutions out there.

SSH has been around since 1995 and is widely used in many Unix environments all over the world. Like Linux, it came out of Finland. Computer scientist Tatu

Ylönen originally created it, and his SSH Home Page (*http://www.cs.hut.fi/ssh/*) is a great place to find SSH information and links to the freeware SSH distributions. SSH development has since been taken up by SSH Communications Security, Ltd. (*http://www.ipsec.com/*), who also create IPSec toolkits so that developers can include IPSec in their TCP/IP products.

SSH contains quite a bit of functionality and many security improvements over the *r* utilities. It allows for secure authentication, including RSA host keys, RSA user keys, and passwords. RSA authentication helps prevent against IP and DNS spoofing and man-in-the-middle attacks. SSH can encrypt transferred data with a choice of ciphers, including 3DES, Blowfish, and IDEA. This means that you can choose a method based on the sensitivity of your data, the speed of your systems, and patent restrictions in your country. Authentication and encryption are covered in more detail later in this chapter.

SSH can also be used to forward X11 connections for secure X Window System sessions. It does this by creating a fake X server on the machine from which the SSH client is run. It then "proxies" the connection and forwards it to a real X server (running the SSH daemon) over a secure connection. SSH also has the capability to redirect arbitrary TCP/IP ports (though only root can redirect privileged ports). It can redirect a port on a local side to a port on the remote side, or redirect a port on the remote side to a port on the local side. When such a connection is in place, any data sent through the redirected ports will be sent through the secure connection.

A freeware version of SSH is available as source code that can be compiled for almost any Unix and Unix-like platform, including Linux, FreeBSD, Solaris, AIX, and HP-UX. Commercial versions for those Unix platforms, as well as Windows 3.x/95/NT and Macintosh, are available from DataFellows. You can also purchase a ready-made SSH-based VPN product from them.

In this chapter, we're going to be using the Unix freeware version of SSH for our examples. In addition, we're going to be using Linux as our Unix flavor of choice because it's also freely available and common, though the examples can be extrapolated to other variants, and we'll mention any platform-specific issues we might be aware of. We'll look at the capabilities of the SSH, how to build and set it up, and its components. We're going to focus on tunneling a PPP connection using SSH to create a secure network, and give you some troubleshooting tips and resources. Finally, we'll do a brief performance evaluation of this solution.

The SSH Software

SSH is both software and a secure communications protocol. It has practically become the *de facto* security standard for Unix remote access. As of this writing, the IETF SECSH working group was advancing the second-generation of the protocol, called SSH 2, and protocol drafts are available. More information can be found at the IETF's web site, SSH Security Communications' web site, or *http://www.ssh.fi/drafts*.

Here are the basics of how SSH works: The SSH server daemon, called *sshd*, runs on its own well-known TCP/IP port: 22. The server listens for connections from an SSH client, for instance, the program called *ssh*. Authentication is accomplished using the RSA key exchange for the client and server (in conjunction with *.rhosts*), or using RSA key exchange for individual SSH users. The keys for hosts and users are typically 1,024 bits in length. The SSH server program also has its own RSA key, which is used in conjunction with the host key for session key exchange. By default, this key is regenerated every hour and is never saved in a file. This transient key makes it more difficult for someone to decipher packets captured previously (or in the future) if they were somehow able to learn the server's current key and host key. The server key is normally 768 bits.

If the user specified a command to run when he invoked the SSH client, that command is run remotely on the server. If no command is specified, a pseudo-terminal is allocated on the remote server and an interactive login session is begun. A pseudo-terminal (or TTY) is just the standard virtual character device Unix systems allocate a user when they log in remotely. Pseudo-terminals under Linux are often denoted as either "ttyp" or "pty," followed by a unique designator. Normally, a pseudo-terminal isn't generated when *ssh* is used to simply run a program remotely unless a certain parameter is specified, which we'll discuss later.

Encryption Capabilities

Encryption algorithms supported as of SSH 1.2.25 are Blowfish, IDEA, 3DES, DES, and arcfour (a free RC4 equivalent). These ciphers are normally all enabled on the SSH client. On the *sshd* server, some are enabled by default and others can be enabled only at compile time with flags added to the *configure* script (see the "Building and Installing SSH" section for more on the *configure* script). Technical descriptions of these ciphers can be found in Chapter 2, *Basic VPN Technologies*. Your choices are:

Blowfish
> The SSH implementation of Blowfish uses a 128-bit key and, next to IDEA, is considered one of the best ciphers to use with SSH. It's enabled by default in *sshd*. To turn it off, add the `--without-blowfish` flag when executing the *configure* script.

IDEA
> The IDEA cipher is enabled by default in *sshd*, and is the one that *ssh* will try to use by default if another isn't specified. It uses a 128-bit key. Use

`--without-idea` to turn it off. It's important to note that IDEA is patented in the United States and Europe, and although it's available in the free version of SSH, it cannot be legally used for commercial purposes within those regions without a license. In fact, the commercial version of SSH comes with IDEA disabled by default, and a separate license must be obtained to use it. Licenses can be obtained from Ascom Systec AG of Switzerland (see *http://www.ascom.com/*).

3DES

Triple-DES is automatically enabled (and can't be disabled) in SSH, because it's also used to encrypt private keys. It uses a 112-bit key, and is the fallback cipher if the client requests one that the server doesn't support.

DES

DES uses a 56-bit key, which is considered too small for commercial purposes, so it's disabled by default on the server. Use `--with-des` to turn it on.

arcfour

The arcfour cipher is supposed to be equivalent to RC4. It uses a 128-bit key length and is the fastest cipher SSH supports. It's disabled by default on the server because there is a security hole in the way it's implemented in SSH 1.x. SSH 2.x does not have this problem. If the client specifies arcfour and the server doesn't support it, the server will automatically switch to Blowfish. To enable it on the server, use the `--with-arcfour` flag at configuration time.

None

This is no encryption, which is disabled by default. It's really used only for testing, so you shouldn't turn this capability on. To turn on no encryption, use `--with-none` when executing the configure script.

Building and Installing SSH

For most Unix systems, the installation of SSH is pretty straightforward. Simply download the gzipped tar file from one of the FTP mirror sites listed at *http://www.ssh.fi/sshprotocols*, for instance, *ssh-1.2.25.tar.gz*. (Note: Typically there's a new version of SSH released every few months.) In order to compile SSH, you need an ANSI C compiler such as *gcc*. The simplest way to build this software is to do the following:

```
# ./configure
# make
# make install
```

The *configure* script should recognize your system type, discover important information about your build environment, and—if everything checks out—create a corresponding *Makefile*. The *make* program uses this *Makefile* to build the software. The *make* install directive installs the SSH components and manual pages in the right places, and generates the initial 1024-bit host key pair (if it doesn't already exist).

The last thing you'll have to do is put *sshd* in an *rc* file, so it will launch at startup. On Linux, you'll want to put it in */etc/rc.d/rc.local*, with a syntax like this:

```
# Start SSH
echo "Starting SSH Daemon..."
/usr/local/sbin/sshd;
```

There are other parameters you can use with *sshd*, and we'll look at some of them in the "SSH Components" section.

You'll also want to enable the port on which you're running SSH. In our case, we're going to use the default port of 22, so we'll have to edit our */etc/services* file and add a line like this:

```
ssh             22/tcp
```

As of this writing, SSH has been known to compile on at least thirty-six different versions of Unix, so most of the time you should be able to build it without a hitch. We have built it on four different Unix systems without problems. If you have problems during the configuration, compilation, or installation stage, the *configure* utility may not have recognized your system type, you may need to make some minor configuration changes by hand, or you may need to upgrade some of the tools in your build environment to newer versions. It's a good idea to read the *INSTALL* text file to look for any specific problems with your system or environment. For example, there are problems compiling with *gcc* prior to release 2.7.2.3, or there may be a problem with schemes that aren't standardized across Unix systems, such as shadow password implementations. If you encounter a problem not covered in the *INSTALL* text and are stumped, use some of the resources in the "Getting Help with SSH" section.

SSH Components

The SSH software is comprised of a small suite of utilities that perform different functions. We're not going to give you an overview of every feature of these utilities. Instead, we're going to look at functions and parameters that you should know in order to operate an SSH VPN—both those you should use and those you might be better off not using. For other functionality, we suggest checking the manpages for each of these tools.

sshd

The SSH server daemon is called *sshd*. As shown in the section "Building and Installing SSH," it's normally started from an *rc* file. When launched, it generates the first instance of the server key pair. Because of this, it's typically not recommended that you start *sshd* from *inetd*, because *inetd* will launch it each time somebody makes a connection. This server key generation adds additional time to the login, sometimes on the order of tens of seconds, depending upon the speed of your machine, its load, and the size of the server key you choose. In some cases this delay will be unacceptable, or at the very least annoying.

sshd has a configuration file called */etc/sshd_config*, which lets you set a number of default runtime and security parameters, including port, server key bits, and the types of authentication allowed.

Useful sshd parameters for our purposes

No parameters are normally needed to launch the SSH daemon, but there are a few that can be useful in making modifications.

-b *bits*

> You can set the length of the server key with this option. The default server key is 768 bits, but this option can be used to set it higher if you're concerned about security at that level. Even though 768 bits is considered relatively safe, key lengths of 1024 bits are generally thought to be safe for the next several years. Using a key length that is shorter than 768 bits is also possible. If you really wanted to start the SSH daemon from *inetd*, you could shorten the key length to shorten the generation time, thereby shortening the login time. Key lengths of less than 512 bits, however, are often considered insufficient for business transactions over the Internet. The server key can also be set with the **ServerKeyBits** parameter in the *sshd_config* file.

-k *seconds*

> Another option you might want to change is the **-k** option, which will adjust the time to live of the server key. Normally, this key is regenerated every 3600 seconds (one hour), but it can be adjusted to shorter or longer regeneration times. A setting of 0 means that the key will never be regenerated, which isn't recommended, as server key regeneration is an important security feature of SSH. This can also be modified with the **KeyRegenerationInterval** parameter in the SSH daemon configuration file.

-p *port*

> *sshd* is normally run as *root* on Unix systems on TCP port number 22, but it is possible to launch it as another user if you use the **-p** option to have it listen on a non-privileged port (ports above 1023), and if you specify a different location for the host key file (the default host key file, */etc/ssh_host_key*, can be read only by *root*). For VPN applications, there shouldn't be any need to run the daemon as anyone other than *root*, though it may be useful in other situations, such as making a secure connection to a system that you don't have

superuser privileges on, and that isn't already running the daemon. The "Port" parameter in the *sshd_config* file can also set the default port.

The types of authentication allowed—password, *.rhosts*, host key, or user key—can be controlled from the *sshd_config* file. We'll go into these settings more when we create a VPN in the "Creating a VPN with PPP and SSH" section.

ssh

ssh is the client program, which can also be invoked as *slogin*. The client can be used either to log in to a host or to execute a program on a remote host, when the host is running *sshd*. The client is designed to be easy to use and to be run by any user. At the minimum, you can use the following command:

```
ssh hostname
```

which will let you log into a host that's running *sshd*. Or, you can execute a remote command with the following syntax:

```
ssh hostname command
```

Understanding SSH authentication

Like the *r* utilities Unix users are familiar with, SSH lets you allow password-free access to a system based on a hostname/username combination in a *hosts.equiv* file or *.rhosts* file. In other words, it doesn't trust network information alone for authentication, as IP addresses and DNS entries can be spoofed. The */etc/ hosts.equiv* file is checked first, and contains hostname and username entries put there by the system administrator. Individual users can also create *.rhosts* files in their home directories that contain hostname and username entries for hosts they commonly log in from. This file is checked after *hosts.equiv*, and *hosts.equiv* can override *.rhosts*. (Note: password-free access for root can't be granted in the *hosts.equiv* file, only in root's *.rhosts* file.) Unlike the *r* utilities, SSH won't allow you to log in password-free based simply on hostname or username. You can specify otherwise at compile time, but this isn't recommended because it strips SSH of secure authentication. Normally, SSH requires an additional, more secure authentication method in order to proceed.

The default additional method is RSA authentication using host keys. These keys are stored in the system's */etc/ssh_known_hosts* file or the user's *$HOME/.ssh/ known_hosts* file.

Another method is RSA authentication based on a user's public/private key pair, where the server knows a user's public key, and the user's client program knows his private key. In this scheme, a user will store his public keys on a remote host in his *$HOME/.ssh/authorized_keys* file. When the user connects to the system using *ssh*, it tells the server which user/key pair it would like to use. The server checks to see if that key pair is in the *authorized_keys* file and, if so, it encrypts a challenge message using the public key and sends it back to the user's SSH client. The client then decrypts the message using the user's private key, and sends the message back to the server—thus verifying that the user is who he says he is, without ever sending the private key over the network.

Additionally, authentication can be made using a Trusted Information Systems (TIS, recently acquired by Network Associates) authentication server. We won't go into this type of authentication in this chapter, but information can be found in the *README.TIS* file that comes with the SSH distribution.

Running ssh in "batch mode"

ssh can also be called from a script in batch mode (see the parameter later in this section) to execute automated commands securely on a remote system. When in batch mode, *ssh* won't ask for a password or passphrase as long as password authentication is not needed (as when you're using RSA user authentication), and as long a passphrase isn't used to protect the user's private key. Although this method is less secure, it's useful in scripts where a user might not be around to supply input. Some security is still maintained because only the user, as the owner of her identity file, can read the private key due to file permissions.

Useful ssh parameters for our purposes

Like *sshd*, *ssh* also has a configuration file, called */etc/ssh_config*. By default, everything in the file is commented out. In addition, there are a number of command-line parameters. We'll look at a few of them here:

-*username:*

> A useful feature of the SSH client is the ability to change the login name you're using when logging into another machine. Like *rsh*, it will normally use the name that you're logged in with on the system you're connecting from. You can override that behavior with this parameter.

-c *cipher:*

> This parameter lets you change the encryption technique the client is using. As we've said, it's IDEA by default. The types of ciphers you can set with this parameter are idea, blowfish, des, 3des, arcfour, and none. You can also change this with the Cipher parameter in the *ssh_config* file.

-p *port:*

> This allows you to change the default port from 22 to something else, just as in *sshd*. The Port parameter in *ssh_config* also controls this.

-o *option:*

> This allows you to enter a command that includes one of the *ssh_config* file options for which there might not be a separate parameter. For example, including the configuration file option **BatchMode yes** will keep the client from asking you for a password or passphrase, which is useful in scripts.

-t:

> This parameter tells the client to force the server to allocate a pseudo-terminal, even if the client is being used to run a command remotely. This parameter is important to our VPN setup.

ssh-keygen

The *ssh-keygen* utility can be used by SSH users to generate their RSA user/key pairs on their client systems, or by an administrator to create a host key pair. It's run straight from the command line, and most users won't need to include any other parameters. It generates the *$HOME/.ssh/identity* file for the private key, and the *$HOME/.ssh/identity.pub* file for the public key. Additionally, it asks for a passphrase, which is used to encrypt the private key with 3DES. This means that if someone happened to get a hold of your private key file, they would not be able to read the key unless they also knew your passphrase. 3DES is still considered safe from brute force attacks.

-b *bits:*

> This sets the number of bits used in the key pair. It's 1024 bits by default, which is also recommended.

-f *file:*

> This parameter can be used to create a different key file from the defaults.

ssh-agent and ssh-add

The *ssh-agent* command is executed by a user on his or her local machine, and is used in conjunction with RSA user authentication. The purpose of *ssh-agent* is to hold the private identity keys for a given user. The *ssh-add* program adds these identity keys to the agent. Running *ssh-agent* and *ssh-add* before executing *ssh* means that you won't have to enter a passphrase each time you want to execute the client. The passphrase is requested when you run *ssh-add*, which then decrypts the private key and stores it in memory, and you're never again asked for it while the agent is running. It can also be used to hold multiple identity keys to enable easy login to multiple machines, where different identities might be used. Why have different identities? One reason might be that security policy at work might dictate the need for a 1024-bit key, while at home or school you can get by with a 512-bit key. In this case you would want an identity for each security level. Another reason is that having multiple identities means that all systems you access won't be vulnerable if a single identity is compromised. When you have multiple identities, *ssh* will try each public key within memory until the server accepts one and sends a challenge response.

ssh-agent can be given a command parameter. This command is usually a shell, or the command to start an X Window System environment. *ssh-agent* will execute this command, and all subsequent commands will be children of the agent. All of these children will have access to the private keys the agent stores, and the keys will be removed from memory once the initial command is exited. In addition, *ssh-agent* can be called from an *eval* statement within a shell script. Using this method, you do not need to provide a shell as a parameter.

When *ssh-add* is invoked without parameters, it loads *$HOME/.ssh/identity*. You can also specify other identity key files (created with *ssh-keygen*) by specifying the location and name of the file. For instance, you might have one private key for school, another for home, and another for work. In this case, you might issue a command like the following:

```
# ssh-agent $SHELL
# ssh-add ~/.ssh/home
# ssh-add ~/.ssh/work
# ssh-add ~/.ssh/school
```

scp

The secure copy program, *scp*, is designed to replace *rcp*. It can be used to securely copy files between computers using the SSH protocol. It has many of the same functions as *rcp*, and can even recursively copy files. The invocation normally looks like this:

```
scp file1 host2:file2
```

make-ssh-known-hosts

The *make-ssh-known-hosts* script can search a domain for all hosts running the SSH daemon, and obtain their public host keys in order to make the */etc/ssh_known_hosts* file easily. There are a number of parameters you can use to control its settings. Running it without any parameters will use the domain the host belongs to.

Creating a VPN with PPP and SSH

It's possible to create a routed secure network over the Internet by creating a PPP connection within an SSH connection. In this scenario, you would have a Linux server connected to each network you would like to include in the VPN. These servers could either be acting as routers/firewalls, or simply be routers sitting behind another firewall. For simplicity's sake, we're just going to use an example where Linux systems are routers behind another firewall. There are a number of firewalls that can be used and we don't want to muddle the description of how to set up the VPN with setting up a firewall.

Figure 8-1 shows our sample setup, which we'll use throughout the rest of this chapter. In this scenario, there's a "master" and a "slave" VPN system. Each of these systems is a Unix system with SSH, PPP, and other needed applications. The designation of master and slave is actually arbitrary. The terms are just used to differentiate between the system that initiates the SSH connection (the master) and the one that accepts it (the slave). Either machine could be both a master and a slave that makes and accepts multiple VPN connections. It's easy to picture this situation as being a branch office that has a master server, making a VPN connection to a central office's slave server. Other branch offices could also call into that same slave server for their own VPNs.

In our example, we have the following interfaces defined:

master-lan (192.168.3.1)
> This is the IP address that the master has on its internal network. It's part of the unregistered CIDR block of Class C networks (192.168.0.0/16, from RFC 1918).

master-gw (1.0.0.1)
> This is an IP address for the master's network interface card on the perimeter (a.k.a. DMZ) network. It's fully Internet routable.

master-vpn (192.168.1.1)
> This is the IP address for the master's PPP interface. It's part of the unregistered block.

slave-lan (192.168.4.1)
> The IP address the slave has on its internal network.

slave-gw (2.0.0.1)
> The IP address the slave machine has on its perimeter network. It's part of a routable set of addresses.

slave-vpn (192.168.1.2)
> The IP address of the slave's PPP interface.

With this setup, if someone on the master's internal network (192.168.3.0/24) using *master-lan* as their gateway address wants to connect to a machine on the slave's internal network (192.168.4.0/24), the traffic will be routed through the VPN connection between the master and slave. All other traffic will be halted (i.e., no other

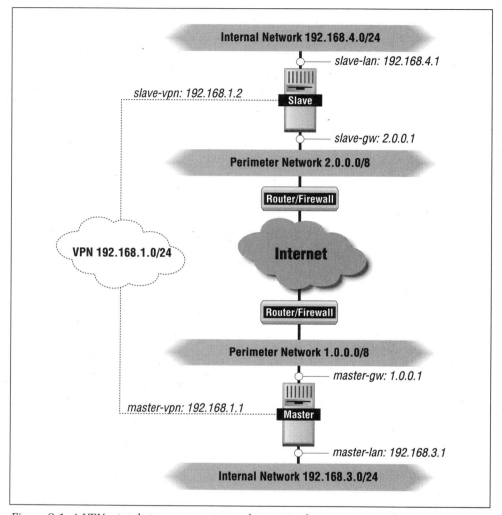

Figure 8-1. A VPN setup between a master and server in the ora-vpn.com domain

Internet traffic is routed) because the 192.168.0.0 networks cannot be routed over the Internet. As an alternative, IP masquerading can be used on Linux routers, which will allow those unregistered addresses to "pass through" the Linux system and access the Internet.

The router/firewalls on both the master and slave sides are set up to allow SSH traffic through TCP port 22 for both the master and server machines. All of these hosts are in a domain called *ora-vpn.com*.

Here are the things that must happen on the master and slave in order to create a VPN using PPP and SSH:

1. We need to launch PPP on the slave. We're going to use *pppd*, which, when launched from a pseudo-terminal without another terminal device (such as a serial line) listed as a parameter, will automatically use the I/O of the tty it was launched from. If you telnet to a machine that has *pppd* and run it from the command line, you'll see PPP protocol character strings (which look like garbage) appear in your telnet window.

2. We want the connection to be secure, so instead of telnet, we install *sshd* on the slave and run *ssh* on the master. Creating an SSH connection from the master to the slave and running *pppd* on the slave will make it secure, but it doesn't complete the PPP connection. The PPP daemon also needs to be run on the master.

3. We need to launch the *ssh* command that runs *pppd* on the slave from a different pseudo-terminal, so that other commands can be run by a script that sets up the VPN. Running *pppd* on the same tty would generate the PPP garbage, and make it difficult to run other commands unattended. We're going to use a program called *pty-redir* to create this new pseudo-terminal. The terminal's identifier (e.g., ttyp1) will also need to be stored for later use by *pppd* on the master.

4. The PPP daemon needs to be launched on the master with a parameter that tells it to direct I/O through the pseudo-terminal we generated with *pty-redir* to connect to the slave using *ssh* and run *pppd*. At this point, the master's *pppd* will create a PPP connection with the slave's *pppd* through the tty of the SSH connection. The master's *pppd* program will also have the local and remote IP addresses of the PPP interfaces as parameters.

5. Appropriate routes need to be set up on the master and slave.

Now we'll actually implement this type of VPN configuration. What follows is based on Arpad Magosanyi's VPN HOWTO for Linux (at *http://sunsite.unc.edu/ LDP/HOWTO/mini/VPN.html*) and our own experiences.

The VPN Components

Creating an SSH VPN requires the Linux operating system and a few other pieces of software, described below. All of these are freely available on the Internet.

Linux

For our setup, we used the Slackware distribution of Linux for x86 processors with a kernel version of 2.0.33. Other distributions are Red Hat, Debian, and Caldera, plus several others. If you don't already have Linux, the Linux Online web site (*http://www.linux.org/*) has links to the distribution sites.

At the time this chapter was written, the 2.0.x kernels were considered the stable releases, while the 2.1.x kernels were development versions. Whatever distribution you choose, we recommend that you use at least the 2.0.33 version of the kernel because it has safeguards against TCP SYN flood and "Teardrop" denial-of-service attacks. You will also need the kernel source, so make sure you have it handy as well.

pppd

We used PPP version 2.3.5. This package includes kernel code and the code for *pppd*. It can be used to build PPP for Linux, Solaris, SunOS, FreeBSD, OSF, and a handful of others. It can be found at *ftp://cs.anu.edu.au/pub/software/ppp/*.

SSH

We used version 1.2.25, which we've already talked about. We recommend using at least 1.2.25 because it contains a security fix that prevents a certain type of man-in-the-middle attack.

sudo

A handy little program that allows a user (granted the appropriate rights) to execute a program as the superuser. We used Sudo 1.5.4. It can be found at *ftp://ftp.uu.net/pub/security/sudo/*.

pty-redir

This program is used to create a new pseudo tty on the master in which to run the SSH client and output the name of the tty (e.g., `ttyp1`) for use later by *pppd* on the master system. You need this utility (or some variant) in order to make the PPP connection through SSH. Arpad Magosanyi, author of the Linux VPN HOWTO, wrote the redirector we used. At the time of this writing, it was at version 0.1. Its home is *ftp://ftp.vein.hu/ssa/contrib/mag/*. The version we used for our setup can be found at *http://www.vpn.outer.net/* under the Tools section.

The VPN Startup Script

Rather than starting up the VPN by hand, we used a modified *VPN* startup script that was also available in the Linux VPN HOWTO. This script is based on a skeleton used to build Unix startup scripts. You can find the script on the HOWTO itself, or the version we modified for our setup, at *http://www.vpn.outer.net/* under the Tools section.

The Slave's Scripts

These are very simple scripts that set up PPP and routing on the slave. Ours are available from the VPN web site.

Setting Up the VPN

Most people wouldn't call setting up the VPN a user-friendly process, but if you're comfortable compiling software and editing configuration files on a Unix system—and are willing to spend the time and effort—you shouldn't have too much trouble. Here is a brief summary of the steps to accomplish this:

1. Set up Linux on both the master and slave system.

2. Set up *pppd* on both systems.

3. Create a user account on the slave.

4. Set up SSH for RSA authentication on both systems.

5. Configure *sudo* on the slave.

6. Install and configure *pty-redir* on the master (modify if necessary).

7. Set up the *VPN* script on the master.

8. Set up a routing and PPP script on the slave.

In the subsections that follow, we'll take you through each of these steps.

Setting up the master and slave Linux systems

On both the master and slave systems, it's recommended that you strip them down to their essentials. It's better not to run something you don't need than to have it become a backdoor for an intruder. It's a good idea to remove the following services from your */etc/inetd.conf* file: *systat, netstat, finger, tftp,* and the *r* utilities. After the system is fully configured, you can also disable the telnet and ftp daemons in this file—the ultimate goal being that SSH is the only way to access the system. You're probably better off not installing *sendmail,* or you should at least keep it from starting by renaming the file to something else. Finally, make sure that you didn't install any other packages you don't need, such as BIND, NIS, NFS, X11, Samba, etc. Be minimalist.

You will need development tools, such as a C compiler (*gcc* is what we used), *make,* and C libraries. You'll also need a copy of the Linux kernel source code and TCP/IP networking utilities installed (e.g., *netstat, ifconfig, route,* etc.). When configuring the kernel for compilation (for instance, when doing a *make config* under Linux), you shouldn't include any other network protocols besides TCP/IP and PPP. It's probably also best to tell the configuration program to optimize the system as a router rather than as a host. Whether or not you want to do IP masquerading or use the host as a firewall will depend on your particular needs. Don't augment the kernel with unnecessary capabilities, such as multimedia sound card drivers.

Setting up the PPP daemon

The PPP daemon is also required on both systems. After you've extracted the source hierarchy, look at the *README* file appropriate to your system. On a Linux system, run the configure program to copy the *Makefiles* into place. Next, run *make kernel*, which will install the updated PPP drivers into your kernel source tree. You'll then have to build a new kernel with these drivers, install it, and reboot. (If you've never built a new kernel before, carefully read the *README* file in the kernel source tree—typically */usr/src/linux/*. The book *Running Linux* by Matt Welsh and Lar Kaufman (O'Reilly & Associates) also describes in detail how to build a kernel.)

On Linux, the PPP drivers can also be built as a kernel module. Modules are typically used to keep the kernel trim, as it doesn't have to load driver modules until they are needed. For this example, since we've already got a small kernel that only needs to do a few things, we just compiled PPP in directly. If the reboot was successful, return to the PPP daemon source tree and run *make* to build *pppd*, auxiliary programs, and the manpages, then run *make install* to put them into place.

 In the version of *pppd* we used, 2.3.5, there was a bug in the Linux kernel driver updates that caused compilation to fail for 2.0.x kernels. While we expect that the authors will have this fixed in future releases, we thought that we would mention it here. If compilation of *ppp.c* fails with complaints about too few arguments in *dev_kfree_skb*, edit line 3079 in *ppp.c*, make VERSION equal to your version of the kernel (e.g., change 2,1,86 to 2,0,33). A good place to go for help on these types of problems is the USENET group *comp.os.linux.networking* or *linux.dev.ppp*.

Once everything is in place, try running *pppd* from the command line on both the master and slave. On the slave, put a file called *.ppprc* in vpn1's home directory containing only the word "passive." You should see a bunch of garbage characters start to scroll across your terminal screen. It should time out after thirty seconds or so, or you can escape from it by pressing Enter, then "~", then Control-Z. Then kill the process with `kill %1`.

If you didn't see garbage, something is probably wrong with the PPP daemon itself. On a Linux system, check the */var/adm/messages* and */var/adm/syslog* files for clues (or check */etc/syslog.conf* to see where your files reside). Typically, the *messages* file will tell you if the daemon started successfully, and *syslog* will give you protocol-specific errors. If the daemon doesn't believe that the PPP drivers are compiled into the kernel, it will give you a message stating so right away. Use the *dmesg* command to see if the PPP drivers were loaded.

Creating a user account on the slave

Because we're going to launch the VPN script on the master from startup it will run as *root*, so there's no need to create a separate VPN account on that box. On the slave, however, it's better to create a separate account for the VPN connection rather than logging in as *root*. This will also allow you to create several accounts for several different VPNs, if different masters are all logging into the same slave. You might have this situation when there are several branch office masters setting up VPNs with one central office slave. For our purposes, we'll call the user account vpn1. Give it a password that's hard to crack, and it doesn't need to be easy to remember—we're going to be using RSA authentication for the SSH login.

Setting up SSH authentication

We've already gone through how to set up SSH on a system. Once you set up the SSH daemon to launch at startup, follow these steps to set up SSH authentication:

1. On the master host, set up a key pair for the root account using the *ssh-key-gen* program. If one already exists, check to make sure no existing services are using it. If not, you might want to go ahead and set one up again in order to make sure the keys are not compromised. This process will create the *$HOME/.ssh/identity* and *$HOME/.ssh/identity.pub* files for *root*. When you're prompted for a passphrase, leave it blank and press Enter. Because the VPN script might start up while the machine is unattended (such as after a remote reboot), we don't want it to have to enter the passphrase in order to connect with the SSH client.

2. Log into the slave as vpn1 or *su* to that user. Run *ssh-keygen* for that user. In that user's home directory, create a *.rhosts* file with the hostname of the master (*master-gw*) and the account that the master is going to be logging in as—in this case it's vpn1.

3. Next you want to add the slave's public host key to the root's *known_hosts* file on the master. The easiest way to do this is to run *ssh* to connect to the slave, and *ssh* will automatically ask you if you wish to add the slave's public key to the file, to which you respond "yes." To add the master's public host key to vpn1's *known_hosts* file, you can either try to connect to it using the SSH client, or copy the key from */etc/ssh_host_key.pub*.

4. Next, copy root's public key from *identity.pub* on the master and put it in vpn1's *authorized_keys* file.

At this point, we have *.rhosts*, RSA host, and RSA user authentication all enabled for this connection, providing maximum security. To further tighten security, we can edit the */etc/sshd_config* file on both hosts and modify or verify the following entries:

```
PermitRootLogin no
StrictModes yes
RhostsAuthentication no
RhostsRSAAuthentication no
RSAAuthentication yes
PasswordAuthentication no
AllowHosts master-gw.ora-vpn.com slave-gw.ora-vpn.com admin.ora-vpn.com
#
```

The `PermitRootLogin` setting of "no" will prevent *root* from logging in to either system using SSH. A `StrictModes` of "yes" means that the SSH daemon will complain if a user's home directory is world-writable.

The next few entries control the types of authentication permitted:

- Setting `RhostsAuthentication` to "no" (which is the default) means that *rhosts* authentication alone is not enough to allow a user to make an SSH connection.

- `RhostsRSAAuthentication` set to "no" means that *rhosts* authentication plus RSA host authentication isn't sufficient either.

- Setting `RSAAuthentication` to "yes" (which is the default) means that RSA user authentication is allowed.

- `PasswordAuthentication` set to "no" means that password authentication (if RSA authentication fails) isn't allowed.

The `AllowHosts` option is usually commented out, but it can be enabled to allow SSH connections only from a specific host. In this case, the slave is allowing connections only from *master.ora-vpn.com*. On the master, you would set `AllowHosts` to allow *slave.ora-vpn.com*. This means that each machine will allow an SSH connection only from the other.

Of course, if you disable telnet completely and allow the other VPN host to connect only via SSH, that's the only machine you'll be able to connect for remote administration. Aside from the chosen remote host, all work will have to be done at the console. Alternatively, you can add other hosts, such as *admin.ora-vpn.com* in our example, or allow every host from your domain to connect with the wildcard **.ora-vpn.com*.

At this point, you should be able to connect to the slave from the master as vpn1 using the SSH client. During this trial, you might want to keep a telnet session open on the slave in case there are problems. Try entering a command like this on the master, but with your slave in place of ours:

```
# ssh -l vpn1 slave-gw.ora-vpn.com
```

It should log you in to the slave machine without asking for a password. If it fails, it's probably due to an authentication error. Try running the same command, but add the −v option. That will give you excellent debugging output and show you whether it's *.rhosts*, RSA host, or RSA user authentication that's failing.

Configuring sudo on the slave

The *sudo* program is set up much like the other programs, using *configure, make,* and *make install*. It is placed in */usr/local/bin*. In order to change the configuration file for *sudo,* called *sudoers*, you need to use the *visudo* tool, which can be run only as *root*. The *visudo* editor uses your selected editor (*vi* by default), but will lock the file to make sure only one person is editing it, and will perform syntax checking against what the user is entering. It will automatically open *sudoers* when invoked.

sudo only needs to be installed on the slave for the vpn1 account, since the VPN script will be run as *root* on the master. The reason is that vpn1 will have to eventually execute the *route add* command, which is privileged. Here are the lines to add to your *sudoers* file:

```
# Cmnd alias specification
Cmnd_Alias VPN=/usr/sbin/pppd,/sbin/route
# User specification
vpn1 ALL=NOPASSWD: VPN
```

The lines beginning with the pound sign (#) are comments and will be ignored. The first command sets up a command alias called VPN that contains the *pppd* and *route* programs. This parameter provides a convenient way to group multiple programs that you want to allow users or groups to execute as superuser. The next entry in the file says that the user vpn1 can execute all of the commands in that alias from any host without a password. Normally, *sudo* requires that you enter your password before executing the command as *root*.

You should now be able to test *sudo* on the slave as the user vpn1. Try the following command:

```
# sudo /usr/sbin/pppd
```

It should launch *pppd* for you as *root*, and you'll see the PPP protocol garbage output again. If you have problems and you know that PPP already works, there might be something wrong with your *sudoers* file. Check the */var/adm/sudo.log* file for errors.

If *sudo* worked, try the following line on the master, logged in as *root*:

```
# ssh -l vpn1 slave-gw.ora-vpn.com sudo /usr/sbin/pppd
```

Once again, you should see the garbage output. This time, it's being delivered across your SSH connection to your local terminal.

Putting pty-redir on the master

The *pty-redir* program allows you to create a new pseudo-terminal on the master in order to run the PPP traffic through it. It comes with a *Makefile*, so all you should have to do is a *make*, then move the binary to your */usr/local/bin* directory. This file needs to be only on the master.

Line 84 of *pty-redir*.c v0.1 controls the name of the pseudo terminals that *pty-redir* uses. This name must match the naming convention of your system. In the original source, the line looked like this:

```
fprintf(stderr,"/dev/pty%c%c",a,b);
```

For our Slackware Linux configuration, we had to change it to look like the line below in order for it to work:

```
fprintf(stderr,"/dev/tty%c%c",a,b);
```

For your particular flavor of Unix, you may have to make modifications as well.

Now you should be able to run everything through *pty-redir*.

```
# pty-redir /usr/local/bin/ssh -1 vpn1 slave-gw.ora-vpn.com \
sudo /usr/sbin/pppd
```

You won't get any output here, so it's probably best to watch the logs and do a *ps* on the slave to see if *pppd* is running. If you enter *ps* on the master, you should see your entire command.

Setting up the VPN script

If you've gotten this far, you're practically there. All that's left is setting up the script that will make the VPN connection. This script resides on the master, and must accomplish the following:

- Allocate a new pseudo terminal on the master.

- Open an SSH connection to the slave.

- Start *pppd* on the slave.

- Start *pppd,* which also assigns IP addresses, on the master through the redirected pseudo-terminal.

- Set up the routing table on the slave (through a second SSH connection).

- Set up the routing table on the master.

The *VPN* script that's part of the Linux HOWTO accomplishes all of these. A listing of the script, along with our modified version, can be found on the Tools section of the authors' web site.

The first thing to do is edit the script and change the appropriate initialization settings for the VPN script. In this case, we're going to want to change the following:

PPPAPP

> Change this to the path of the *ppp* script in the home directory of the master's account on the slave server. In our case, it's */home/vpn1/ppp.*

ROUTEAPP

> Likewise, change this to the path to the routing script. For us, it's */home/vpn/ route.*

MYPPPIP

> This is the IP address of the VPN interface on the master. For us, it's 192.168.1.1.

TARGETIP

> The is the IP address for the VPN interface on the slave. We have it set to 192.168.1.2.

TARGETNET

> This is the network address (not the IP address) for the LAN side of the slave. It's 192.168.4.0 for us.

MYNET

> This is the network address for the LAN side of the master (192.168.3.0).

SLAVEWALL

> This is the hostname of the slave. We have it set to *slave-gw.ora-vpn.com.*

SLAVEACC

> This is the login name for the master's account on the slave. For us, it's vpn1.

PPPD, REDIR, SSH

> Check the location of these utilities to make sure the paths match those on your system.

When we were finished editing the file, our settings looked like this:

```
PATH=/usr/local/sbin:/sbin:/bin:/usr/sbin:/usr/bin:/usr/bin/X11/:
PPPAPP=/home/vpn1/ppp
ROUTEAPP=/home/vpn1/route
PPPD=/usr/sbin/pppd
NAME=VPN
REDIR=/usr/local/bin/pty-redir
SSH=/usr/local/bin/ssh
MYPPPIP=192.168.1.1
TARGETIP=192.168.1.2
TARGETNET=192.168.4.0
MYNET=192.168.3.0
SLAVEWALL=slave-gw.ora-vpn.com
SLAVEACC=vpn1
```

The next useful item to look at in the script is the line that actually starts up *pppd* on the slave. It looks like this:

```
$REDIR $SSH -o 'Batchmode yes' -t -l $SLAVEACC $SLAVEWALL\
sudo $PPPAPP >/tmp/device
```

As you can see, this is similar to what we did by hand earlier. The `-o Batchmode yes` option has been added to *ssh* to let it know it's in a script and shouldn't ask for passwords or passphrases. The `-t` option forces *ssh* to allocate a pseudo terminal on the slave which, as we said earlier, doesn't normally occur when *ssh* is used solely to execute a remote command. The pseudo tty on the slave is required for *pppd*'s I/O. The *pty-redir* program generates a new pseudo-terminal on the master, which is used to actually run the *ssh* program. The name of the pseudo- terminal is redirected into the file called */tmp/device*, which is used later by the master-side *pppd* in the script. Note that *pty-redir* outputs the tty name using STDERR. In order for us to get the script to redirect the STDERR output to the */tmp/device* file, we had to change it to look like this (the 2 is the number for the standard error output):

```
$REDIR $SSH -o 'Batchmode yes' -t -l $SLAVEACC $SLAVEWALL\
sudo $PPPAPP 2>/tmp/device
```

Another thing to note is that there's a ten-second sleep period after this command is run before execution continues. This is to give the SSH connection time to open, and the slave long enough to start the PPP daemon. This value can be adjusted for your environment.

Once the VPN script is configured, you can place it in a startup directory, such as */etc.rc.d*. You'll want to change the permissions so that only *root* can execute it (`rwx------`). It can be called from the *rc.local* file with the following command:

```
/etc/rc.d/VPN start
```

It can also be started by hand this way.

Setting up the slave's scripts

On the slave, there are only two simple scripts. The first is called *ppp*, and the second is *route*. These both reside in the home directory of the master's account on the slave, in our case */home/vpn1*.

The *ppp* script is very simple, and has this single line:

```
#!/bin/bash
/usr/sbin/ppp
```

Remember that you've already put a *.ppprc* file with the single line of "passive" in the vpn1 user's home directory.

The *route* script simply contains the route that's going to be added so that the slave machine knows how to get back to the master's LAN. For us, it will look like this:

```
#!/bin/bash
/sbin/route add -net 192.168.3.0 gw 192.168.1.1
```

The permissions on both scripts should be changed so that vpn1 is the owner and has full permissions to both files, while nobody else does:

```
-rwx------   1 vpn1    users         27 Jun  6 01:30 ppp*
-rwx------   1 vpn1    users          1 Jun  6 01:40 route*
```

Testing the Connection

Now that everything is in place, you can test your VPN connection. The first thing to do is start up the VPN script by hand. You should see something like this:

```
# VPN start
setting up vpn
tty is /dev/ttyp1
#
```

That's it. It should be up and running now. From the master, attempt to ping the slave's VPN interface address of 192.168.1.2. You should get a reply. Next, attempt to ping the LAN interface on the slave, and you should also get a reply. Finally, attempt to ping another machine on the slave's LAN, from which you should also get a reply.

Doing *ifconfig* on the master or slave should show you the PPP interface being used for the VPN. For instance, here is the output from our master:

```
ppp0      Link encap:Point-Point Protocol
          inet addr:192.168.1.1  P-t-P:192.168.1.2  Mask:255.255.255.0
          UP POINTOPOINT RUNNING NOARP MULTICAST  MTU:1500  Metric:1
          RX packets:61 errors:1 dropped:0 overruns:0
          TX packets:61 errors:0 dropped:0 overruns:0
```

Similarly, the *route* command should show you all of the routes that have been added to whatever system you run it on.

Troubleshooting Problems

Now let us assume that everything didn't go as smoothly as planned. There are several points of failure along the way, but fortunately there are some good ways to pinpoint the problem.

Errors from the VPN Script

The following are errors that might occur when you execute the *VPN* script. All of these errors should appear directly on the screen. When looking at these errors, it's important to remember the essentials of what the *VPN* script does: it redirects a pseudo-terminal, launches the PPP daemon on the slave using SSH, launches the PPP daemon on the master, and sets up routing on both the master and slave.

FAILED!

If you see this message, *pty-redir* failed to get a valid pseudo-terminal. You should check the contents of the */tmp/device* file and see if it's empty. If it exists but is empty, and you actually saw *pty-redir* spit out a device name when you ran it by hand earlier, STDERR output may not be redirected to that file. You will have to add a 2 as we showed under "Setting up the VPN script."

SIOCADDR: Network is unreachable

This is a message from one of the *route* commands. It can mean there is a mistake either in one of the IP addresses or networks in the VPN script settings, or in the slave's *route* script. Or it could mean that a PPP connection was never successfully started, in which case you'll need to check the logs (see "Connection Problems").

SIOCADDRT: Operation not permitted

This is also a message from one of the *route* commands. It means that you're not allowed to execute the *route* command in order to add a route, and is probably taking place on the slave. You should double-check your *sudoers* file on the slave to make sure that your master account has permission to execute the *route* command as root.

Connection Problems

If you get the "Network is unreachable" error from the *VPN* script, you might want to look at a process list on the slave using the *ps* command to see if the PPP daemon is running. If it isn't, either the SSH connection wasn't completely successful, or the PPP daemon failed to start up. The best place to look for problems with both of these is in */var/adm/messages* on the slave. A normal *ssh* and *pppd* startup on the slave should look like this in the logs:

```
Jun  6 04:01:40 slave-lan sshd[18745]: log: Connection from 1.0.0.1 port 1
Jun  6 04:01:41 slave-lan sshd[18745]: log: RSA authentication for vpn1
accepted
Jun  6 04:01:41 slave-lan sshd[18747]: log: executing remote command as user
vpn1
Jun  6 04:01:41 slave-lan sudo:      vpn1 : TTY=ttyp1 ; PWD=/home/vpn1 ;
USER=root
Jun  6 04:01:41 slave-lan pppd[18747]: pppd 2.2.0 started by vpn1, uid 0
Jun  6 04:01:41 slave-lan pppd[18747]: Using interface ppp0
Jun  6 04:01:41 slave-lan pppd[18747]: Connect: ppp0 <--> /dev/ttyp1
Jun  6 04:01:53 slave-lan pppd[18747]: local  IP address 192.168.1.2
Jun  6 04:01:53 slave-lan pppd[18747]: remote IP address 192.168.1.1
```

As you can see, the SSH daemon output says that authentication is accepted, and *sudo* successfully launches the PPP daemon as root for vpn1. The PPP daemon is started up on the slave, then it's started up on the master (communicating with *ttyp1,* which is the SSH connection), which also assigns IP addresses.

Debugging an SSH connection

A failed SSH connection will give you the following error in the *messages* log: `fatal: Connection closed by remote host`. If this log indicates problems with the SSH connection, try connecting to the master from the slave using `ssh -l vpn1 -v`. That will give you verbose output of what's going on when you attempt to connect. Here are some common errors:

Server refused our key

> This means that the public key of the account on the master attempting to make the connection (e.g., root) doesn't exist in the *authorized_keys* file of the account on the slave (e.g., vpn1). The solution is to copy the public key from root's *identity.pub* file into vpn1's *authorized_keys* file.

Server refused our rhosts authentication or host key

> This means that the server isn't in the *.rhosts* file or found in a *known_hosts* file. Add the server to either one, or both.

As we said earlier in "Building and Installing SSH," some implementations of shadow passwords may not work with SSH. Although it's compatible with most of the major methods, including those used by Solaris, Ultrix, SCO, Irix, and Linux, there may be some that it doesn't recognize or know how to handle. You may not notice any problems at compile time, and will only see them when you attempt to make a connection using password authentication and are denied login. At this point your two options are to attempt to add the appropriate code yourself (found in the *configure.in* and *auth-passwd.c* files), or to send a query to the SSH mailing list or the program's author. See the upcoming section "Getting Help with SSH" for more on this.

Debugging a PPP connection

If it looks like SSH has started successfully, but PPP never starts, there are two things you need to check: *sudo* and *pppd*.

The first thing to do is see if *sudo* executed successfully in the *messages* file. If you need more information, check for failures in *syslog*, which will typically look like this:

```
Jun  6 04:33:26 slave-lan sudo:       vpn1 : user NOT in sudoers ; TTY=ttyp0 ;
PWD=/home/vpn1 ; USER=root ; COMMAND=/sbin/route
Jun  6 05:32:12 slave-lan sudo:       vpn1 : command not allowed ; TTY=ttyp0 ;
PWD=/home/vpn1 ; USER=root ; COMMAND=/sbin/route
```

In the first entry, the user isn't found in the *sudoers* file and should be added. In the second, the user is found, but isn't allowed to execute that particular command as root. Again, *sudoers* should be edited and that command added to the Cmnd_Alias line shown earlier.

You can also check to see if the PPP daemon executed correctly. If, in the *messages* file, it looks like it was never executed on the slave, try starting it up by hand and see if it works. You should at least see that it says it was started in the *messages* file. You can also check the *syslog* file for errors such as "This system lacks kernel support for PPP." This, of course, means that you should recompile PPP into your kernel.

On the master, you should check for similar PPP daemon errors in *syslog*, especially for messages such as this:

```
Jun  4 20:51:41 master-lan pppd[19786]: Failed to open /dev/ptyp1: I/O error
```

This means that the PPP daemon is trying to start on a pseudo terminal that doesn't actually exist. It might be that your system uses a different naming convention for pseudo ttys from the one *pty-redir* is using. In this case, you'll want to check our tip in the "Putting pty-redir on the master" section. Another possibility is that the SSH connection between the master and slave had not finished opening and the PPP daemon hadn't started completely on the slave, in which case you'll want to increase the sleep time in the *VPN* script from 10 seconds to something higher. Finally, it could be that the SSH connection closed before PPP daemon started on the master. It should take longer than 10 seconds for the PPP daemon to time out, so you should probably look to SSH itself for the problem.

Getting Help with SSH

Because of its popularity, there is an enormous number of SSH users out there, so finding someone who has an answer to your particular question shouldn't be a problem. The best place may be the SSH mailing list, *ssh@clinet.fi*. To join the list, send email to *majordomo@clinet.fi* with "subscribe ssh" in the body of the message. You may want to first check the list archive at *http://www.cs.hut.fi/ssh-archive/*. There's also a USENET newsgroup, *comp.security.ssh*, that is gatewayed with the mailing list. Other resources can be found at the SSH Home Page. If you think you've found a bug in SSH, you can report it to *ssh-bugs@cs.hut.fi*.

A Performance Evaluation

We tested the performance of this method of creating a VPN to better give everyone an idea of the performance degradation caused by the various encryption methods of SSH, as well as the PPP connection. We used two 133 MHz Pentium systems (slow by today's standards, but we're looking only for relative values) each with 10Base-T (10 Mbps) Ethernet cards. The two systems were on the same switched-Ethernet backplane.

In our test, we transferred a 7 MB compressed binary file using the FTP protocol. We first did it ten times with just straight FTP to get a baseline. Next, we set up the VPN and did it with no encryption for ten trials. Finally, we performed ten trials each on three different ciphers: IDEA, Blowfish, and 3DES. The highest and lowest numbers were thrown out for each type of transfer, and an average was taken. We didn't test DES or arcfour, since they're disabled by default and aren't recommended by SSH's authors.

Table 8-1 shows the results of the test in the average amount of kilobytes per second transferred and the average percent efficiency versus plain FTP. The fourth column is the percent efficiency versus a VPN with no encryption. The term "VPN" just describes the PPP connection through SSH, with the type of encryption used in parentheses.

Table 8-1. VPN Performance Showing Average Kbytes/Second Transferred and Percent Efficiency

Connection Type (encryption type)	Kilobytes/second	% Efficiency vs. Plain FTP	% Efficiency vs. VPN with no Encryption
Plain FTP (none)	480	—	233%
VPN (none)	206	43%	—
VPN (Blowfish)	174	36%	85%
VPN (IDEA)	124	26%	60%
VPN (3DES)	96	20%	47%

As you can see, the VPN connection of just PPP through SSH causes a considerable amount of performance degradation. This performance degradation is due to just the PPP and SSH protocols overhead. It's interesting to note that, overall, adding encryption to the connection doesn't cause that much of an additional bottleneck. Obviously, though, some ciphers are more efficient than others, with Blowfish edging out over IDEA, and leaving 3DES in the dust.*

---

* Note that the percentage efficiencies versus no encryption that we calculated in our test are roughly equal to the percentages given by the SSH authors in the *README.CIPHERS* file that comes with the SSH distribution.

9

The Cisco
PIX Firewall

One of the most efficient and convenient options when creating a VPN is to install a network security device on your perimeter network to provide LAN-to-LAN tunneling, roaming, and authentication. Already, the major routing and network vendors have their own offerings in the field. In this chapter we will delve into the configuration of the Cisco PIX firewall product to give you an idea of how these devices are used and what benefits you can expect to gain from using them. We chose the Cisco PIX product because it was one of the first entrants into the market, it was backed by one of the largest and most trusted vendors (Cisco Systems), and we started work on this book at a time when integrated VPN products were few and far between and IPSec was not even fully formed by the IETF (the Internet Engineering Task Force).

The Cisco PIX Firewall

The PIX provides three basic VPN requirements: it separates the packet filtering functions from the main gateway router, it dynamically shares a pool of Internet addresses among many internal users, and several PIX units can be combined to create a VPN tunnel session between sites. In this chapter we will explore how the PIX firewall can be used in your network, and we will cover some basic installation and configuration techniques.

The PIX has two Ethernet ports: one for the internal (or private) network and one for the external (or public) network, which is normally the Internet. The PIX uses two Intel 10/100 Ethernet cards to handle high-capacity sites. It is essentially like other Cisco router products, although it does not run Cisco's popular IOS operating system. The PIX can also be deployed redundantly to create a fail-safe router, so that a failure in one PIX automatically causes a transfer of traffic to the other.

The PIX provides firewall protection by completely isolating the private (or internal) network from an outside one. The internal network uses private addresses, such as those in the 192.168.*n.n* range defined by RFC 1918, and the PIX translates them dynamically to a range of external addresses used on the Internet using NAT (Network Address Translation).

More current information about the Cisco PIX firewall can be reviewed at *http:// www.cisco.com/warp/public/751/pix/.*

The PIX in Action

Figure 9-1 is a diagram of where to install the PIX firewall on a standard network topological map.

Functionally, the PIX firewall is set up much like a packet filtration router. The two Ethernet interfaces are labeled "outside" and "inside" for the two networks that you will need to connect it to. In Figure 9-1, the PIX firewall is situated on the "perimeter network" between the internal router and the external router. You will notice that the only machine connecting both networks is the PIX firewall. By funneling traffic through the PIX, you can construct an effective security gateway.

For the purpose of illustrating some of the sample configurations in this chapter, we will assume that the topology of our network looks like the one depicted in Figure 9-2.

ISP Assigned Addresses (Global Pool)

To create the dynamic address translation slots that we referred to earlier, which will be used to map internal addresses into external ones, we need to get a NIC registered network allocated to us, and have it routed to the PIX firewall. In Figure 9-2, the global pool our Internet service provider has provided to us for our tests is a small network comprised of only eight machines. We also have eight machines on our perimeter (outside) network. We will explain how this network is to be entered into the PIX's configuration in a moment. Let us first discuss how that global pool will work conceptually, and why it is needed in the first place.

The PIX firewall, as you can see, has three different network address ranges associated with it, but only two interfaces. The notation we will be using for the network ranges is used to depict Classless Interdomain Routing networks. The number after the slash indicates how many bits are used to define the network part of the range. The host part of the range can be determined by subtracting the number after the slash from 32 (the number of bits total in a TCP/IP address). For example, a /29 network would have 29 bits of network and 3 bits of hosts. Since

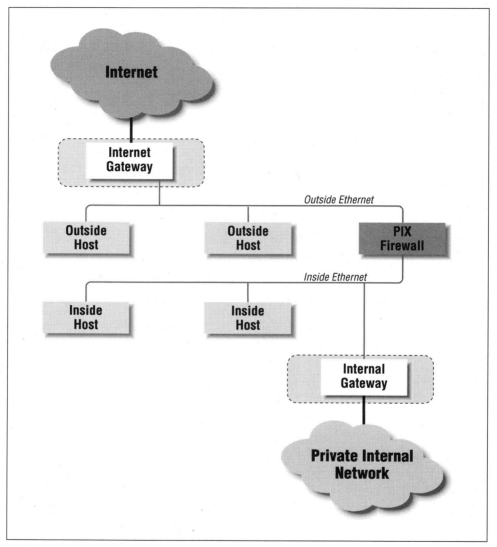

Figure 9-1. A typical PIX firewall setup

2^3 is 8, we know that we have been assigned an eight-machine network. Here are the ranges we will be using in our examples:

- Outside Ethernet: 1.251.174.152/29
- Inside Ethernet: 192.168.2.0/24
- Global pool: 2.241.11.248/29

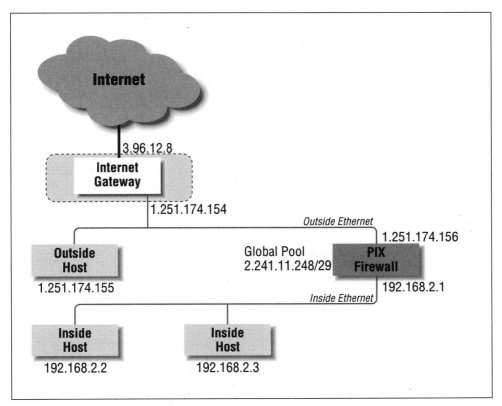

Figure 9-2. A test network for our initial configuration

The PIX uses a feature called *Dynamic Address Translation* to map the Internal address range (192.168.2.0/24) into the Global range (2.241.11.248/29) as connections are opened and addresses are needed. When not in use, as when a machine is turned off or the user has left for the night, the addresses in the global pool that may have been assigned to the user are returned to an open status and assigned to another user. The global pool must be a separate network from both the internal and external networks.

As we briefly touched on before, using a global pool and dynamic addressing to assign network addresses has two benefits. It results in good protection by hiding the internal machine needing Internet access. It also allows hundreds of sites to share a 32-machine or smaller network, if the site doesn't have too many users trying to connect to the Internet at any one time.

For everything to work as expected, your Internet service provider needs to add a routing table entry on their backbone to route your global pool of addresses to you. In this case, the ISP added a route that pointed network 2.241.11.248/29 to the 1.251.174.156 interface on the PIX firewall. The ISP could have also pointed this network to the gateway router (3.96.12.8), in which case we would have needed to add a further route from 3.96.12.8 to the PIX's external interface to complete the connection.

Advantages of the PIX Firewall

One of the PIX's strongest points is that it is a single-point hardware solution that is easy to configure and to administer. Dynamic address translation allows a large network to share a small amount of address space. Most importantly for our purposes in this book, two or more PIX boxes provide an encrypted tunnel across the Internet.

Hardware solution

One of the biggest advantages of using the PIX firewall is that it is a separate piece of hardware from the servers that host your critical services. Physical hardware solutions, if they are made well and are easy to configure and maintain, are excellent ways for creating firewalls and VPNs. Network coordinators and their staffs can easily install many PIX firewalls in a large, non-homogenous, world-wide WAN. Hardware implementations are generally more reliable; they have been through more rigorous testing than software solutions, and are sometimes faster in operation since much of the core microcode can be burned onto chips.

Superior to Unix and other router firewalls

The PIX runs an operating system unlike those on either the "normal" Cisco routers or traditional Unix machines, which run routing or gateway software. While Cisco is known for robust software, it is quite complex because it is designed for a variety of routing and connectivity needs. For instance, most versions of Cisco's IOS software support a wide variety of routing protocols, such as RIP, IGRP, BGP, AppleTalk, and IPX. This support, which is perfect for the management of any large network, is considerable overkill if all you need is the single function of packet filtration. By removing all of that extra overhead, the PIX makes an excellent choice for a firewall.

As the PIX was designed with only one purpose in mind, that of securing a private network by both filtering traffic and establishing secure links across an unprotected Internet, it is an excellent place to establish logging controls on the network. Further, the PIX machine is a fine encryption device, protecting valuable communication with tried and true cryptographic techniques.

Single point of control/failure

When network trouble is at hand, a clear delineation between the outside world and one's local world is an immense asset. By using a single unit to handle the network's entire firewalling needs, the network coordinator has a clear starting point for troubleshooting. The PIX provides such an architecture.

By having a single unit handle all network traffic in this manner, equipment malfunction and software misconfiguration could cause a great amount of havoc in one fell swoop. But Cisco has anticipated this problem with a fail-over, hot-standby mode, whereby two units can be configured in parallel. Should some fault occur to one of the units, the other can support the firewall by maintaining operation transparently.

Dynamic address translation

The dynamic translation feature, which allows users to "pick up" a free address from the Internet pool whenever they need one, does more than just allow many people to share a few NIC registered addresses. It also provides adaptive security to the hosts using the internal addresses. The PIX unit has two interfaces, one for the exterior network and one for the interior one. Because of this, the internal address range is hidden by translating the internal address into the dynamic pool of addresses for Internet exchange. This method provides a high level of security because a threat is much less likely when an attacker doesn't know the architecture, network range, or setup of the internal network

PIX acts like a proxy server

Unix-based proxy servers are commonplace in today's world, and most of them serve their function well. Proxy servers do essentially what the PIX firewall was engineered to do: they hide a machine or a network of machines from the outside world by masquerading as the client in network conversations with unknown or unverifiable parties.

The PIX is more robust than the standard proxy servers because it provides a quick session bypass once the authenticated parties have shaken hands. Traditional proxy servers maintain state information for the duration of the session, and handle their packet control at the top of the protocol stack. Moreover, because software-driven proxy servers perform packet filtering, they prevent the use of almost all the VPN solutions on the market today.

Ease of configuration and maintenance

For the most part, the PIX is very easy to handle in everyday use. Once the configuration is applied and tested, it handles its job silently and without complaint. As is popular in today's world, to further assist the network coordinators that will be installing the device, Cisco has made an HTML front end for configuration. There is of course the old standby option of the command-line–driven interface, which could be used by those more familiar with Cisco's prevalent IOS software.

High-speed access

For those with ultra-high–capacity lines, such as fractional or full DS3s (T3s), the PIX, with its two 100-megabit Ethernet cards, can easily handle a significant amount of Internet traffic. Although we wouldn't recommend piping a T3's full load of traffic through only one machine, the fact that the capacity is there is quite a benefit.

Links

By using an additional card that comes separately, the PIX firewall can be used to create an encrypted channel between itself and another such unit somewhere out on the public side of the PIX. This "private link encryption" feature gives the PIX firewall its most tremendous benefit: it lets organizations link private Internets securely using the public networks, with very simple configuration. That's what this book is all about. One slight disadvantage is that the PIX firewall supports only IP traffic. (We suppose this could be considered an advantage as well.)

Limitations of the PIX Firewall

Even though the PIX is a nearly complete solution to the development of a virtually private network, it does have some drawbacks in terms of maintenance, network address translation limits, and price.

Hardware solution

Hardware can be tricky if mismanaged, difficult to debug if misconfigured, and hard to replace quickly if broken. Hardware like the PIX is provided by only one vendor, and you can't be sure what will happen to the vendor in the future.

Dynamic address use

There is a limited pool of addresses that the PIX can assign to hosts on your internal network that want to communicate with the outside. Cisco sells a few different varieties of the product, allowing for 32, 256, or 1024 sessions simultaneously. Remember that one user could be using many different sessions at once, so there is a definite limit on how much a PIX can handle when it's connected to a huge network.

Budgetary considerations

A whole squadron of Cisco PIX units might be prohibitively expensive to widely distribute across your network. The PIX firewall has a suggested retail price in the tens of thousands of dollars, and the encryption cards required to create VPN tunnels go for a few thousand each.

Maintenance

As with any new equipment, you have to consider the need for ongoing maintenance and growth. The PIX firewall, which may be initially easy to configure, could grow to have a complex configuration even if there are no other firewalls providing a similar function. The persons in charge of coordinating network activity need to establish a plan for how traffic needs to be restricted, and to which networks these restrictions apply. Subtle mistakes in the configuration could lead to potentially large security holes.

Configuring the PIX as a Gateway

The PIX firewall comes standard with two switchable 10/100 Megabit Ethernet cards, a serial console port, a failover control card, some required cabling and mounting parts, and possibly a secure encryption card, depending on the bundle purchased. In this section we will set up a PIX unit right out of the box, configure it for basic operation, and set up an average firewall. Beyond that, we will illustrate the setup of multiple PIX units so that they may link to one another across the Internet, thus creating a VPN.

In this section, we show you how to connect to the PIX so you can configure it, how to set up your firewall on the PIX, and how to do some initial testing. Configuration of the PIX doesn't affect configuration of any other hosts on the inner or outer networks, which you can still set up using traditional rules. The configuration examples in this chapter were set up using the 4.1.6 version of the PIX operating software.

Connecting to the PIX

Example 9-1 shows the PIX boot screen, which is sent to the console port when the unit powers on. A serial console cable, supplied with the unit, must be attached to a personal computer, and the terminal software must be configured as follows before any commands may be input into the system:

- 9600 baud

- 8 bits, no parity, 1 stop bit

To confirm that the connections are made properly and that the terminal software
is set up right, simply booting the PIX firewall should produce the output seen in
Example 9-1.

Example 9-1. PIX Console Startup Screen

```
Copyright (c) 1996-1998 by Cisco Systems, Inc.

              Restricted Rights Legend

Use, duplication, or disclosure by the Government is
subject to restrictions as set forth in subparagraph
(c) of the Commercial Computer Software - Restricted
Rights clause at FAR sec. 52.227-19 and subparagraph
(c) (1) (ii) of the Rights in Technical Data and Computer
Software clause at DFARS sec. 252.227-7013.

              Cisco Systems, Inc.
              170 West Tasman Drive
              San Jose, California 95134-1706

Type ? for help
armadillo 0>
```

A Sample Configuration

The configuration of the firewall is pretty straightforward. Given our test scenario
featured in Figure 9-2, we have developed a configuration that meets those
requirements. Here are the configuration parameters we entered into our PIX:

```
nameif ethernet0 outside security0
nameif ethernet1 inside security100
enable password testing
password testing
hostname lab-test-1
no failover
names
pager lines 24
syslog output 20.3
no syslog console
syslog host 192.168.2.2
interface ethernet0 auto
interface ethernet1 auto
ip address outside 1.251.174.156 255.255.255.248
ip address inside 192.168.2.1 25.255.255.0

arp timeout 14400
global (outside) 1 2.241.11.249-2.241.11.251
global (outside) 2 2.241.11.252-2.241.11.254
nat (inside) 2 192.168.2.128 255.255.255.128
age 10
route outside 0.0.0.0 0.0.0.0 1.251.174.154 1
```

```
no rip outside passive
no rip outside default
no rip inside passive
no rip inside default
timeout xlate 24:00:00 conn 12:00:00 udp 00:02:00
timeout rpc 00:10:00 h323 00:05:00 uauth 00:05:00


no snmp-server location
no snmp-server contact
snmp-server community public
telnet 192.168.2.2 255.255.255.255
mtu outside 1500
mtu insde 1500
```

The two *nameif* commands assign short names to the two interfaces: outside
and inside. Then, the two *interface* commands define the speed at which the
interfaces operate. We used the **auto** keyword to have the hardware automatically sync to the Ethernet it is attached to. The *ip address* commands use the
assigned names to establish the network configuration for the internal and external networks. The internal network we chose was part of the unroutable RFC 1918
network 192.168.0.0, which is traditionally used for hosts requiring Network
Address Translation (NAT) on an interior network protected by a firewall such as
the PIX.

As Figure 9-1 depicts, we don't have an internal router. The network that we used
for testing was very small and an internal router was not necessary. You can see
this in the configuration by studying the *route* command entry, which points the
default route (0.0.0.0) to the gateway to which the PIX would send external traffic
(1.251.174.154). Logically enough, you are always required to specify an outside
router.

The *rip* command sets whether the PIX should or should not broadcast default
routing information (using the RIP protocol) to either the inside or outside
interface. Our sample configuration disables all RIP route propagation since we
had such a small example. Should you have an internal router that extends the
network to other locations, you would need to set the default internal route mentioned above to the router responsible for accessing the rest of the network, and
you may be required to set up RIP routes on the PIX so that it can see everything
that may need access to the outside network.

The *timeout* commands are used to set how much time must pass before a translation slot or a connection slot is cleared. The timeout is specified in the format
hours:minutes:seconds. The PIX derives strength in its security by creating dynamic
translations between internal hosts on unroutable networks to external routable
hosts and disguising this process from the external peer. By lengthening the timeouts to several hours or even days, you lose some of the security because outside

attackers have longer to study a peer-to-peer connection and could have enough time to stage a compromise. Further, if you lengthen the timeouts, internal hosts that are vying for external addresses may find addresses not available and hence connections could be slowed down or ceased. It is up to the network administrator to analyze the network for average use patterns and to adjust the timeouts appropriately.

The *telnet* and *syslog host* commands set a host address from which telnets may connect to the PIX and where logging information is to be sent. Only inside network addresses may be used to connect to the PIX. As in our example, we set up the administrator's workstation at IP address 192.168.2.2 as our only point of access into the PIX. The configuration allows for a mask to be entered after the address so that a whole range may be allowed telnet access. In our example, our PIX is connected to a DMZ network in address range of 1.251.174.152/29. Our ISP assigned us the range of 2.241.11.248/29, routed to our PIX's address at 1.251.174.156 (as per the `ip` address definition above).

We decided to split this network into two ranges, some for dynamic NAT translation slots, and some for use with static translation slots called *conduits* (described later in this chapter). From the configuration we presented, you can see that the two `global` commands define these two ranges. We will be using range 1 (2.241.11.249–2.241.11.251) for our conduits, and range 2 (2.241.11.252–2.241.11.254) for our dynamic NAT hosts. The NAT configuration is accomplished by the `nat` command in the example configuration. Thus, the internal hosts in the range 192.168.2.128–192.168.2.254 will be able to obtain dynamic NAT addressing from the PIX in the second range (2.241.11.252–2.241.11.254).

Firewall Configuration on the PIX

Although PIX access control is somewhat similar in form to the IOS-based access lists, the PIX uses a combination of the keywords `outbound`, `apply`, and `show outbound` to accomplish the same types of tasks. While standard Cisco routers require explicit commands to shut out incoming traffic, the Dynamic Address Translation feature of PIX normally blocks inbound traffic to machines on the inside network by default. Because of this, there are no *inbound* packet filtering commands. There are inbound commands, however, that allow connections, even though the firewall is in place. We will cover these shortly.

We tested the default behavior of the PIX by using the configuration previously illustrated and carrying out several tests, the results of which are summarized here.

We logged on to a machine on the outside network (1.251.174.155) and tried to ping one of the translation table addresses: one of the test machines we set up on the inside network that was dynamically given a NAT address in the second global pool (2.241.11.254). The connection was denied. The PIX also barred us from opening a connection to a known port on the inside machine, even directly after an outbound connection was made from that unit. A machine on the Internet was found to exhibit the exact same behavior. The Cisco PIX firewall provides a level of protection right out of the box without complex configuration, testing, or troubleshooting.

By using the *conduit* and/or *static* commands (covered later in this chapter), we can set up special configurations that allow inbound connections to occur through the firewall. Thus, our mail server, web server, and FTP server can be contacted and deliver information to or from the outside world.

Before we foray further into the practice of "punching holes" in the PIX firewall, we will take our sample configuration and add some more restrictions to our inside Ethernet hosts. Let's say that we have decided, in our role as the network administrators, that we wish to deny outbound web access from the single internal host 192.168.2.100 and from the range of hosts from 192.168.2.128 to 192.168.2.254. Further, we have deemed the telnet protocol to be troublesome and wish to deny all hosts on the inside network telnet access, except our own workstation (192.168.2.2). The following configuration parameters accomplish these tasks:

```
outbound 11 deny 192.168.2.100 255.255.255.255 80
outbound 11 deny 192.168.2.128 255.255.255.128 80
outbound 11 permit 192.168.2.2 255.255.255.255 23
outbound 11 deny 192.168.2.0 255.255.255.0 23
apply (inside) 11 outgoing_src
```

The "11" following the **outbound** command refers to the access list used to group the firewall instructions. The masks following the IP addresses, such as the 255.255.255.128 following 192.168.2.128, refer to a netmask, or a whole range of hosts, rather than just to an individual node.

Some immediate differences appear when you compare the preceding access lists to those that would be found on any ordinary Cisco routing product running IOS. Most noticeable is that PIX Firewall uses a single host/network pair to control access, whereas IOS uses a double host/network pair. For example, you might find something like the following on an Internet-connected serial interface on a Cisco 7500 to produce the same results as the first line in our PIX firewall:

```
access-list 101 deny tcp 192.168.2.100 0.0.0.0 0.0.0.0 255.255.255.255 eq 80
```

Also, the PIX uses the **apply** keyword to activate or deactivate the access control provided by the **outbound** directives.

In addition to checking where packets come from, as in our example, we can check the destinations of our packets. To illustrate, let's say that site 1.1.1.1 on the

Internet has unsavory materials on it and you wish to block all access to this site from your network. The following configuration accomplishes this:

```
outbound 12 deny 1.1.1.1 255.255.255.255
apply (inside) 12 outgoing_dest
```

You'll notice a couple of things. First, we used another outbound access list (numbered 12) to handle the new configuration. We feel it best to separate the outgoing destinations' firewalls from the outgoing source destinations. Although not required, it does help keep things more orderly when these access lists get large, which is certainly going to happen over time. Second, we left off the port parameter. By doing so, we effectively cut all communication attempts with host 1.1.1.1 on *any* port.

By using the principles we illustrated in the two firewall configuration examples, you can construct large and sometimes complicated firewalls, granting access and denying access to as granular or as wide an audience as you desire. Keep in mind that the shorter the list of access items, the faster the machinery handles packets, and the easier it will be for you when a problem with the firewall eventually explodes. Remember to use as large a network as possible (grouping related machines in a single network), so that there is no need to enter 32 separate commands where one would have sufficed.

Testing, Tracing, and Debugging

To facilitate debugging and testing, the PIX firewall comes with a suite of test utilities. We will cover in brief the operation of the major ones.

debug

The *debug* command can be used to test the configuration of the PIX firewall and to check the ongoing operation of the unit whenever you suspect a connectivity problem. To enable the tracing function, execute the command **debug trace on** to the PIX firewall. Results will be echoed to the console as ICMP packets are received or transmitted. For instance, using a machine on our inside network (192.168.2.2) to ping a machine on our outside network (1.251.174.155) produced the following output:

```
1.251.174.155 <- 2.241.11.254 (192.168.2.2)
1.251.174.155 -> 2.241.11.254 (192.168.2.2)
```

Each ping packet is represented by a pair of log entries: one for the initial ICMP request and one for the returning response.

Pinging from the inside network to the outside PIX interface address will not produce a response, nor will pinging from a machine on the outside network to the PIX's inside interface address. This is normal behavior. Using our sample networks, if we were to ping from 192.168.2.2 to 1.251.174.156, we would *not* get a response. Likewise, pinging from 1.251.174.155 to 192.168.2.2 or 2.241.11.254 will fail.

xlate

The *xlate* command stands for "translate," and displays the current assignments of the inside network addresses to the global pool of addresses. Since these assignments are temporary and will eventually disappear, the status reported by *xlate* can be different from minute to minute. The command is of great assistance when debugging problems with connectivity across the PIX firewall. It provides some very comprehensive output, including the idle time of a connection, the bytes transferred, and the ports used to build it. Here's some output after we started a telnet session across the PIX as well as launching Netscape Navigator:

```
$ sh xlate
Global 2.241.11.254 Local 192.168.2.2 nconns 10 econns 0 flags pvA
   TCP out 3.96.12.2-80 in 192.168.2.2-1700 idle 0:00:17 Bytes 365 Flags E
   TCP out 3.96.12.2-80 in 192.168.2.2-1699 idle 0:00:18 Bytes 365 Flags E
   TCP out 3.96.12.2-80 in 192.168.2.2-1698 idle 0:00:19 Bytes 365 Flags E
   TCP out 3.96.12.2-80 in 192.168.2.2-1697 idle 0:00:19 Bytes 365 Flags E
   TCP out 3.96.12.2-80 in 192.168.2.2-1696 idle 0:00:22 Bytes 370 Flags E
   TCP out 3.96.12.2-80 in 192.168.2.2-1695 idle 0:00:22 Bytes 371 Flags E
   TCP out 3.96.12.2-80 in 192.168.2.2-1694 idle 0:00:22 Bytes 367 Flags E
   TCP out 3.96.12.2-80 in 192.168.2.2-1693 idle 0:00:22 Bytes 371 Flags E
   TCP out 3.96.12.2-80 in 192.168.2.2-1692 idle 0:00:30 Bytes 323 Flags E
   TCP out 3.96.12.2-23 in 192.168.2.2-2049 idle 0:00:03 Bytes 1086 Flags
UFHIO
```

As you can see, there were a ton of port 80 connections established. Most of these are single graphic files located at the web server's main page (3.96.12.2). Netscape, as with most of the other popular browsers, initiates many requests for each graphic after it has pulled down the contents of the main HTML page. The last line of the output is our telnet session, as evidenced by the port 23 hanging on the end of the address.

arp

Sometimes when debugging network configurations, such as those involving the PIX firewall, you need to determine "what the PIX can see." Using the address resolution protocol, which handles the translation of Ethernet addressing into IP addresses, the PIX provides a fine tool for tracking down the physical machinery to which the PIX firewall is talking. The *arp* command, logically enough, provides a list of Ethernet and IP addresses for both of the PIX's interfaces. When things get confused as to what host is doing what on the network, and what access permissions it should be allowed to have through the PIX to the Internet, the *arp* command becomes helpful.

Here's an example of the output of our rather tiny example world detailed earlier in the chapter:

```
# sh arp
        outside 4.96.12.9 00:34:08:93:1b:76
        outside 4.241.10.209 00:77:70:62:5b:ee
        outside 4.96.12.100 00:05:02:65:27:fb
        outside 2.96.12.1 00:00:0c:65:de:10
        outside 2.96.12.2 00:20:af:67:8c:77
        outside 2.96.12.62 00:e0:1e:33:33
        outside 2.96.12.43 00:32:9a:00:33:9f
        outside 2.96.12.23 00:32:97:0e:23:56
        outside 3.96.12.33 08:00:07:4f:23:c5
        inside 192.168.128.1 00:10:4b:45:1b:12
        inside 192.168.129.2 00:40:22:33:3a:3d
        inside 192.168.129.3 00:a0:22:4c:c6:23
        inside 192.168.128.4 00:05:f2:28:23:7b
        inside 192.168.129.5 00:40:32:31:33:1c
        inside 192.168.129.6 00:de:08:bf:ec:05
        inside 192.168.129.7 00:60:8c:dd:c0:89
```

show interface

To check the physical Ethernet interfaces on the PIX, the **show interface** command provides some summary information. Here is the output of the command for illustration:

```
# sh interface
interface ethernet0 "outside" is up, line protocol is up
  Hardware is i82557 ethernet, address is 00:a0:c9:48:33:23
  IP address 1.251.174.154, subnet mask 255.255.255.248
  MTU 1500 bytes, BW 100000 Kbit half duplex
        2053034 packets input, 486927215 bytes, 0 no buffer
        Received 1068648 broadcasts, 0 runts, 0 giants
        269 input errors, 124 CRC, 145 frame, 0 overrun, 124 ignored, 0 abort
        1014642 packets output, 98109936 bytes, 26 underruns
interface ethernet1 "inside" is up, line protocol is up
  Hardware is i82557 ethernet, address is 00:a0:c9:34:23:23
  IP address 192.168.128.1, subnet mask 255.255.252.0
  MTU 1500 bytes, BW 10000 Kbit half duplex
        1095847 packets input, 103598967 bytes, 0 no buffer
        Received 95886 broadcasts, 0 runts, 0 giants
        22 input errors, 22 CRC, 0 frame, 0 overrun, 22 ignored, 0 abort
        975558 packets output, 387229999 bytes, 0 underruns
```

Configuring the Other VPN Capabilities

So far, in our discussion of the PIX firewall, we have demonstrated its use and configuration as a packet filtration firewall and as a dynamic lookup and translation mechanism that hides the identity of internal machines. In this section we will briefly discuss how to build a virtual private network between two PIX units, thus connecting private networks with the Internet as a transport medium.

Offering Services to the Internet Through Conduits and the static Command

The *conduit* command is a short-circuit mechanism that lets hosts on the outside network bypass the PIX's adaptive security mechanism to connect to hosts on the inside network. This isn't really as scary as it may sound. It is frequently required and actually very normal to punch holes in the firewall for specific, known services, the security of which can be monitored and tested before the hole is opened.

You can put in an exception to the PIX's adaptive security system either by using the *conduit* command or as the last parameter of the *static* command (an example of which is detailed below). But Cisco recommends that the *conduit* command be used.

Let us say that we have a mail-exchanging Unix host on our outside network (1.251.174.155) and an SMTP/POP host on our inside network (192.168.2.3). We wish to accomplish two things:

1. Map the address of our internal SMTP server statically to the translation table address 1.241.11.254 (the first one chosen by PIX).

2. Create a conduit that allows SMTP traffic to flow from that static address to our outside mail-exchanging host.

Here's the pair of commands needed to produce the desired effect:

```
$ static 2.241.11.254 192.168.2.3
$ mailhost (inside, outside) 2.241.11.254 192.168.2.3 32 24
```

The `static` command merely assigns a fixed address so that the mail server won't continually get a NAT-assigned address from the pool. It is difficult to send mail to a machine whose address is always changing. The `mailhost` command is a variant of the `conduit` command that allows incoming port 25 traffic to the static translation slot assigned to the mail server at 192.168.2.3. It is different from `conduit` because it actually looks at the directive and arguments being passed to the mail server (HELO, MAIL, RCPT, DATA, RSET, NOOP, or QUIT). It allows only the most basic of commands, thereby reducing the threat of an outsider sending unwanted commands in attempts to compromise the machine.

Now let's assume that we have a web server that we want to assign a fixed address to and create a conduit for, much like the mail host in the previous example. We would perform essentially the same tasks to allow only port 80 traffic to the unit:

```
$ static 2.241.11.257 192.168.2.99
$ conduit (inside, outside) 2.241.11.257 80 tcp 0 0
```

The "0 0" part on the end is a PIX shorthand for the default network pointing to everything. Hence, this pair of commands would allow any host anywhere on the outside interface to come in through the PIX only using tcp port 80, but only to the address at 2.241.11.257, which is statically linked to internal host 192.168.2.99.

Tunneling with the link Directive

The most stellar application of the PIX firewall is to create a ready-made tunnel. To create a virtual private network per the guidelines detailed in this book, a private encrypted tunnel needs to be created between two separate sites. The PIX firewall, in addition to its deployment as a packet restriction firewall and a dynamic translation mechanism, can also be used in this capacity through the *link* command. Of course, at least two PIX units are required to create the link.

The *link* command establishes an encrypted link between two PIX units, thus letting the two sites carry on secure communications over their "outside" networks. Currently, you can link together up to 64 different PIX firewall sites in this fashion. Cisco calls this security mechanism a *private link* feature, and requires the installation of a separate encryption card in the PIX unit, along with the appropriate PIX software. All PIX firewalls that you intend to use for tunnels must be installed with both of these components.

The private link operates by scanning packets that arrive at its inside interface. Packets that match the PIX's list of "route link" configurations are encrypted and encapsulated in a UDP frame, then sent off across the outside interface. The PIX uses port 1123 to exchange its private link information. When the encrypted bundle arrives at the destination unit, the packet is unwrapped, decrypted, and forwarded on to the inside interface.

As an example using our networks, let's assume that we added another PIX firewall to our San Francisco office. The networks the service provider allocated were 5.182.95.248/29 for the outside interface and 6.242.188.0/24 for the global pool. Our administrator in San Francisco decided to assign the address 5.182.95.250 to the PIX's outside interface. The configuration of the rest of the machine is similar to the first site we discussed. In the configuration example below, we link together the two PIX units using their outside Ethernet interfaces with a special secret key shared by both systems.

Here are the commands we would enter on the PIX that we originally set up:

```
$ link 5.182.95.250 1 A6B5C02
$ link path 6.242.188.0 255.255.255.0 5.182.95.250
```

Here are the commands for the new San Francisco PIX:

```
$ link 1.251.174.156 1 A6B5C02
$ link path 192.168.2.0 255.255.255.0 1.251.174.156
```

The *link* command itself is used to associate one PIX unit with another one, and also serves to set the key that the two units will use to encrypt and decrypt packets. The *link path* command is used to explicitly tell the PIX that packets destined for another "internal network" on a friendly PIX should *not* be forwarded or translated as other packets are, but instead encrypted and tunneled. As you can see, setting up multiple PIX units in a large array is very simple. By duplicating the pair of commands above for every private link communication channel the PIX has, an administrator can simply and easily add, change, or remove whole tunneled sites.

The PIX's encryption, which uses a separate piece of hardware, is currently restricted to a key size of 56 bits. Although no official announcement has been made, it is our guess that Cisco will provide a beefier version of its encryption card for those most paranoid about security, and for those with ultra-sensitive data to share and protect.

10

Managing and Maintaining Your VPN

Now your VPN is up, and remote users and sites are connecting to it over the Internet. This doesn't mean that you're in the clear and can tuck this book onto your shelf and never think about VPNs again. Now begins the battle to keep your VPN upgraded and monitor its security—not to mention dealing with problems when users call to complain that they can't connect. Some of these problems can be taken off of your hands by using an ISP that will manage your VPN for you. Even if you go this route, a good working knowledge of what can go wrong is essential. That's what this chapter is about.

Unlike a firewall or proxy server, where you may set it up once and not touch it for months, your VPN is a more dynamic security mechanism. The main reason for this is that users rarely realize that they're interacting with a firewall or a proxy, while logging into a VPN server may take some interaction on their part. Users with various types of equipment may access your VPN from any point on the Internet at any hour or day. Anyone who has ever run a remote access server knows the various problems dial-up users can have. Many of the same problems that apply to remote users also apply to remote access VPN users. Remote sites that are connecting to a corporate LAN might require less maintenance, however, because with a LAN you often need to set them up once, have them dial in, and that's it. In this chapter, we'll go over the problems that can occur and look for possible debugging information and solutions, as well as list what you should be armed with when working with an ISP on VPN issues.

While this chapter can't address the specifics of your network, we can give you some general security suggestions. It's important to remember that no level of authentication or encryption can protect you if you don't have a sound security policy in place. We briefly touched on this in Chapter 1, *Why Build a Virtual Private Network?*, and Chapter 2, *Basic VPN Technologies.*

Finally, you'll want to keep up with the latest trends, standards, and security holes in VPN technologies, so that you can ensure that your VPN is up-to-date. We'll go over a list of resources you can use at the end of this chapter and in Appendix B, *Resources, Online and Otherwise.*

Choosing an ISP

Choosing the right ISP for your VPN connection may be one of the most important things you do. To provide the most reliable connection you possibly can, you should use the same ISP for each end of the VPN connection. The first thing to take into consideration is geography. You will want to choose an ISP that has points of presence in all of the places you need. Although local and regional ISPs might be perfect for connections within the same city or even the same state, if you need connectivity across the country you should choose a larger, national provider.

Another consideration for a reliable VPN is a quality of service (QoS) guarantee. This is an agreement between a customer and an ISP that guarantees a certain amount of availability and bandwidth on an ISP's network. Typically QoS guarantees a certain amount of latency for your traffic on the ISP's network, typically measured in tens of milliseconds. Most national ISPs guarantee 99.5% availability on their network. QoS guarantees will appear in your ISP's service level agreement (SLA) with you.

There are also VPN services that ISPs are selling, including GTE, UUNET, and others. With these services, they operate and manage your VPN for you. Prices are variable, and are typically based on the number of sites and the total amount of bandwidth used.

Solving VPN Problems

There are numerous points of failure with VPNs. This makes tracking down the cause of a problem more difficult than it might be for a normal WAN or remote access connection. Among the possible problems are connectivity problems, authentication errors, and routing problems.

Connectivity Problems

Anyone familiar with maintaining or dialing into remote access servers—or into an ISP for that matter—is also familiar with the frustration of trying to pinpoint the problem of a bad connection. The main difficulty with connectivity problems is that they have so many causes. Here are a few possibilities:

- Telco problems
  - Bad lines
  - Busy switch
- ISP problems
  - Busy signals (probably from a user-to-modem ratio that's too high)
  - Bad modem or router
- End-user problems
  - Bad modem or router
  - A modem or router that's incompatible with the ISP's
  - Configuration problem

Besides these general communication problems, you may discover problems with port usage on firewalls. As you've seen, several VPN packages use specific TCP or UDP ports in order to communicate (for example, PPTP uses TCP port 1723). If these ports aren't open, you may not be able to make a VPN connection or transport data across the VPN. It's possible that these ports may be blocked at your ISP or on your own routers.

Authentication Errors

Authentication problems are common in the realm of dial-up connections, even when VPNs aren't involved. Here are the two most common authentication problems:

- A mismatched username or password, which occurs when either the connecting machine or the far end thinks that the username or password is something other than what it is. This is sometimes caused by a simple typographical error. Likewise, there could be mismatched keys in a public key system.

- The connecting system and the destination are using different authentication methods. For instance, the connecting machine might be attempting PAP authentication, while the destination system is expecting CHAP.

There is a third level of authentication problems involving public key infrastructures. It's important to use the same key exchange protocol. For example, some IPSec products allow for a number of key exchange options: Manual, SKIP, or IPSec. In a public key infrastructure there could also be problems with certificate authorities and certificates.

Routing Problems

Routing problems occur when you're able to connect successfully to your ISP, but have trouble getting to certain hosts over the Internet, or getting out to the Internet at all. These problems are commonly due to configuration errors. Either the IP address, netmask, or gateway on your system is set incorrectly, or your ISP doesn't have a route for you.

Chances are that any one of the problems discussed in this chapter—authentication, connectivity, or routing—is caused by a configuration mismatch on your equipment, the ISP's equipment, or the equipment on the far end of the connection. The routing problem, however, could also be due to any one of the numerous connection points on the Internet backbone between you and the destination. You, and your ISP, will have little control over these problems, but it's nice to know where the problem is so that you can report it to the proper people.

In Chapter 5, *Configuring and Testing Layer 2 Connections*, in the section "Troubleshooting Problems," we mentioned two useful utilities for testing routes: *ping* and *traceroute*. Both of these tools can be used to troubleshoot problems on other VPNs as well. *ping* is a utility found on Unix, Windows 95/98, and Windows NT systems. It sends packets to a given destination and awaits a return. It doesn't tell you what route the packets take, but it does tell you if they get there at all and if there's any packet loss. *traceroute* is a program on Unix systems. The Windows 95/98/NT equivalent is TRACERT. *traceroute* will actually show you the path packets take to their destination. This information can be useful to pinpoint exactly where a problem is occurring.

traceroute information can sometimes be confusing. Be sure to read up on what the various latencies mean, as well as asterisks, exclamation marks, and other symbols. A good TCP/IP networking book will explain how to read *traceroute*'s output, as will its manual page on a Unix system. Also keep in mind that an ISP or company may be blocking *traceroute*'s UDP packets at their firewall for security reasons, so you may want to contact them and find out if this is the case. If the problem appears to be with a backbone provider, the best thing to do is still to contact your ISP. They can then contact the backbone provider and see what the problem is.

Dealing with an ISP

Working with an ISP to solve a VPN problem may prove difficult, especially if the ISP doesn't support VPNs. As a network administrator, therefore, you'll want to know your VPN product inside and out. The most important thing to remember when troubleshooting a problem with an ISP is to give them as much information as possible. At a minimum, give them this information:

- What VPN product you're using.

- What the IP address of your system should be.

- What the IP address of the destination VPN server or router should be (e.g., the address of your PPTP server).

- The TCP or UDP ports that your VPN product uses, in case your ISP has those ports blocked at a firewall.

- Any *ping* or *traceroute* output you may have that demonstrates the problem.

Make sure your ISP is someone you trust. During the course of the troubleshooting session you may have to give them security information about your network, or set up a test account for them to attempt to dial into. Here are some suggestions for finding a trustworthy ISP, or building trust with your current one:

- Use a well-established ISP: either a well-known national provider, or a local one that has a good reputation and operating history. Your local Better Business Bureau is a good place to start.

- If possible, always deal with the same support person. This will not only assure you better service—as they'll be familiar with your past problems—but will also keep the number of people you might give sensitive network information to at a minimum.

Compatibility with Other Products

Other products on your network may interfere with the performance of your VPN. Before investing the time and money to set up a VPN, you should do some research to ensure that your system and network configuration will work with it—especially if you have an elaborate security setup. Here are some caveats when setting up a VPN or adding a new product to your network:

- Some routers may block certain TCP ports out-of-the-box as a security measure. Find out which ports it blocks and make sure that they're not ports your VPN uses. You can usually turn this filtering off.

- As we've already said, some VPN products won't work through a proxy server. Versions of the Microsoft Proxy Server before 2.0, for instance, don't work with PPTP. If you already have a proxy server and want to implement a VPN, you may want to multi-home the VPN server between the Internet and your LAN, just as you have the proxy server set up. (See Figure 10-1.) VPN-only traffic routes through the VPN server, while all other traffic routes through the proxy server.

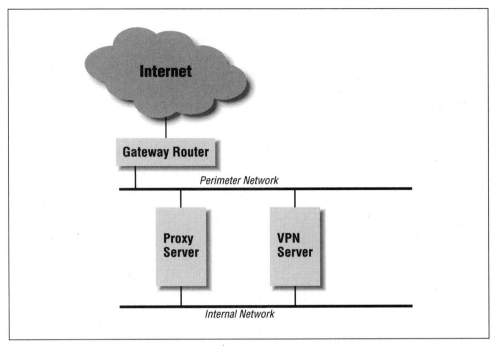

Figure 10-1. Running a proxy server with a VPN server

- Network Address Translation (NAT) is a protocol many routers support that allows machines to access the Internet even though they have internal IP addresses (set aside in RFC 1918) that are not usable on the wider Internet. Essentially, each machine is given a nonroutable address, while the router has a routable IP address. When each of the machines behind the router wants to access the Internet, it pretends to have the IP address of the router.

If you want to use NAT, we suggest a double-router setup, as shown in Figure 10-2. It shows a gateway router to the Internet and a perimeter network with Internet-routable IP addresses. On the perimeter network is a NAT-capable router multi-homed to have interfaces to both the perimeter network and the internal network. The machines on the internal network have only non-Internet routable IP addresses. The VPN server is also multi-homed between the perimeter and internal networks, and will route only VPN traffic to and from those networks.

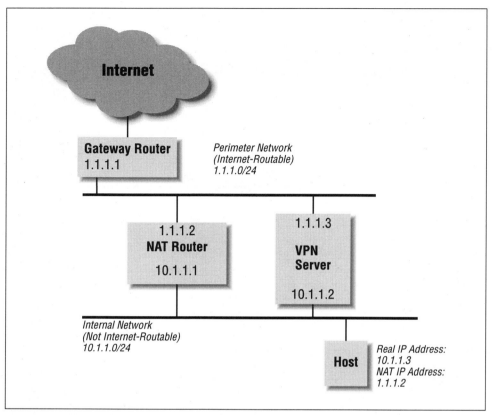

Figure 10-2. Running a Network Address Translation router with a VPN server

Delivering Quality of Service

We have already spoken about QoS in reference to choosing an ISP. This section will discuss creating QoS for your own connectivity. QoS gives you the ability to manage your bandwidth. It does this by allowing you to assign priorities to certain types of network traffic based on user, application, host, network, or protocol. With a VPN, you might be using your VPN Internet connection for normal Internet traffic as well, such as email, web browsing, file transfers, etc. Since a VPN connection is business-critical, you might want those users to have less latency time compared to some other services. In this case, you could bump up the priority of your VPN traffic, while lowering the priority of traffic that is not necessarily business oriented, such as PointCast, NNTP, or access to certain URLs.

The Resource Reservation Protocol (RSVP) is a proposed Internet QoS standard that can be used to manage IP traffic. It is already available on some routing and

VPN equipment, and some operating systems. In addition, there are a number of bandwidth management products available from vendors such as Packeteer and Check Point.

Security Suggestions

Our primary security suggestion is to make the VPN the only entry point to your network from the Internet. That is, make sure all of your systems are blocked or otherwise inaccessible from the Internet unless outside users connect to it via a VPN. Chapter 2 describes the use of firewalls to do this, and the subsequent implementation chapters go into more detail.

Restrict Who Has VPN Access

It's not a good idea to give out VPN access to just anyone. If your organization is undergoing constant change, or you are running a virtual corporation where everybody works from home, you may find it difficult to limit the users who have access. You may want to only allow people who really need remote access to have it. Here are some examples of people who might need remote VPN access:

- Traveling sales or marketing people who need access to email and files.

- Employees who work from home, or who need access to network servers after hours. Examples might be software developers, testers, documentation writers, or managers. Unless someone is permanently working from home or has a constant need for such access, it might be a good idea to grant them access only while they need the account, such as when they're ill or unable to come into work. For example, an employee who breaks her leg badly and has to stay at home for several months might still be able to dial in and work.

- Network or systems administrators.

We also suggest that you create an acceptable-use policy governing your VPN accounts, which you should distribute to anyone with VPN access. Here are some suggested guidelines:

- The VPN account is not a generic Internet account that an employee can use for anything he or she wants. It's virtually an extension of the corporation's own network and the account the user has on the corporate system, even though it might go through an ISP. The user shouldn't give the account information to kids, relatives, friends, or even fellow employees.

- The user shouldn't be routing a multi-homed connection to the VPN and another ISP. (See the sidebar for an example of why.)

- The user should direct all technical support problems regarding the VPN to the network administrator rather than directly to the ISP involved. If needed, the network administrator can contact the ISP. There should be no reason for the user to give his or her password or the internal network domain to the ISP.

- VPN users should change their passwords more often than other users of the internal network domain. They should also be sure to choose meaningless passwords, possibly containing nonalphanumeric characters, that can't be easily guessed. Examples: "xf3Kr!" or "bat*CORE."

- Finally, when employees leave, remember to take away their VPN access just as you do their accounts on the local system. Even though tracking them should be easy if they attempt to use it, they could still cause enough havoc and confusion to make life miserable for the rest of the employees—not to mention that VPN access makes it easier for them to leave with trade secrets or software licensed to your company.

Why You Shouldn't Route a Multi-Homed Connection Between a Corporate VPN and Another ISP

The second item of our acceptable use policy for VPNs mentions not allowing users to multi-home between the corporate VPN and another ISP. Here's an example of why they shouldn't: Bob the software engineer has two ISDN boards in his Windows NT system, one of which he uses to call his favorite ISP, the other he uses to connect to his office's VPN. Each ISDN interface has a separate IP address: one from the ISP, the other for the corporate network. Bob also has routing (IP forwarding) enabled on his NT box. This type of setup allows someone from the Internet to use Bob's machine as a gateway router to the corporate LAN. This effectively bypasses any type of firewall or proxy the company might have set up to prevent Internet access to the internal network. We've heard stories of software developers who have set up their systems this way so that they could work from home, dialed into the corporate LAN, and surfed the Internet using their own ISP. When it was discovered that they were doing this, their employment was terminated.

Restrict What VPN Users Can Get To

On large corporate LANs, network administrators often create several network segments separated by routers, which can limit network traffic to certain segments and provide firewall capabilities. For instance, there's no need for anyone in the manufacturing division to reach the human resources payroll server—whether they have a password or not.

Likewise, you can use internal routers and firewalls to limit where the VPN users can go. If the resources are available to you, we highly recommend doing this. Since VPN routers or servers are often open to the outside, it's the most vulnerable point on your network, and it makes sense to curb access as much as possible. You can start by limiting general access only to servers that VPN users would need most, such as email servers and a few application servers. Here are some examples of information you might never want accessible from a VPN user or remote access user:

- Security and encryption information, such as RSA private keys and SSL certificates

- Username and password information

- Top-secret research and development information

- Payroll information

- Private information on employees, including psychological or health information

- Any information your customers have entrusted you to keep private (for instance, if you're a hospital, then you'll want to keep medical records extremely secure)

You can then grant further access on a case-by-case basis. Software engineers will need to get to development servers, for instance. The ideal thing to do in this case would be to set up multiple VPN servers—one for each department—and limit who can use them.

Avoid Public DNS Information for VPN Servers and Routers

Since your VPN server will be an accessible entry point to your network, it's better not to let attackers know what it is or what it does. The simplest thing to do is not assign a DNS hostname to your VPN server at all. If you must assign one (for internal use, for instance), look into setting up a "fake" DNS server with meaningless information that's accessible to the greater Internet, while you have a server with specific information to use inside your LAN.* At any rate, don't let the outside world see a meaningful name for your VPN server, such as *avtunnel.caffeine.net*, *pptp-gw.caffeine.net*, or even *win-nt.caffeine.net*. Any one of these tells an attacker what type of system it is, and what vulnerabilities can be exploited. That's why many network administrators will follow some theme, such as Dr.

---

* A discussion of how to set up a "fake" DNS host can be found in *Building Internet Firewalls*, by D. Brent Chapman and Elizabeth D. Zwicky (O'Reilly & Associates).

Seuss characters, when naming hosts. It's a good way to give meaningless (yet easy to remember) names to systems—not just an attempt to be cute. We recommend you set up an alternate DNS server for internal use anyway; this way you can give all servers more meaningful names for Intranet users.

Keeping Yourself Up-to-Date

It's a good idea to keep your VPN up-to-date, but don't be in a rush to upgrade just because you're looking for a new feature or two. New software is notorious for introducing as many problems as it patches. Here are the primary reasons to upgrade your VPN software:

• There's a security hole in the product you currently use.

• There's a bug that causes system problems (such as crashes, memory leaks, or networking problems).

• The current version isn't compatible with another product on your network, or a product that the remote users have, and the new version improves interoperability.

• The new version has several features essential to the operation of your VPN.

Finding information on VPNs is currently like trying to stargaze in the middle of Las Vegas—there's a lot of marketing hype out there, but practical information tends to get washed out. Nonetheless, we've compiled into Appendix B a short list of things to keep up with in the world of VPNs.

11

A VPN Scenario

If you haven't gotten enough of the virtual private network yet, this chapter will cover a real, live, up and running VPN. We've covered the theory and some general cost-to-benefit analysis, and now we move on to some actual products working in a production environment. Though we have used specific products here like Ascend and Cisco, you may well find that other solutions better fit your enterprise. In other words, this chapter isn't VPN law, just an example.

The Topology

We'll call the company in this case study Immediate PC. It manufactures and sells computer parts and peripherals.

About a year ago, Immediate PC made the commitment to standardize its network communications between its various sites over the Internet. Naturally, their main concerns were security, cost, and reliability.

Communication needs at Immediate PC are like those at most companies. Sales agents in the field must communicate with manufacturing managers at the factories to order and ensure production of needed stock. The retail store arm of the company also communicates with shipping, manufacturing, and several other departments on a daily basis. Various factories and other divisions across the country must send and obtain data to keep their operations flowing.

Several different platforms are used at various levels of the organization. The main corporate network is comprised of Windows NT servers and Windows NT or Windows 95 workstations. Additionally, there are several Unix servers of various flavors. Remote access users employ a variety of operating systems, and a few departments within the main corporate networks use Macintosh systems.

Without the Internet, the flow of data and the cost associated with private lines and dial-up access were crippling operations and eating into profits. Having decided to use advanced technology to remedy the situation, Immediate PC migrated gradually from private lines and remote access to a controlled use of the Internet. Research, training, and various levels of approval preceded the move to virtual private networks.

After this move, the company reduced the cost of network communication and resolved several communications problems. What emerged was the virtual private network detailed in the network diagram at the end of this chapter. The chosen architecture links a central corporate office with various remote offices, large and small, in addition to a gaggle of remote access users.

The following sections detail what was needed in connections to the Internet, equipment, software, and virtual private network solutions.

Central Office

The central office is the natural source of information about products and operations. Security is critical. Besides the VPN, several other Internet services are centralized here, including the corporate web, email, and FTP servers. The company web-based Intranet is also centralized at the main office.

Network Connections

The central office maintains two T1 connections through two separate national Internet providers. This provides redundancy and gives other connecting sites a variety of network paths over which they can reach the central office. The T1 connections allow enough bandwidth for all sites to connect to the central network with adequate response time over the VPN, in addition to supporting these other services.

Hardware and Operating System

Routing traffic from the T1, the company has a Cisco 4500 Internet router. This is a robust and expandable router that can handle up to four T1s for a large network. Likewise, it can encapsulate and route a variety of protocols, from IP to Apple-Talk. For broad coverage of VPN solutions, the main office is running PPTP on Windows NT servers. Secondarily, there is a Unix server and an Ascend MAX remote access hub, both running PPTP.

VPN Package

The central office must run three VPN servers to give their connecting networks a variety of solutions. The large branch offices require a stable and fast network-to-network VPN. For this high-bandwidth task, the Cisco PIX firewall was chosen. In addition to being a robust firewall solution, the PIX enables the various large networks to encrypt data traffic from one network to the other. This, combined with the routing power of the Cisco routers, allows each network a variety of protocols, while maintaining a secure connection. Other network-capable VPNs like the AltaVista Tunnel didn't provide the robust and fast VPN solution for these large remote networks. Other remote users dialing in either to the Internet or one of the branch offices are using PPTP.

Large Branch Office

Other Internet services are maintained at some of the large branch offices, such as web and FTP servers.

Connection

Large branch offices around the country are connected to the Internet via fractional T1 or full T1, depending on the size of their networks and the level of network activity. Their network connections are through one of the two national providers that connect the central office to the Internet. This allows for a faster connection to the central office. This strategy lessens the amount of "hops" necessary to reach corporate office Internet connections.

Hardware and Operating System

A Cisco 2500 router is needed to support fractional to full T1 connections for these networks. Sites use PPTP and Windows NT or Unix servers for dial-up users and smaller connecting networks.

VPN Package

The Cisco PIX Firewall is implemented at these locations for connections to the central office and to provide network security against Internet-based attacks. These branch offices also use PPTP for their remote access users, and for incoming connections from the small branch offices. Users run PPTP client on their Windows NT, Windows 95, or Macintosh workstations.

Small Branch Offices

Small branch office sites host very few resources to share—certainly not major web pages that are expected to get lots of hits—but they need continuous and reliable access to the larger offices.

Connection

The smaller branch offices maintain either dedicated or dynamic ISDN connections to their Internet service providers. Some offices use the same national service provider as the corporate office, while others use providers who maintain upstream connections through the same networks as the corporate office. Though this does not affect the basic functionality of the VPN, it does increase the speed and reliability of the connection between sites.

Hardware and Operating System

Small branch offices use the Ascend Pipeline 50 ISDN router for their Internet connection. The Ascend supports PPTP, and routes Internet traffic for up to 255 IP addresses. A Windows NT or Unix server is utilized at each site to validate incoming PPTP users and to connect to the VPN.

VPN Package

A PPTP server and client are used at each site for accessing the VPN.

Remote Access Users

Remote access users include those on the road and those working off-site.

Connection

A variety of connection methods are used, from ISDN to analog phone lines and modems. Again, the best scenario is to have all remote access users connect through the same national provider as the rest of the corporate network or through a provider who is on the same network.

Hardware and Operating System

Individual users can have a variety of platforms, from Windows NT or Windows 95 workstations to Unix to MacOS. ISDN routers, terminal adapters, or analog modems could all be in use.

VPN Package

The PPTP client is used by end users to access the VPN.

A Network Diagram

Figure 11-1 shows connections from the Internet to the central office to a large office, a small office, and a remote user. It is important to note the flow of traffic throughout the VPN. PPTP servers validate incoming traffic. This encrypted traffic passes through interposing firewalls and is relayed directly to the PPTP server. The traffic is then routed to the desired internal network node. The Cisco PIX firewall, on the other hand, immediately directs authorized traffic to the network and thus provides a faster backbone for the VPN.

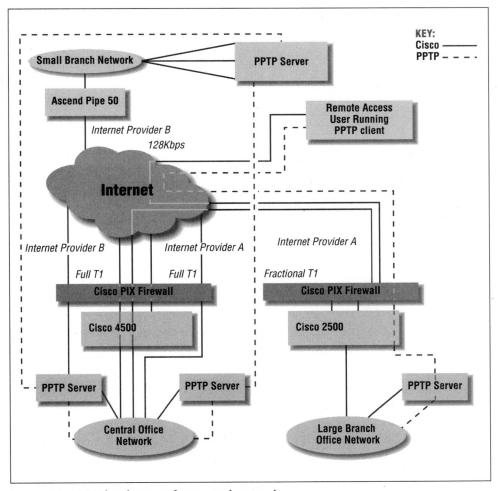

Figure 11-1. VPN hardware, software, and protocols

Regardless of the need or resources available, if your enterprise requires secure network connections over the Internet, there is a solution available. Other solutions, such as IPSec, L2F, SSH, or L2TP, would work just as efficiently. What should be noted is that your organization's needs should result in the VPN network solution chosen.

Emerging Internet
Technologies

IPv6

Because VPNs ultimately use the Internet as their transport medium, they are subject to the advantages and disadvantages associated with using the Internet Protocol (IP). As you are probably aware, the mechanics of the Internet (the TCP/IP protocols) rely not exactly on the familiar names that we are used to seeing in URLs, such as *www.ibm.com* and *ftp.uu.net*, but rather on a lower level addressing scheme that uses IP addresses or "dotted quads." An IP address, such as 207.25.97.8, specifies precisely one computer. The IP address is the lowest common denominator separating one machine from another.

A hot topic among networking professionals is that the current pool of IP addresses is drying up. Since the IP address is formed by putting 4 bytes together, with each byte having 256 combinations (2^8), there is a limited number of IP addresses available (2^{32}, or 4,294,967,296, to be exact). You may be thinking that four billion addresses is nothing to sneeze at, which is true, but the explosive growth of the Internet world-wide has caused a great strain on the system for deploying those addresses. One reason for this is that huge blocks have already been given out and the system for assigning new ones is antiquated and difficult to administer.

The current version of the IP protocol is Version 4, and Version 5 disappeared while still under discussion. IP Version 6 (IPv6 for short) is a project supported by networking companies, technology professionals, and organizations (such as the Internet Engineering Task Force [IETF]), to increase the size of the IP address pool to accommodate the massive growth expected on the Internet over the next several decades. Rather than simply increasing the size of the IP address pool, the ongoing work with IPv6 addresses a whole host of architectural issues. There is a virtual mountain of Requests for Comments, or RFCs, devoted to the design and implementation of IPv6. From RFC 1887 we can see a few of the topics being explored:

- Topological information included to significantly reduce routing protocol overhead

- Additional levels of hierarchy with anchors built in to ease future growth

- Standards for mapping service providers and subscribers to components of an IPv6 address

- Address assignments for all network entities based on growth and need

- Allocation of the IPv6 addresses by the Internet Registry

- Multi-homing and multiple domain routing choices

- IPv4 address space mapping into IPv6

- Multicast addressing

- Mobile host addressing

- Administrative addressing

- Mechanisms for publishing routing information to third parties

- A division of routing policies into host-to-router, router-to-router inter-domain, and domain-to-domain

In summary, IPv6 is analogous to what the phone company was required to do to handle long distance calling. When the user prefixes an area code to the already existing number, the telephone exchange can route to that area from the outside simply by consulting the first three numbers and looking up the city/area to which the call should be routed. Hence, a call placed from San Diego to the 212 area code would go to New York, regardless of where exactly in New York that call would terminate. The IPv6 initiative is following a similar strategy.

Because IPv6 is in its infancy (much like VPNs), there is always some new information bubbling to the surface. We suggest that you check out the popular search engines and newsgroups for any new updates or advancements.

IPSec

Another very important topic to VPN administrators is the IETF IPSec project, which is a working group committed to the design requirements necessary for Internet Protocol security. IPSec provides cryptographic security methods to undergird authentication, integrity, access control, and confidentiality. Current thoughts on the implementation of IPSec will include both the IPv4 realm and the newer IPv6 one. For the greatest flexibility, the specific protocol formats are independent of the cryptographic algorithms used to protect the data.

Most of the VPN implementations that we cover in this book all use a software, host-based encryption scheme, which places the bulk of the burden to protect the data right on a person's desktop. The goals of IPSec coincide nicely with those of future VPNs: to elegantly integrate the security underpinnings used to protect privacy with routing machinery and to provide security in a simple way to an entire class of hosts or networks. Further, by utilizing authentication and access control, a true VPN can be established between almost any two devices or subnets without the need for specialized software, configuration, and firewalling.

The best place to read up on the continued work done on IPSec is the IETF's web site at *http://www.ietf.cnri.reston.va.us/html.charters/IPSec-charter.html.*

S/WAN

Of the new technologies emerging on the horizon, the S/WAN initiative—based on the fundamentals of IPSec—may make the biggest news. RSA Data Security is coordinating closely with most of the leading TCP/IP networking vendors to create a full range of interoperable VPN and security products. The S/WAN objective is to use the IPSec protocol suite to allow customers to mix and match virtually any firewall, stack, and router products into different configurations of a VPN. The various solutions we have covered, like the AltaVista Tunnel and the Cisco PIX firewall, are all single-vendor solutions. S/WAN would allow users and administrators the flexibility to deploy a network-wide VPN solution without having to retool the whole network and without a big outlay of capital equipment expenditures.

As with IPSec, S/WAN incorporates security encryption at the IP level, which is fundamentally more secure than higher level protocols in the TCP/IP suite like the SSL (Secure Sockets Layer). To guarantee interoperability, which is the primary goal of S/WAN, vendors must adhere to a common set of resources, software code, and implementations.

The S/WAN proposal utilizes RSA's most advanced block encryption algorithm, the RC5 symmetric block cipher. RC5 keys can range from 40 bits to 128 bits and provide a fantastic degree of security, judging by the number of MIPS-years required to brute force attack a datagram. To accommodate backward compatibility and the U.S.'s restriction on exporting cryptography, the S/WAN code can be effectively implemented with almost any encryption algorithm (3DES, DES, RC2-RC5, RSA, etc.).

Expect to see a wealth of new S/WAN products over the next few years from vendors of equipment that you currently deploy in your shop. We expect this to be an exciting time for new VPN products and services.

B

Resources, Online and Otherwise

Software Updates

Whatever VPN product you purchase, be sure to keep up with any software updates. As with any new product, yours is bound to have its share of bugs and security holes that need to be patched. In addition, updates may offer necessary new features and interoperability that weren't available in the original release. For instance, many VPN products are just now including IPSec, or the IKE key exchange standard.

The best place to look for updates is the product's web site. Sometimes updates will be available for free directly from the site. The authors maintain a web page about new and updated products at *http://www.vpn.outer.net.*

U.S. corporations that develop VPN products have limits on the grade of encryption they are allowed to export. As competition opens up and computing power increases and redefines what's "commerce-grade" and "military-grade," U.S. companies will be allowed to export stronger encryption packages. If you're outside of the U.S., this means that you'll be able to make your VPN even more secure, so be on the lookout for these upgrades.

The IETF

Monitoring the activities of the Internet Engineering Task Force (IETF) is a good way to keep up with emerging standards related to VPNs. IPSec, for instance, is an IETF working group attempting to create a standard for secure IP communication, which can be used in VPNs. See *http://www.ietf.cnri.reston.va.us/1id-abstracts.html* for a draft index.

Remember that most of these drafts haven't been implemented outside of experimental environments yet, so look to this site to provide you with information on "up-and-coming" Internet technologies. RFCs are informational documents on technologies that may already be in place. An index of actual RFCs can be found at *http://ds.internic.net/ds/rfc-index.html.*

CERT Advisories

The Computer Emergency Response Team Coordination Center (CERT-CC) acts as a focal point for information pertaining to security on Internet hosts. In addition to providing assistance to Internet users whose systems or networks have been compromised, it's an information center storing known product vulnerabilities. This information is distributed in what are known as CERT-CC Advisories. You can have new advisories emailed to you by subscribing to *cert-advisory-request@cert.org.* New advisories are also posted to the *comp.security.announce* newsgroup. An archive of the advisories is kept at *ftp://info.cert.org/pub/cert_advisories/.*

Although most of these advisories pertain to Unix systems, there are many that cover Internet security in general (such as IP spoofing). Newer advisories have also covered problems with web browsers, Java, and JavaScript.

The Trade Press

Since VPNs are such a new technology, the best place to keep up with the current trends is in the network and Internet industry press. Good places to find articles about VPNs are in magazines such as *Communications Week, Network World, Info World, CIO,* and *LAN Times.*

Networking and Intranet-Related Web Sites

The best way to find the most current information about VPNs is on a web site with information on Intranets or networking. The online presences of the magazines previously mentioned are a good place to start, as are the web pages of companies that make VPN products. We've compiled a short list of web sites that have VPN information:

The Internet Week VPN Source Page
   http://techweb.cmp.com/internetwk/VPN

Virtual Private Networks Resource Page
   http://www.vpn.outer.net

IPSec Working Group Page
http://www.ietf.cnri.reston.va.us/html.charters/ipsec-charter.html

Microsoft PPTP Information
http://www.microsoft.com/communications/PPTP.htm

Microsoft Security Updates
http://www.microsoft.com/security

Cisco L2TP Information
http://www.cisco.com/warp/public/779/servpro/solutions/vpn/l2tun_ds.htm

Cisco L2F Information
http://www.cisco.com/warp/public/728/General/vpdn_wp.htm

Aventail's VPN Guide
http://www.vpnguide.com

RSA Data Security, Inc.
http://www.rsa.com

Counterpane Systems
http://www.counterpane.com

RSVP Charter
http://www.ietf.cnri.reston.va.us/proceedings/96mar/charters/rsvp-charter.html

Usenet Newsgroups

There are many Usenet newsgroups that may contain articles on VPNs and VPN products. We've come up with a list of groups that contain discussions about VPNs:

comp.dcom.sys.cisco
This group often contains discussions about L2F, L2TP, and the PIX firewall.

comp.security.firewalls
A group where many VPN announcements and articles are posted; it's also a great place for firewall information in general.

comp.os.ms-windows.networking.ras, microsoft.public.windowsnt.protocol.ras, and *microsoft.public.windowsnt.steelhead*
All of these newsgroups have regular discussions of Microsoft VPN products.

comp.protocols.tcp-ip
This group sometimes contains articles relating to VPNs, tunneling, and IPSec.

sci.crypt
A newsgroup that deals specifically with cryptography issues.

Mailing Lists

The Firewalls Mailing List
> A firewall list founded by Brent Chapman. You can subscribe at:
> *http://lists.gnac.net/firewalls/*

Firewall Wizards Mailing List
> Another firewall list with discussions of firewalls and VPNs:
> *http://www.nfr.net/firewall-wizards*

The VPN Mailing List
> A relatively new list that deals specifically with VPN issues. Send email to *majordomo@listserv.iegroup.com* with "subscribe vpn" in the message.

Index

About the Authors

Charlie Scott is the Senior Vice President of OuterNet Connection Strategies, Inc., an Internet service provider and outsource company based in Austin, Texas, and specializing in innovative and emergent technologies. At OuterNet, he helps create and implement new products for their network operations center and co-location facilities. While an undergraduate at the University of Texas at Austin, Charlie was a research assistant in a cognitive science lab, and planned on going to graduate school in that field. He was eventually able to get his B.A. in Psychology. But he always enjoyed working with computers, and his exposure to the Internet at U.T. deviated him enough to abandon all plans for graduate school and start working with computer networks. The next few years saw him at Texas Instruments, IBM, and Wayne-Dresser before he helped found OuterNet.

Charlie has also co-authored a half-dozen Internet-related books (many with Mike and Paul), on topics ranging from electronic commerce to CGI programming. He has an MCSE and is working towards Cisco and other certifications. When he finds spare time, Charlie likes to write and read fiction. He also enjoys spending time with his wife Mary and their four beautiful felines.

Paul Wolfe has done everything from drive M1A1 tanks in Desert Storm to sling computer chips for Motorola. He now divides his time between his family and his job, as well as writing. He has written four books in the last two years, covering such topics as Windows NT web servers, Internet commerce, VRML, and virtual private networks. Paul is currently a team leader for system builds, hardware inventory, and ISDN deployment for Tivoli Systems, an IBM company. He dreams of restoring his 1986 Toyota Tercel to its former glory and racing it on the stock car circuit.

Mike Erwin is the President and Chief Executive Officer of OuterNet Connection Strategies, Inc. Mike has served in these posts for the last four years, while also working for Apple Computer, Inc., architecting and implementing connectivity, application, scripting, and development support for Apple's Worldwide Support Center. Mr. Erwin is the co-author of several other works, including the *CGI Bible*, *Building Web Commerce Sites*, and the *60 Minute Guide to VRML*. Mike's technology-related interests involve encryption algorithms, super computing, distributed operating systems, universe game simulations, and building secondary securities markets on the Net.

Before becoming completely immersed in work, Mike used to find that his hobbies included playing hearts, drinking cheap vodka, staying up until dawn, and doodling with oil paints with his left hand. Mike's current favorite things include dabbling with theoretical and particle physics, martial arts training, gambling, securities prospecting, and, of course, sleeping.

Colophon

The animals featured on the cover of *Virtual Private Networks, Second Edition,* are puffins. Puffins are small, unusual-looking birds with large triangular bills, short necks, and stocky bodies. They live in colonies, sometimes tens of thousands of birds together, along the icy shores of the northern regions of the globe. Though they are rarely seen outside of the northern regions, there are approximately 15 million puffins in the world today. Despite their short wings, puffins can fly, although they spend most of their time swimming or walking erect on land. While flying, they make a purring sound.

Here's some more puffin stuff: puffins' primary food sources are small fish and marine animals. They dive for fish and use their wings to swim underwater to catch them. They can carry as many as 30 fish in their mouth at one time, to bring back to shore for their young. Puffin pairs often mate for life. Usually one egg is laid per pair, and both mother and father incubate the egg and feed the young hatchling.

Edie Freedman designed the cover of this book, using a 19th-century engraving from the Dover Pictorial Archive. The cover layout was produced with Quark XPress 3.3, using the ITC Garamond font. Whenever possible, our books use Rep-Kover™, a durable and flexible lay-flat binding. If the page count exceeds RepKover's limit, perfect binding is used.

The inside layout was designed by Nancy Priest and implemented in FrameMaker by Mike Sierra. The text and heading fonts are ITC Garamond Light and Garamond Book. The illustrations that appear in the book were created in Macromedia Freehand 7.0, and screen shots were created in Adobe Photoshop 4.0 by Robert Romano. This colophon was written by Clairemarie Fisher O'Leary.

More Titles from O'Reilly

Network Administration

DNS and BIND, 2nd Edition

By Paul Albitz & Cricket Liu
2nd Edition December 1996
438 pages, ISBN 1-56592-236-0

This book is a complete guide to the Internet's Domain Name System (DNS) and the Berkeley Internet Name Domain (BIND) software, the UNIX implementation of DNS. This second edition covers BIND 4.8.3, which is included in most vendor implementations today, as well as BIND 4.9.4, the potential future standard.

TCP/IP Network Administration, 2nd Edition

By Craig Hunt
2nd Edition December 1997
630 pages, ISBN 1-56592-322-7

A complete guide to setting up and running a TCP/IP network for practicing system administrators. Beyond basic setup, this new second edition discusses the Internet routing protocols and provides a tutorial on how to configure important network services. It now also includes Linux in addition to BSD and System V TCP/IP implementations.

The Networking CD Bookshelf

By O'Reilly & Associates, Inc.
1st Edition January 1999 (est.)
Features CD-ROM
ISBN 1-56592-523-8

Network administrator alert! Six bestselling O'Reilly Animal Guides are now available on CD-ROM, easily accessible with your favorite Web browser: *TCP/IP Network Administration, 2nd Edition; sendmail, 2nd Edition; sendmail Desktop Reference; DNS and BIND, 3rd Edition; Practical UNIX & Internet Security, 2nd Edition;* and *Building Internet Firewalls.* As a bonus, the new hardcopy version of *DNS and BIND* is also included.

sendmail, 2nd Edition

By Bryan Costales & Eric Allman
2nd Edition January 1997
1050 pages, ISBN 1-56592-222-0

sendmail, 2nd Edition, covers sendmail Version 8.8 from Berkeley and the standard versions available on most systems. This cross-referenced edition offers an expanded tutorial, solution-oriented examples, and new topics such as the #error delivery agent, sendmail's exit values, MIME headers, and how to set up and use the user database, *mailertable*, and *smrsh*.

Cracking DES

By Electronic Frontier Foundation
1st Edition July 1998
272 pages, ISBN 1-56592-520-3

The Data Encryption Standard withstood the test of time for twenty years. *Cracking DES: Secrets of Encryption Research, Wiretap Politics & Chip Design* shows exactly how it was brought down.
Every cryptographer, security designer, and student of cryptography policy should read this book to understand how the world changed as it fell.

Security

Building Internet Firewalls

By D. Brent Chapman &
Elizabeth D. Zwicky
1st Edition September 1995
546 pages, ISBN 1-56592-124-0

Everyone is jumping on the Internet bandwagon, despite the fact that the security risks associated with connecting to the Net have never been greater. This book is a practical guide to building firewalls on the Internet. It describes a variety of firewall approaches and architectures and discusses how you can build packet filtering and proxying solutions at your site. It also contains a full discussion of how to configure Internet services (e.g., FTP, SMTP, Telnet) to work with a firewall, as well as a complete list of resources, including the location of many publicly available firewall construction tools.

Security

Web Security & Commerce

By Simson Garfinkel with Gene Spafford
1st Edition June 1997
506 pages, ISBN 1-56592-269-7

Learn how to minimize the risks of the Web with this comprehensive guide. It covers browser vulnerabilities, privacy concerns, issues with Java, JavaScript, ActiveX, and plug-ins, digital certificates, cryptography, web server security, blocking software, censorship technology, and relevant civil and criminal issues.

Protecting Networks with SATAN

By Martin Freiss
1st Edition May 1998
128 pages, ISBN 1-56592-425-8

SATAN performs "security audits," scanning host computers for security vulnerabilities. This book describes how to install and use SATAN, and how to adapt it to local requirements and increase its knowledge of specific security vulnerabilities.

Stopping Spam

By Alan Schwartz & Simson Garfinkel
1st Edition October 1998
204 pages, ISBN 1-56592-388-X

This book describes spam—unwanted email messages and inappropriate news articles—and explains what you and your Internet service providers and administrators can do to prevent it, trace it, stop it, and even outlaw it. Contains a wealth of advice, technical tools, and additional technical and community resources.

Computer Security Basics

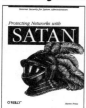

By Deborah Russell & G.T. Gangemi, Sr.
1st Edition July 1991
464 pages, ISBN 0-937175-71-4

Computer Security Basics provides a broad introduction to the many areas of computer security and a detailed description of current security standards. This handbook describes complicated concepts like trusted systems, encryption, and mandatory access control in simple terms, and contains a thorough, readable introduction to the "Orange Book."

PGP: Pretty Good Privacy

By Simson Garfinkel
1st Edition January 1995
430 pages, ISBN 1-56592-098-8

PGP is a freely available encryption program that protects the privacy of files and electronic mail. It uses powerful public key cryptography and works on virtually every platform. This book is both a readable technical user's guide and a fascinating behind-the-scenes look at cryptography and privacy. It describes how to use PGP and provides background on cryptography, PGP's history, battles over public key cryptography patents and U.S. government export restrictions, and public debates about privacy and free speech.

Computer Crime

By David Icove, Karl Seger & William VonStorch
(Consulting Editor Eugene H. Spafford)
1st Edition August 1995
462 pages, ISBN 1-56592-086-4

This book is for anyone who needs to know what today's computer crimes look like, how to prevent them, and how to detect, investigate, and prosecute them if they do occur. It contains basic computer security information as well as guidelines for investigators, law enforcement, and system administrators. Also includes computer-related statutes and laws, a resource summary, detailed papers on computer crime, and a sample search warrant.

Practical UNIX & Internet Security, 2nd Edition

By Simson Garfinkel & Gene Spafford
2nd Edition April 1996
1004 pages, ISBN 1-56592-148-8

This second edition of the classic Practical UNIX Security is a complete rewrite of the original book. It's packed with twice the pages and offers even more practical information for UNIX users and administrators. In it you'll find coverage of features of many types of UNIX systems, including SunOS, Solaris, BSDI, AIX, HP-UX, Digital UNIX, Linux, and others. Contents include UNIX and security basics, system administrator tasks, network security, and appendices containing checklists and helpful summaries.

How to stay in touch with O'Reilly

1. Visit Our Award-Winning Web Site

http://www.oreilly.com/

★ "Top 100 Sites on the Web" —*PC Magazine*
★ "Top 5% Web sites" —*Point Communications*
★ "3-Star site" —*The McKinley Group*

Our web site contains a library of comprehensive product information (including book excerpts and tables of contents), downloadable software, background articles, interviews with technology leaders, links to relevant sites, book cover art, and more. File us in your Bookmarks or Hotlist!

2. Join Our Email Mailing Lists

New Product Releases
To receive automatic email with brief descriptions of all new O'Reilly products as they are released, send email to:
listproc@online.oreilly.com
Put the following information in the first line of your message (*not* in the Subject field):
subscribe oreilly-news

O'Reilly Events
If you'd also like us to send information about trade show events, special promotions, and other O'Reilly events, send email to:
listproc@online.oreilly.com
Put the following information in the first line of your message (*not* in the Subject field):
subscribe oreilly-events

3. Get Examples from Our Books via FTP

There are two ways to access an archive of example files from our books:

Regular FTP
- ftp to:
  ftp.oreilly.com
  (login: anonymous
  password: your email address)
- Point your web browser to:
  ftp://ftp.oreilly.com/

FTPMAIL
- Send an email message to:
  ftpmail@online.oreilly.com
  (Write "help" in the message body)

4. Contact Us via Email

order@oreilly.com
To place a book or software order online. Good for North American and international customers.

subscriptions@oreilly.com
To place an order for any of our newsletters or periodicals.

books@oreilly.com
General questions about any of our books.

software@oreilly.com
For general questions and product information about our software. Check out O'Reilly Software Online at **http://software.oreilly.com/** for software and technical support information. Registered O'Reilly software users send your questions to: **website-support@oreilly.com**

cs@oreilly.com
For answers to problems regarding your order or our products.

booktech@oreilly.com
For book content technical questions or corrections.

proposals@oreilly.com
To submit new book or software proposals to our editors and product managers.

international@oreilly.com
For information about our international distributors or translation queries. For a list of our distributors outside of North America check out:
http://www.oreilly.com/www/order/country.html

O'Reilly & Associates, Inc.
101 Morris Street, Sebastopol, CA 95472 USA
TEL   707-829-0515 or 800-998-9938
       (6am to 5pm PST)
FAX   707-829-0104

International Distributors

UK, EUROPE, MIDDLE EAST AND NORTHERN AFRICA (EXCEPT FRANCE, GERMANY, SWITZERLAND, & AUSTRIA)

INQUIRIES
International Thomson Publishing Europe
Berkshire House
168-173 High Holborn
London WC1V 7AA
United Kingdom
Tel: 44-1-71-497-1422
Fax: 44-1-71-497-1426

ORDERS
International Thomson Publishing Services, Ltd.
Cheriton House, North Way
Andover, Hampshire SP10 5BE
United Kingdom
Tel: 44-1-264-342-832 (UK)
Tel: 44-1-264-342-806 (outside UK)
Fax: 44-1-264-364-418 (UK)
Fax: 44-1-264-342-761 (outside UK)
Email: itpint@itps.co.uk

FRANCE

GEODIF
61, Bd Saint-Germain
75240 Paris Cedex 05, France
Tel: 33-1-44-41-46-16 (French books)
Tel: 33-1-44-41-11-87 (English books)
Fax: 33-1-44-41-11-44
Email: distribution@eyrolles.com

ORDERS
SODIS
128, av.du Mal de Lattre de Tassigny
77403 Lagny Cédex, France
Tel: 33-1-60-07-82-00
Fax: 33-1-64-30-32-27

INQUIRIES
Éditions O'Reilly
18 rue Séguier
75006 Paris, France
Tel: 33-1-40-51-52-30
Fax: 33-1-40-51-52-31
Email: france@editions-oreilly.fr

GERMANY, SWITZERLAND, AUSTRIA

INQUIRIES
O'Reilly Verlag
Balthasarstr. 81
D-50670 Köln, Germany
Tel: 49-221-973160-0
Fax: 49-221-973160-8
Email: anfragen@oreilly.de

ORDERS
International Thomson Publishing
Königswinterer Straße 418
53227 Bonn, Germany
Tel: 49-228-970240
Fax: 49-228-441342
Email: order@oreilly.de

CANADA (FRENCH LANGUAGE BOOKS)

Les Éditions Flammarion ltée
375, Avenue Laurier Ouest
Montréal (Québec) H2V 2K3
Tel: 00-1-514-277-8807
Fax: 00-1-514-278-2085
Email: info@flammarion.qc.ca

HONG KONG

City Discount Subscription Service, Ltd.
Unit D, 3rd Floor, Yan's Tower
27 Wong Chuk Hang Road
Aberdeen, Hong Kong
Tel: 852-2580-3539
Fax: 852-2580-6463
Email: citydis@ppn.com.hk

KOREA

Hanbit Media, Inc.
Sonyoung Bldg. 202
Yeksam-dong 736-36
Kangnam-ku
Seoul, Korea
Tel: 822-554-9610
Fax: 822-556-0363
Email: hant93@chollian.dacom.co.kr

SINGAPORE, MALAYSIA, THAILAND

Addison-Wesley Longman Singapore Pte., Ltd.
25 First Lok Yang Road
Singapore 629734
Tel: 65-268-2666
Fax: 65-268-7023
Email: Daniel.Loh@awl.com.sg

PHILIPPINES

Mutual Books, Inc.
429-D Shaw Boulevard
Mandaluyong City, Metro
Manila, Philippines
Tel: 632-725-7538
Fax: 632-721-3056
Email: mbikikog@mnl.sequel.net

TAIWAN

O'Reilly Taiwan
No. 3, Lane 131
Hang-Chow South Road
Section 1, Taipei, Taiwan
Tel: 886-2-23968990
Fax: 886-2-23968916
Email: benh@oreilly.com

CHINA

China National Publishing
Industry Trading Corporation
504 AnHuiLi, AnDingMenWai
P.O. Box 782
Beijing 100011, China P.R.
Tel: 86-10-6424-0483
Fax: 86-10-6421-4540
Email: frederic@oreilly.com

INDIA

Computer Bookshop (India) Pvt. Ltd.
190 Dr. D.N. Road, Fort
Bombay 400 001 India
Tel: 91-22-207-0989
Fax: 91-22-262-3551
Email: cbsbom@giasbm01.vsnl.net.in

JAPAN

O'Reilly Japan, Inc.
Kiyoshige Building 2F
12-Bancho, Sanei-cho
Shinjuku-ku
Tokyo 160-0008 Japan
Tel: 81-3-3356-5227
Fax: 81-3-3356-5261
Email: japan@oreilly.com

ALL OTHER ASIAN COUNTRIES

O'Reilly & Associates, Inc.
101 Morris Street
Sebastopol, CA 95472 USA
Tel: 707-829-0515
Fax: 707-829-0104
Email: order@oreilly.com

AUSTRALIA

WoodsLane Pty., Ltd.
7/5 Vuko Place
Warriewood NSW 2102
Australia
Tel: 61-2-9970-5111
Fax: 61-2-9970-5002
Email: info@woodslane.com.au

NEW ZEALAND

Woodslane New Zealand, Ltd.
21 Cooks Street (P.O. Box 575)
Waganui, New Zealand
Tel: 64-6-347-6543
Fax: 64-6-345-4840
Email: info@woodslane.com.au

SOUTH AFRICA

International Thomson South Africa
Building 18, Constantia Park
138 Sixteenth Road
(P.O. Box 2459)
Halfway House, 1685 South Africa
Tel: 27-11-805-4819
Fax: 27-11-805-3648

LATIN AMERICA

McGraw-Hill Interamericana
Editores, S.A. de C.V.
Cedro No. 512
Col. Atlampa
06450, Mexico, D.F.
Tel: 52-5-547-6777
Fax: 52-5-547-3336
Email: mcgraw-hill@infosel.net.mx

O'REILLY®

O'REILLY®

O'Reilly & Associates, Inc.
101 Morris Street
Sebastopol, CA 95472-9902
1-800-998-9938

Visit us online at:
www.oreilly.com
order@oreilly.com

O'REILLY WOULD LIKE TO HEAR FROM YOU

Which book did this card come from?

_____

Where did you buy this book?
- ❏ Bookstore
- ❏ Direct from O'Reilly
- ❏ Bundled with hardware/software
- ❏ Computer Store
- ❏ Class/seminar
- ❏ Other _____

What operating system do you use?
- ❏ UNIX
- ❏ Windows NT
- ❏ Macintosh
- ❏ PC(Windows/DOS)
- ❏ Other _____

What is your job description?
- ❏ System Administrator
- ❏ Network Administrator
- ❏ Web Developer
- ❏ Programmer
- ❏ Educator/Teacher
- ❏ Other _____

❏ Please send me O'Reilly's catalog, containing a complete listing of O'Reilly books and software.

Name _____ Company/Organization _____

Address _____

City _____ State _____ Zip/Postal Code _____ Country _____

Telephone _____ Internet or other email address (specify network) _____

Nineteenth century wood engraving
of a bear from the O'Reilly &
Associates Nutshell Handbook®
Using & Managing UUCP.

POST CARD

BUSINESS REPLY MAIL
FIRST CLASS MAIL   PERMIT NO. 80   SEBASTOPOL, CA

Postage will be paid by addressee

O'Reilly & Associates, Inc.
101 Morris Street
Sebastopol, CA 95472-9902